DECENT WORK:
OBJECTIVES AND STRATEGIES

DECENT WORK: OBJECTIVES AND STRATEGIES

Edited by Dharam Ghai

International Institute for Labour Studies
International Labour Office   Geneva

ISBN 92-9014-785-7 (print)

ISBN 92-9014-786-5 (web pdf)

First published 2006

ILO publications can be obtained through major booksellers or ILO local offices in many countries, or direct from ILO Publications, International Labour Office, CH-1211 Geneva 22, Switzerland. Catalogues or lists of new publications are available free of charge from the above address, or by email: pubvente@ilo.org. Visit our website:www.ilo.org/publns.

Photocomposed in Switzerland
Printed in Switzerland

WEI
PCL

Preface

The main purpose of this book is to provide an introductory text on the concepts, strategies and policies pertaining to decent work. The papers presented in the volume explore the evolution and content of the concept of decent work and its key components, and show their relevance and applicability in diverse institutional settings and at different stages of development.

The first chapter by Dharam Ghai, *Decent work: Universality and diversity*, provides an analytical introduction to the concept and substance of decent work, drawing on research carried out by the ILO to address a number of questions and issues. A discussion on the intellectual contribution of the decent work paradigm is followed by consideration of the universality of its goals and a typology of models. The author then discusses the goals and features of the four decent work components, namely: rights at work, employment, social protection and social dialogue.

The decent work framework draws attention to the relationships between its different components in at least three distinct ways.

First, it points to the different domains of operation of these components. For instance, rights at work are closely linked with the domain of norms and legislation, although their implementation depends heavily upon adequate capacity, institutions and resources. Likewise, social dialogue is in the first instance a matter of providing a suitable legislative and institutional infrastructure. In contrast, the achievement of employment and social security objectives requires substantial economic resources, in addition to an enabling policy and institutional environment. The different domains of decent work components thus bring together questions relating to rights and standards, voice and representation, and human security and employment, which place differential demands on scarce resources. These are key to the formulation of plans to achieve decent work goals.

Second, the decent work framework exposes and invites an analysis of the complementarities and trade-offs among its different components. For instance, does the extension of social security affect the volume of employment? Does social dialogue lead to higher productivity and improved remuneration? Is there a conflict between the quality and quantity of employment? What is the impact of collective bargaining on the volume of employment? The decent work framework seeks to provide policy and institutional options that increase the synergy among its different components.

Third, the decent work paradigm provokes questions about universality and particularity. It is sometimes argued that the ILO's work on standards, employment, social security and industrial relations is largely derived from industrial market economies, and is applicable at best only to the formal sectors in other countries, so excluding large swathes of their economics and working people. Regardless of the validity or otherwise of this argument, it is clear that the overall approach and terminology of the decent work framework lends itself more easily to the analysis of structural and institutional diversity, thus facilitating a universalistic approach to the world of work.

Chapter two by Bob Hepple, *Rights at work*, provides a framework for understanding the evolution, typology and content of rights at work. It starts with a discussion of the basic concepts of rights, goals, obligations, principles and standards. Four historical and comparative models of rights at work are critically assessed. These models are: (a) protection and toleration in the liberal state; (b) equality, security and other rights in the social democratic welfare state; (c) market regulation in the neo-liberal state; and (d) rights-based regulation in the emerging development model. The author considers a number of controversial questions: (a) can rights at work be reconciled with competitiveness? (b) what is the relationship between workers' rights and human rights? (c) how can these rights contribute to the alleviation of poverty and inequality? And (d) how can these rights be progressively realized? The chapter concludes with a discussion of policy options for realizing rights at work.

Chapter three by Martin Godfrey, *Employment dimensions of decent work: Trade-offs and complementarities*, discusses the typology of employment problems in different institutional and developmental settings, and considers the main approaches to strategies for employment promotion. The context within which the decent work objective is approached will differ from country to country. What is possible will depend in part on the type of economy in question, in terms of income per head, importance of wage employment and government role – whether industrialized, transition

or developing. It will also depend on the nature of the labour market
– whether it is more or less flexible. The author therefore suggests a six-
category typology of countries for the discussion of policy. The focus of
the policy discussion is on the demand for labour, an approach that puts
increasing productivity at the centre of a decent work strategy. At the same
time it is necessary to improve the "integrability" of labour-market outsiders to enable them to take advantage of any increase in labour demand.
How this may work differs between the six categories of country. In the
industrialized countries the prospects for growth in demand for labour are
extremely uncertain and macroeconomic policies that are "supportive of
activity" are needed. In transition countries, whether flexible or inflexible,
the prime means of increasing demand for labour is further overall economic reform. Among the developing countries ways of increasing demand
for labour are likely to vary widely. The author stresses the importance for
a decent work strategy of workers gaining (or regaining) control of their
own destiny, and emphasizes the relevance of the ILO Declaration on
Fundamental Principles and Rights at Work of 1998 for this objective.

Chapter four by Ashwani Saith, *Social protection, decent work and development*, points out that the decent work concept can embrace the agendas of
poverty reduction, human development and social integration. The concept makes it possible to address the full range of development concerns
and to question the nature of the structures and processes that reproduce
the cycles of poverty and exclusion. The author considers the issue of a
trade-off between decent work and economic growth. An understanding
of the synergetic and sequential relationships could inform the phasing of
policies addressing various decent work components. This chapter argues
that the notion of decent work needs to be considered within a broad
development context, rather than in a narrow focus on the workplace or
enterprise alone. Hence the agenda for decent work, and for universalizing social protection, must engage with wider processes and policies of
development.

Chapter five by Sarosh Kuruvilla, *Social dialogue for decent work*, explores
the concept of social dialogue and proposes a number of indicators to
measure its nature and strength. The guiding principles are as follows:
measures of the rights underpinning social dialogue are clearly necessary
but they are not sufficient, as we need good measures of the actual practice
of social dialogue as well; there is also a need for interpretations of the
elements involved by experts with an intimate knowledge of the national
system concerned; the measures must take account of the large number
of people who have no representation rights, as well as those who are not
in traditional employment relationships; the measures must be dynamic,
comprehensive, valid and transparent; and, finally, the costs involved in
collecting data for the measures and the actual assessment exercise must

be sufficiently low. The methodology advocated by the author involves the creation of "National Social Dialogue Data Sheets", that incorporate information on 28 quantitative and qualitative indicators /measures of social dialogue. The approach taken in developing this framework deals with the conceptual issues noted above, as well as the problems with earlier approaches. The chapter concludes with a discussion on the trade-offs between validity and reliability in the measures proposed.

The contents of the present volume were commissioned as a set of special studies on decent work by the Education and Outreach Programme of the International Institute for Labour Studies. Thanks are due to A.V. Jose for organizing and managing this work, and for his substantive contributions. This volume consists of signed articles, under the responsibility of their authors, rather than a definitive ILO statement, and indeed the concept of decent work is still being deepened and elaborated. But the contributions in this book aim to help clarify the concept and make it more accessible. The volume is addressed to officials in government, trade unions and employers' organizations, as well as to academics and policy-makers interested in the well-being of all in the world of work.

I would also like to record my appreciation of the contribution made by Dharam Ghai, who helped in organizing the studies and acted as general editor of the publication. In addition, Barbara Cooper, Sophie Lièvre and Vanna Rougier provided valuable assistance in the production of the present volume.

Gerry Rodgers
Director
International Institute for Labour Studies

November 2005

Contents

Chapter II
Rights at work   *Bob Hepple*

Chapter III
Employment dimensions of decent work:
Trade-offs and complementarities   *Martin Godfrey*

Tables

Figures

Boxes

Chapter IV
Social protection, decent work and development   *Ashwani Saith*

Chapter V
Social dialogue for decent work   *Sarosh Kuruvilla*

Chapter I
Decent work:
Universality and diversity

Dharam Ghai

Summary

This paper seeks to discuss a few of the analytical issues posed by the decent work paradigm. The first point relates to the theoretical and conceptual contributions made by the paradigm. We argue that its principal contribution consists in providing a unified framework for analysis of work integrating issues of rights, the quality and quantity of employment, social security and voice and representation. This framework clearly reveals potential complementarities and conflicts among the different components of decent work, thus throwing light on the complex issues of priorities and sequencing in attaining decent work objectives. The paper also proposes a typology of models to take account of country diversity with regard to decent work concepts and policies.

The paper then discusses the four components of decent work, focusing on their objectives and policies for advancing rights at work, opportunities for remunerative employment and access to social security and for strengthening social dialogue. The last section of the paper focuses on decent work indicators and performance. It discusses the nature and type of indicators, difficulties encountered in the choice of indicators, the construction of indices of decent work and of its components, and the use and results of such indices in mapping the patterns and performance of decent work in different countries.

A distinguishing feature of the discussion throughout the paper is the attempt to relate these issues to diversity among countries in their economic structure, institutional configuration and stage of development. This brings out the universality and richness of the decent work paradigm.

Introduction

The ILO Director-General Juan Somavia introduced the concept of decent work, in his first report to the International Labour Conference in June 1999, in the following words:

The primary goal of the ILO today is to promote opportunities for women and men to obtain decent and productive work, in conditions of freedom, equality, security and human rights (ILO, 1999, p.3).

Since its formulation in 1999, ILO has undertaken a considerable number of conceptual, empirical and operational studies on the decent work paradigm. The studies have comprised an elaboration of models, strategies and policies; the development of indicators and indices on decent work; empirical investigation of interrelationships among different components of decent work; and promotion of decent work approaches at the country level.

The purpose of this paper is to provide an analytical introduction to the concept and substance of decent work. It draws upon the research carried out by ILO to address a number of questions that are often raised in discussions on decent work. What is the intellectual contribution of the decent work paradigm in the ILO context? Is the concept of decent work applicable only to countries with a certain economic structure and institutional configuration, or is it valid across countries with different development levels, economic structures and socio-economic institutions? Can the different country situations be grouped into typologies or models of decent work sharing common characteristics?

What are the goals and main features of the various dimensions of decent work? Are the different components interrelated, and if so, in what ways? Is there an appropriate sequencing of steps that need to be taken to achieve the goals of decent work? Is it possible to develop indicators and map the performance of decent work in different countries? It is of course not possible to give definitive answers to all these questions but their discussion illuminates some crucial dimensions of the goals and strategies of decent work.

Two cross-cutting themes also receive some attention in the paper. The first concerns the ways in which gender issues fit into the concept and policies of decent work. The second relates to how accelerating globalization in the last two decades affects efforts to attain the objectives of decent work.

The structure of the paper reflects the sequence of issues raised above. The discussion on the intellectual contribution of the decent work paradigm is followed by a consideration of the universality of its goals and a typology of models of decent work. The paper then discusses the goals and features of the four decent work components namely, rights at work, employment, social security and social dialogue. This leads to an analysis of the interrelationships among the decent work components. The paper concludes with a discussion of indicators and measures of decent work performance.

1. The contribution of the decent work concept

The decent work concept reflects both continuity and innovation in ILO thinking on work-related issues. At a minimum, it may be regarded as a device to capture in a simple and succinct manner the essence of ILO's mission and areas of work. Since its foundation in 1919, ILO has focused its efforts on promoting rights at work, employment, social security and industrial relations. This is reflected not only in its thematic reports, policy advice, training and operational activities, but most of all in the numerous Conventions and Recommendations the Organization has promulgated over the past 85 years. These labour standards provide the legislative framework for policies relating to all four components of decent work in countries around the world.

But the intellectual contribution of decent work goes beyond giving an elegant expression to ILO's objectives and areas of work. Substantively, it lies above all in providing a unified framework for its major areas of work. Without this framework, it is all too easy and tempting to treat ILO efforts in the four areas in a separate and self-contained manner. This indeed has been the general practice in the functioning of the Office for most of the time. The decent work framework draws attention to the relationships between its different components in at least three distinct ways.

First, it points to the different domains of operation of these components. For instance, rights at work pertain primarily to the domain of norms and legislation, although their implementation depends heavily upon adequate capacity, institutions and resources. Likewise, social dialogue is in the first instance a matter of providing a suitable legislative and institutional infrastructure. In contrast, the achievement of employment and social security objectives requires substantial real resources, in addition to an enabling policy and institutional environment. The different domains of decent work components thus bring together questions relating to rights at work, voice and representation, and human security and employment. Their differential demands on scarce resources are pertinent to the formulation of plans to achieve decent work goals.

Second, the decent work framework exposes and invites an analysis of the complementarities and trade-offs among its different components. For instance, does social security have an adverse effect on the volume

3

of employment? Does social dialogue lead to higher productivity and improved remuneration? Is there a conflict between the quality and quantity of employment? What is the impact of collective bargaining on the volume of employment? The decent work framework seeks to provide policy and institutional options that optimize the synergy among its different components.

Last, the decent work paradigm provokes questions about its universality and particularity. A criticism that has been leveled against ILO's traditional work on standards, employment, social security and industrial relations is that it is based on the model of industrial market economies and is applicable at best only to the formal sectors in other countries, thereby excluding large swathes of their economies and working people. The overall approach and terminology of the decent work framework lends itself more easily to analysis of structural and institutional diversity, thus facilitating a universalistic approach to the world of work. The next section elaborates on this point.

2. The decent work paradigm

The decent work paradigm is in principle applicable to all working people in all societies. The objectives of decent work are valid across the full spectrum of institutional and developmental diversity. Working people in all societies desire freedom of association and oppose discrimination, forced labour and child employment in hazardous and harmful situations. They wish to participate through social dialogue in decision-making affecting their work and lives, both at the level of the enterprise and the nation and at regional and global levels. Likewise, all people and all societies desire work in conditions of dignity and safety and with adequate remuneration. Finally, a modicum of social and economic security in work and life is a universal aspiration.

Thus the objectives of decent work are of universal aspiration. But the institutional and policy framework for achieving these objectives must necessarily depend in each country and region on its history and traditions, the level and distribution of resources, the economic and social structure, the stage of development and a host of other specific circumstances. While each country needs to formulate its own decent work policies in the light of these specificities, it may be useful for purposes of discussion to group countries into a few categories whose members share some distinctive socio-economic characteristics.

One such categorization, drawing upon a classification by international agencies, divides countries into three groups or "decent work models".

These may be described as the "classical model" comprising industrialized countries; the "transition model" consisting mainly of countries that have transformed or are in the process of transforming from communism to a market economy; and finally, the "development model" incorporating developing countries. While there is quite considerable diversity within each category, the developing country group is quite exceptional in this respect. It may therefore be more illuminating to divide this group further into semi-industrialized and least developed sub-categories.

From the decent work perspective, the defining features of these models relate to the work status and sectoral distribution of their labour force or working population; the organization of the labour force into trade unions and other structured groups; and public expenditure and social security expenditure as a proportion of gross domestic product (GDP). The full relevance of these socio-economic features will become evident in our discussion on the goals and policies of decent work in the next section.

The classical model countries have a high proportion of their labour force in wage employment (typically 75 to 90 per cent); the great majority of the workforce is found in services (generally between 60 and 80 per cent) and industry (between 10 and 20 per cent). A relatively high proportion of workers are trade union members (typically between 25 and 50 per cent), but this proportion has declined considerably in most countries over the past two to three decades, due in part to the impact of sectoral changes in employment, technological advance and intensifying globalization.

Another feature of these economies is that public expenditure and social security expenditure represent a relatively high proportion of GDP – typically between 35 and 45, and 20 and 30 per cent respectively. But, as with union density, the proportion of overall government and public social expenditure has been declining in recent years in most countries – a reflection of the shift towards the privatization of social security and of budgetary pressures caused, inter alia, by growing global economic integration.

The European transition model countries, despite their relatively low per capita incomes, characteristically have a high proportion of their labour force in wage employment (typically between 70 and 90 per cent) and in industry and services (between 60 and 80 per cent). Likewise, a relatively high proportion of the labour force are trade union members (typically between 30 and 50 per cent). These proportions have of course declined sharply with the collapse of communism and are still in a state of flux. Again, we find that in relation to their per capita incomes, the proportion of government and social public expenditure is relatively high (between 30 and 40 per cent and 15 and 25 per cent for most countries). These unusual features of the transition model countries are for the most part legacies of their communist past. As these economies shift further from the communist patterns, they increasingly display features that are more typical of countries in their range of per capita income.

In the development model countries, a higher proportion of the labour force is found in "atypical" work situations: a relatively high proportion work as self-employed or family members, or in the informal sector – typically ranging between 30 and 50 per cent in semi-industrialized economies and 70 and 90 per cent in the least developed countries. The proportion of those in agriculture is also relatively high – in the range of 20 to 40 per cent and 40 to 70 per cent for the two sub-categories. Trade union density (the proportion of the workforce organized in unions) varies between 5 and 15 per cent, with only a few countries showing much higher proportions. Finally, government and social security expenditures generally constitute a relatively low proportion of GDP – between 20 and 30 per cent and 5 and 10 per cent for the semi-industrialized economies and between 10 and 25 per cent and 2 to 5 per cent for the least developed countries.

Some observers have suggested flexibility of the economy and labour markets as another way of categorizing countries. This criterion cuts across the four-fold classification proposed above. Flexibility refers to the range and extent of regulations pertaining to wages, employment, working conditions, social security, trade unions and collective bargaining, and to the prevalence of resource allocation by administered or quantitative methods. The fewer the government regulations in these domains, the more flexible the economy. In recent decades, there has been a worldwide trend towards liberalization, deregulation and privatization resulting in greater flexibility in national economies. The expansion in the scope and intensity of globalization has been an important contributory factor to this trend. The relevance of the flexibility criterion for decent work, as well as the other socio-economic characteristics reflected in the typology of models proposed above, is brought out in the following section.

3. Goals and features of decent work components

In this section we look at the four components of decent work with regard to their objectives, content and relevance in different country situations and the ways in which they might be promoted.

a) *Rights at work*

Rights at work constitute the ethical and legal framework for all elements of decent work. Their objective is to ensure that work is associated with dignity, equality, freedom, adequate remuneration, social security and voice, representation and participation for all categories of workers. Rights at work form part of the broader agenda of human rights, which in turn derive from a long tradition with deep philosophic, theological and juridical roots. Human rights have been variously regarded as natural rights deriving from nature, as supernatural with divine ordination, as moral and ethical rooted in humanistic philosophy, and as legal entitlements based on national legislation and international agreements. Their content has also tended to vary according to different schools of thought and ideological trends, evolving from the classical rights to life, liberty and property to a wider notion embracing political, civil, cultural, social and economic rights. The Charter of the United Nations and the Universal Declaration of Human Rights gave a powerful fillip to the human rights movement, endowing it with a universal meaning.

Evolution of rights at work

Rights at work have evolved through various phases in different countries starting with the industrialized world in the nineteenth century. Over time, they have expanded in content and geographical coverage. They now cover both the classical rights of freedom of association, non-discrimination and abolition of forced labour, as well as social and economic rights of collective bargaining, the provision of benefits on cessation of work, adequate remuneration, social security and safety and health at work. These rights resulted from prolonged struggles waged by trade unions, political parties and supportive movements as well as sympathetic individuals. They were facilitated by the establishment of the rule of law, increasing political franchise and related civil and political rights.

Some of the earliest rights related to the freedom to form trade unions, the abolition of forced and child labour, and the prohibition of work for women and children in dangerous and physically demanding occupations. This was the case for instance in the United Kingdom and some other

European countries. A social right such as the retirement pension was pioneered by Germany, where it applied in the first instance to state functionaries. In the early twentieth century, and more especially after the Second World War, the social and economic rights expanded rapidly in the industrialized world as well as in communist and developing countries.

Countries have adopted different approaches to the promotion of workers' rights according to their legal traditions and dominant ideologies. In continental Europe with its Roman law tradition, the preference has been for incorporating these rights in constitutions or formal legislation. The Latin American countries have also followed this route to establishing rights at work. In the Anglo-Saxon countries with their common law tradition, emphasis has often been placed on case law and customary law. The state has shown a preference for a legal framework creating conditions for the main parties – workers and employers and their representatives – to conclude agreements on matters of mutual concern, including social and economic rights. Many other countries in Asia, Africa and the Caribbean influenced by the Anglo Saxon countries have followed these approaches to establishing workers' rights.

Promotion of rights by international agencies

While the ultimate responsibility for creating and implementing rights at work rests with the national authorities, the international agencies have played an increasingly important role in this area. The UN Charter, the Universal Declaration on Human Rights and the Covenant on Economic, Social and Cultural Rights have acted as landmark documents in the struggle for human rights. In addition, a whole series of conventions, norms and declarations on women, children, migrants and indigenous people and on other themes by the UN and specialized agencies, have played a critical role over the past 60 years in shaping the approach and content of human and workers' rights worldwide.

But it is the International Labour Organization, created in 1919, that has had the greatest impact on the corpus of rights at work throughout the world. Its work in this field has been the more effective and realistic because of its unique tripartite structure with its Governing Body consisting of member States and representatives of employers and workers. At its very first session in 1919, the ILO adopted two Conventions relating to child labour and hours of work. Over the past 85 years, the Organization has adopted 185 Conventions and 195 Recommendations covering all the issues of interest to workers and employers. These have included matters relating to employment, wages, hours and conditions of work, social security, industrial relations, multinational enterprises, health and safety at work, and many others. They have also provided protection to vulnerable groups such as migrants, women workers, indigenous people and children against hazardous occupations, exploitation and discrimination. Likewise, many Conventions and Recommendations have been promulgated to lay down standards for specific industries such as transport, maritime, mining, agriculture, textiles, printing, telecommunications and home-based work.

Through its work over the past eight decades, the ILO has developed an impressive body of international labour law. This work has been characterized by a distinctive methodology and process. The first step usually consists of a general discussion on a thematic issue paper prepared by the Office. These discussions form the basis of a draft Convention or Recommendation that is scrutinized carefully by the tripartite constituency and legal experts. After adoption of the labour standard by the Governing Body and the Conference, the Convention or Recommendation must be incorporated into national legislation for it to have legal force. Once a country has ratified a particular labour standard, its compliance becomes subject not only to national judicial processes but also to ILO supervision and surveillance.

The states are required to submit periodic reports on their implementation of labour standards and the aggrieved parties can lodge complaints at the ILO, if in their judgement these standards have been violated. The ILO has established a Committee of Experts to examine the reports and consider the complaints. Separate machinery has been established for the Conventions relating to freedom of association. The ILO also has the possibility of sending experts to independently investigate a situation and report to the Governing Body.

Although there is provision for sanctions in the ILO Constitution in the event of persistent violation of ratified Conventions, this is resorted to only in extreme situations such as the practice of apartheid in South Africa or of forced labour in Myanmar. For the most part, compliance is secured through persuasion, pressure and shame. Thus the process is characterized by three features: achieving consensus through discussion, voluntary assumption of obligations with regard to labour standards, and compliance through persuasion and pressure, with rare recourse to sanctions.

Applicability and implementation of rights at work

Although no formal attempts have been made to rank rights at work by their importance, certain rights have been regarded as fundamental to the well-being of workers. The Declaration on the Fundamental Principles and Rights at Work adopted by the International Labour Conference in 1998 may be considered as a statement of such rights. These relate to freedom of association and collective bargaining, forced and child labour, and discrimination at work. These rights are considered so basic that their acceptance is regarded as a prerequisite of ILO membership. Certainly, they form the core of the rights component of decent work.

Although rights at work embodied in ILO Declarations, Conventions and Recommendations are considered of universal validity and relevance, it is clear that their applicability is conditioned by political systems, economic structures and stages of development. For instance, in communist and authoritarian political systems where power is monopolized by an entity or an individual, it is difficult, if not impossible, to achieve freedom of association, embodied for example, in representative and independent trade unions and employers' organizations.

Likewise, most of the rights at work assume an economic system where the bulk of the workers are wage employees. While, as noted above, this situation is approximated in developed countries, the developing and increasingly many transition countries display a more complex picture with a preponderance of workers in the self-employed, informal and home-worker categories. In the same way, some of the workers' rights, especially those pertaining to social security and adequate remuneration, may be more feasible in high income than in middle or low income countries.

The pattern of ratification and implementation of rights at work bears out to some extent the qualifications noted above. In this regard, it should be noted that the ratification of different Conventions is only a very rough index of the achievement of rights at work. The implementation of the provisions of ratified Conventions tends to vary a good deal by countries. While adequacy of resources and of institutional capacity are often the main explanations of such variations, the priority accorded by political authorities to the ratified Conventions, often reflecting the distribution of power among various social and economic groups, is also a key determinant of the performance of different countries.

b) Employment and work

Employment is a vital component of decent work. Employment in the decent work paradigm refers not just to wage jobs but to work of all kinds – self-employment, wage employment and work from home. It refers to full-time, part-time and casual work and to work done by women, men and children. For decent work to obtain, certain conditions must be satisfied. There should be adequate employment opportunities for all those who seek work. Work should yield a remuneration (in cash or kind) that meets the essential needs of the worker and the family members.

Work should be freely chosen and there should be no discrimination against any category of workers, such as women, migrants or minorities. Workers should be protected against accidents, unhealthy and dangerous working conditions, and excessively long hours of work. They should have the right to form and join representative and independent associations to represent their interests and engage in collective bargaining and in discussions with employers and government authorities on work-related issues. An essential minimum of social security also forms part of decent work. Some of these attributes of employment are discussed further under rights at work, social security and social dialogue.

Work that meets the above conditions is a source of dignity, satisfaction and fulfilment to workers. It motivates them to give their best efforts and furnishes a sense of participation in matters affecting their livelihood. It provides a propitious foundation for skills enhancement, technological progress and economic growth. It also contributes to harmonious working relations, political stability and the strengthening of democracy.

Diversity of employment situations

The employment situation varies sharply among different groups of countries. Often the major factor determining these differences is the level of development, or per capita income. But other factors can also be important such as the share of public sector expenditure and assets, and the amount and distribution of factor and resource endowments. For instance, countries with large public sectors often have a higher proportion of the labour force in wage employment. The relative importance and distribution of cultivable land and mineral resources can also have an important impact on employment structures, reflected in the relation between labour force and natural resources. For instance, countries where land is abundant and relatively evenly distributed are likely to have a higher proportion of the labour force in self-employment than those where land is scarce and the bulk of it is appropriated by large landlords or plantations.

Customary practices or legal regulations bearing on different sections of the population may affect their labour force participation. For instance, in many countries, social and legal constraints on women often confine them to working from home and reduce their opportunities in wage employment. Similar factors may affect the patterns of work of ethnic minorities or children.

Government economic and labour policies play a central role in influencing the pattern of work opportunities. Policies affecting the rate and pattern of economic growth, labour intensity of production and labour flexibility and mobility have an important impact on work opportunities and their distribution among different types of employment. Higher economic growth focused on labour intensive activities should generate greater employment opportunities than low growth dependent on capital intensive sectors and methods of production.

As noted above, a key difference among countries concerns the distribution of the workforce by status – wage employees, further broken down by formal and informal economy, part-time or full-time, self-employed and family members. Another important dimension relates to the sectoral distribution of employment in agriculture, industry and services.

The factors noted above affect the nature of the employment problem faced by a country. Analytically, one may distinguish between four main types of employment problems, encountered in varying degrees in most countries. The one most often referred to is the problem of open unemployment i.e. of unemployed persons looking for full-time or part-time jobs. This problem is found in all categories of countries – industrialized, transition and developing. Open unemployment gets worse during cyclical downturns, but it also has structural dimensions. Exceptionally, most industrialized countries experienced nearly three decades of full employment in the post-war period. But in many countries, the open unemployment problem reappeared in the 1970s and in some has persisted over the past two to three decades with only limited periods of low unemployment rates.

Two groups of industrialized countries have been relatively successful in limiting unemployment – those with highly flexible labour markets and meagre unemployment and welfare benefits, and those with a tradition of strong unions, social dialogue and generous income support and welfare provisions. The former are usually characterized by relatively high income inequalities and absolute poverty, while the latter have succeeded in combining relatively egalitarian income distribution with active labour market policies. A third group of industrial countries have limited income inequalities and poverty through generous social security policies but at the cost of high and persistent levels of unemployment.

Many developing and transition countries also suffer from high unemployment rates, often concentrated in urban areas and among the youth. However, in the absence of unemployment benefits and other social security measures, the employment problem often manifests itself in "underemployment" in the informal sector. Unable to get jobs in the organized sector, people are forced to eke out a living in overcrowded petty occupations either working for informal enterprises or setting themselves up as hawkers and providers of casual services. Typically, they have low incomes and little real work.

The third type of employment problem, encountered mostly in poor countries, including the transition economies, is the opposite. In this situation people work for long hours but for extremely low returns, inadequate to meet the essential needs of their families. This is typical of small farmers, rural workers and employees of petty enterprises. Women are often overrepresented in this category. The problem is essentially one of low productivity caused by antiquated technologies and limited skills.

The fourth type of work problem and possibly the most serious, concerns the excessive working hours for home-based women workers. The work load consists not only of household duties – bringing up children, cooking and looking after the sick and the aged – but also of fetching water and wood, and engaging in some income-generating activities within or outside the household to meet cash needs for food, clothing or medicines. The heavy work load takes a serious toll on health and generates excessive stress. In terms of numbers and gravity, this is far and away the most serious "employment" problem in the world, though seldom recognized as such.

Employment promotion

An effective employment strategy needs to be based on the integration of a host of economic and social policies. This is not only because of the multiple dimensions of work but also because employment is affected by an extensive range of macro- and micro-economic policies. These include macro-economic stability, trade and exchange rate policies, agricultural and industrial development and technology, credit, labour market, training and education policies, to mention some of the more important areas.

While appropriate domestic policies still play a crucial role in generating full and productive employment, the global environment is becoming increasingly important in determining growth and employment prospects. If the world economy is in recession, it is extremely difficult to follow successful employment policies, especially for smaller countries, which are ever more dependent upon the world market for economic growth and employment promotion. This brings out the vital importance of coordinating macro-economic policies at the global level, especially on the part of major economic players, to maintain high levels of aggregate demand and to pursue counter-cyclical policies.

Given the diversity of employment problems in different countries, it goes without saying that each country needs to fashion its own specific employment promotion policies. In some countries, the primary area of focus may be increasing the productivity of small farmers through such measures as security of tenure, access to credit, new technologies, improved marketing and better transport. In other countries, the priority area might be raising the productivity of the non-farming informal sector through better credit, marketing and training in business management. For other countries again, the primary bottleneck to productive employment expansion might be a labour force lacking appropriate skills or poor physical infrastructure – transport, power and communications.

In practically all countries, there is a need to devise women-friendly employment and work policies. These can comprise a wide swathe of social and economic policy. In some countries, it is necessary to combat legal and cultural barriers to women working outside the home. Almost everywhere, there is a need to eliminate open or disguised discrimination against women workers in recruitment, remuneration, promotion and training. Beyond that, states and enterprises must seek to adapt working conditions to the specific needs of women workers, including hours of work, crèche facilities and adequate maternity leave. There is also a need for a package of policies supportive of the efforts of women's groups engaged in income-generating and productivity-enhancing policies. As emphasized above, many women are overburdened with household and outside work. Their overwhelming need is for measures that will reduce the work burden, improve working conditions and increase productivity and remuneration.

While each country needs to devise its own policies to respond to the specificity of its employment problems, there are some general policy stances that seem relevant to a wide range of developing countries. There is increasing recognition of the importance of macro-economic stability and the use of market forces for sustainable growth and efficiency in resource allocation. Through its impact on the rate of growth, the volume of investment is an important determinant of the expansion of employment opportunities. Equally important is the labour intensity of the pattern of growth. A labour-intensive industrial and export-oriented strategy can be quite important for countries with appropriate factor endowments.

Small and medium enterprises generally use more labour per unit of output than big ones. An agrarian structure with a more even distribution of land and water provides more employment opportunities than one where land and related resources are concentrated in a few hands. A strategy based on infrastructural development – irrigation, roads, power, and improvement of the rural and urban environment – can make a significant contribution to employment creation. Similarly, policies that stress the provision of primary health care, literacy and basic education and elementary social security on a universal basis can generate appreciable employment opportunities for an educated labour force.

c) Social protection

The purpose of social protection is to provide security against a variety of contingencies and vulnerabilities. These include ill-health, maternity needs, accidents, unemployment, destitution, extreme economic fluctuations, natural disasters and civil conflicts. A sound social protection strategy should also address the needs of vulnerable groups such as orphaned or abandoned children, single mothers, female-headed households, widows, old persons in need and the disabled. Social protection policies should thus aim to reduce suffering, anxiety, insecurity and material deprivation. They should promote health, confidence and a willingness to accept technical and institutional innovations for higher productivity and growth.

The above definition of social protection goes beyond the more limited notion of security for work-related situations in at least two ways. First, the coverage of protection extends beyond the workers and even their family members to embrace vulnerable and insecure persons outside paid employment and indeed the labour force. Second, the contingencies and vulnerabilities are redefined beyond the conventional insecurities identified in the ILO Conventions on Social Security to include destitution, extreme economic fluctuations and natural and human catastrophes. This more comprehensive definition of social security has the advantage of covering the full range of vulnerabilities of all members of society, not just those of limited sections of the population, who are often among the more privileged groups in some countries.

The conceptually more adequate notion of social protection does not imply of course that all countries are in a position to design and implement the requisite policies and measures. The items and levels of social protection furnished to the population will naturally depend upon their past traditions, stages of development and resource mobilization. But starting with a more comprehensive definition of social protection should at least enable countries to make choices on priorities through a consideration of the entire spectrum of contingencies, hopefully through a democratic process.

Strategic elements in social protection

Historically, the responsibility for providing social security has devolved upon a variety of institutions such as families, clan members, charitable institutions, employers and local and central authorities. Even now the coverage of social protection in most societies is assured through these institutions, although the relative importance of each entity varies a good deal from one country to another and over time. In general, the more economically advanced a country, the greater the responsibility assumed by public authorities. In the poorer countries, the most important sources of institutional support for social protection continue to be families, community groups and charitable bodies.

In designing its social protection strategy, a country needs to address at least three interrelated issues: the coverage of social protection in terms of items and individuals; the organizational and institutional means of providing social protection; and arrangements for financing social support. With regard to the first issue, the list of contingencies and vulnerabilities is quite extensive, as seen above. Even the richest countries may find it difficult to finance all the potential items of social protection. It is therefore necessary to make choices through democratic means about priority items to be covered. The level and range of support provided can of course be increased over time with economic progress. The choices made by countries reflect their political traditions, the intensity of social solidarity, the level of development and institutional means for delivering social protection.

In rich countries, the problems of absolute destitution have been largely overcome. The emphasis of social security policies is therefore on mitigating work-related risks by providing unemployment benefits, pensions for the retired, compensation for victims of accidents, maternity leave, children's allowances, and health insurance. Welfare policies have also been designed to cater for the specific needs of vulnerable groups and those living in poverty. Changing work patterns, family structures and demographic profiles, together with intensifying globalization, have led to a critical evaluation of past social policies. The debates have focused mostly on the level of benefits and the balance between public and private means of financing.

In most developing countries, especially the low income ones, social protection policies must perforce focus on ensuring survival, relieving destitution and mitigating livelihood risks. Their needs can be grouped into three categories. The first comprises basic needs such as access to adequate nutrition, primary health care, primary education, clean water, sanitation and shelter. The second category relates to contingencies such as sickness, accident, death of the principal breadwinner, disability, old age, and the needs of vulnerable groups such as orphaned or abandoned children and widows. The third category includes natural disasters and civil conflicts that can result in massive destruction of property, livelihood and sources of support.

Apart from the identification of priority needs and of individuals and groups suffering from deprivation, social protection strategies must set up an institutional framework for the delivery and financing of social policies and measures. Social security may be financed through public resources or through voluntary or compulsory private contributions or a mixture of the two. The balance between the two alternative methods of financing social protection in a country evidently depends upon historical traditions, political forces and the structure and level of development of the economy. But their economic and social effects are profoundly different.

A system based largely on private financing has a minimal impact on the existing patterns of income distribution. Thus by definition, the scope and level of social protection enjoyed by different individuals and families will vary enormously. In particular, the poorer and the most vulnerable groups will be unable to meet even their essential needs such as adequate nutrition, basic health care, primary education and access to shelter, water and sanitation. Universal access to these services can only be ensured through public financing. Furthermore, in most countries, public financing of social protection services is, in combination with a progressive tax system, one of the most effective instruments of income redistribution and poverty reduction.

The extent of public financing is constrained by three factors. First, the level of development of a country, represented for instance by its per capita income, places limits on the resources that can be mobilized through taxation. Second, the political opposition to heavy taxation on the part of affluent and powerful groups sets further limits on a country's taxable capacity. Third, the disincentive effects of excessive taxation are an effective deterrent to ambitious social security schemes. In many cases, even if the resources could be mobilized, the limited institutional and technical capabilities of the public sector may constrain the effectiveness of its social policies. However, it is worth stressing that the public financing of a service or benefit does not imply public sector delivery or implementation. It is perfectly possible and is indeed quite common for voluntary and charitable bodies, community organizations and even the private sector, to deliver the services that are paid for by public authorities.

As noted earlier, in many rich countries, the past two to three decades have seen a reduction in the share of GDP devoted to social protection expenditure. There has also been a trend towards increased private financing of social security items such as pensions and health care. This is a general reflection of the trend towards neo-liberal policies. Many factors have contributed to these shifts in social protection expenditure, including the resistance to high rates of taxation, real or perceived inefficiencies in the public provisioning of social services and the pressures exerted by more intense competition associated with the quickening pace of globalization.

Similar trends have been visible in many developing countries. Apart from the global influences mentioned above, many of these countries have suffered from declining or negative growth since the 1980s, increasing debt burdens and growing budgetary imbalances. There is, however, growing consensus now about the importance for human well-being and sustained development of universal access to basic services and benefits. There is also increasing realization that these services can best be provided on a universal basis by a strengthened public sector.

There have been attempts in many developing countries to increase access to health, pensions and disability benefits as well as loans and credit through voluntary and community-based schemes. While such initiatives have made a positive contribution to social security coverage, their reach is inevitably limited. For effective universal access to basic services and benefits, there is no feasible alternative to state leadership in planning, financing and ensuring their implementation, even if the responsibility for their organization and delivery is shared with other institutions such as communities, local authorities, voluntary agencies or the private sector.

d) Social dialogue

Social dialogue provides voice and representation to participants in the production process. It is a means for them to defend their interests, to articulate their concerns and priorities and to engage in negotiations and discussions with other actors in the production system and with the public authorities on social and economic policies. It serves to empower the weaker partners in the economy and to bring about a better balance of bargaining power in the market place. Social dialogue can thus be a vital element in a representative and participatory democracy.

Diversity in work situations and priority concerns

Much of the literature on industrial relations focuses on the situation in economically advanced countries where the bulk of the labour force work as wage employees in the formal sector. Even in these countries the importance of the self-employed, the informal sector, part-time and casual employees, especially among women workers, and the unemployed, has tended to rise in most countries over the past 25 years. The classical system of industrial relations deals with the structures and methods of collective negotiations between the unions and the employers' organizations. There is a place for government intervention under certain conditions to facilitate negotiations or prevent economic damage resulting from strikes and lockouts. Typically, there is also provision for tripartite bodies to discuss social and economic policies, especially those relating to the production system.

For most of its existence the ILO has been primarily concerned with helping countries with the establishment and development of such systems of industrial relations. Although present in some form in most countries of the world, it should be stressed that this system of industrial relations is only one method of social dialogue, although the most important and the most discussed and written about. It is important to recall that it does not incorporate the majority of the world's workers, most of whom remain without institutional representation. Even within the framework of the dominant model, there is considerable diversity among countries on the coverage of workers and employers, centralization and coordination between their organizations, the collective bargaining systems and the role played by their respective organizations both in the production process and in social and economic policy-making in the tripartite councils.

A more general framework of social dialogue should accommodate the diversity of production systems and of organizational arrangements of the participants in these systems. As brought out in the preceding sections, in low income countries the predominant forms of employment comprise self-employment in farming and other sectors, home-based work and wage employment in the informal economy. A good deal of this work is carried out on a seasonal, part-time or casual basis. Many of the workers lack autonomous and representative organizations to articulate their interests and engage in collective bargaining and consultations on matters affecting their livelihood. But all over the world, new forms of organization have emerged to cater to the specific interests of workers in the non-formal sector.

These interests cover both direct livelihood issues as well as broader questions of social and economic policy. While wage earners in the informal economy, women workers and part-time and casual employees share most of the concerns of their fellow workers in the formal economy, the specificity of their situation may call for different priorities, different forms of organization and different ways of meeting their needs. For instance, women workers may give priority to flexible hours which make it possible to combine paid work with domestic and child-rearing responsibilities. They also need maternity leave and children's allowances as well as child care facilities. Women working from home are interested in rates of remuneration but also in arrangements for credit, raw materials, equipment, training and marketing. Most workers in the informal economy work for small enterprises with complex arrangements for apprenticeship and compensation and hours of work. All these need to be reflected in their organizational arrangements and negotiation priorities.

The self-employed sector exhibits vast diversity in most countries, ranging from highly paid professionals to hawkers plying their trade in overcrowded streets. In agriculture, the differences are equally striking, ranging from large prosperous farmers to insecure tenants working their tiny holdings. Once again these differences must be reflected in the nature of organizations and the agenda for negotiations. For instance, independent professionals may have a special interest in tax provisions, while "entrepreneurs" in the tiny informal sector are more concerned with government regulations affecting their activities. They need credit facilities and assistance with improving their technical skills, and the design and marketing of their products. Large farmers are likely to press for better prices for their products and access to new technology and better roads, while share-croppers and tenants may be concerned with security of tenure, crop sharing arrangements and access to credit.

Diversity of organizations and social dialogue

A large variety of organizations has emerged to cater to the specific needs of atypical workers and employers. Trade unions have been, and are still, the most important organization for wage employees. They pioneered the principles and forms of organization that have continued to influence all organizations of workers. These include democratic representation, autonomous organization, accountability to members and non-discrimination. The trade unions have historic achievements to their credit in promoting the bargaining power of workers, improving their remuneration and working conditions and ensuring their participation in work-place decisions and in national economic and social policy.

Cooperatives are another tried form of democratic organization with a long history in many countries. Unlike the trade unions, cooperative members jointly own enterprises and provide common services such as marketing, credit and training. However, like the unions, cooperatives are based on the principles of democratic representation, accountability and autonomy. Cooperatives are to be found in all sectors – agriculture, industry and services. They may concern direct production or services such as trade, marketing and credit. Cooperatives can consist of single enterprises, or a federation of enterprises spread across or even beyond a country. Membership may be drawn from a given locality or from across the country. Apart from the direct production or service function, cooperatives engage in consultations and negotiations with other enterprises and public authorities on such issues as taxation, credit, transport, marketing and purchase of goods and services.

Other forms of organizations have emerged to cater to other categories of workers and employers. There has been an explosive growth of informal economy entrepreneurs, stimulated above all by the expansion of micro-credit schemes. Informal economy operators have come together to form their own organizations to negotiate with governments, suppliers, credit institutions and marketing and trading firms. These organizations give members an opportunity to participate in formulating common stands on these issues. They also provide an opportunity to launch joint schemes such as credit and savings programmes, health and life insurance and other types of mutual help activities.

Women workers are especially active in such ventures. In addition, women entrepreneurs and workers have formed their own organizations in different sectors. These cover all sectors and services. Typically, they are multipurpose organizations combining production with trading, and credit and savings with social insurance and social services such as family planning, nutrition, child care, literacy and training. Again there is enormous variation in their size ranging from a few members to hundreds of thousands, although most are relatively small. The organizational structures exhibit considerable variety. Some are quite informal, with no written constitution or regular meetings. Others, mostly large ones, have elaborate structures, providing for general assemblies, executive committees and autonomous management of different enterprises and services.

Community organizations bringing together producers or workers from a given area, rural or urban, have a long history in some countries. The members may be organized around economic activities or social projects. Generally, such organizations seek to combine economic, social, cultural and political roles in representing the interests of their members. In rural areas, peasants or farmers' associations are widespread in all countries. In some there may be separate organizations of tenants, share-croppers and workers.

Recent decades have witnessed the emergence of voluntary agencies working directly with small producers, and workers in unorganized sectors. Although they are not organizations of producers or workers, they play an important role in organizing them, furnishing material or advisory assistance and representing their interests in negotiations with local, national and international bodies, and with other enterprises. They have been important in promoting organizations of peasant farmers, informal sector operators and women workers and entrepreneurs.

Promoting social dialogue

Organizations of enterprises and workers are a vital part of a full-fledged and participatory democracy. They provide a channel for their members not only to work together on immediate issues affecting their businesses and livelihoods, but also to interact with other segments of society on issues of broader concern. They facilitate consultations with public authorities on a wide range of social and economic questions. Governments can play a vital part in promoting such organizations by providing an enabling environment and a suitable policy framework.

The single most important requirement is the existence of effective freedom of association for all citizens to form organizations of their own choosing. This in turn requires not only a suitable legal framework but also its full implementation in terms of appropriate procedures and facilities at all levels, as laid down in the ILO Conventions on freedom of association. Governments can also do much to ensure the autonomy, representativity and accountability of such organizations.

Further, they could create institutions and mechanisms such as tripartite bodies, national economic and social councils and planning commissions with full representation of all significant organizations of workers, enterprises and voluntary agencies. It is particularly important to ensure that women in all their roles, including domestic responsibilities, are fully represented in these bodies. This should contribute to improved policy-making and implementation and a more effective representation of the interests of the weaker and vulnerable segments of society.

4. Decent work components: Interdependencies and priorities

The four components of decent work influence each other in a myriad of ways. This section looks at these interdependencies and potential complementarities and at the conflicts between them. The essence of the decent work approach is to maximize the synergies among its different elements and find policy and institutional options to overcome conflicting relationships and constraints.

Illustrations of interdependencies

Rights at work affect all aspects of work. For instance, rights to a minimum wage and a healthy working environment affect the form and volume of employment. The right to freedom of association and collective bargaining has consequences for the degree and pattern of social protection. It also affects the nature and substance of social dialogue.

Social dialogue provides a vehicle for negotiations on rights at work such as social security, minimum wages and conditions of work. Social dialogue also makes it possible to influence the implementation of these rights, as well as to monitor achievement. Collective bargaining has an obvious impact on the structure, level and conditions of employment. It also provides a forum for negotiations on the form and content of social security. Tripartite and broader forms of social dialogue involving governments, enterprises, workers and civil society agencies exercise an influence on all dimensions of decent work through their impact on macro-economic and other key social and economic policies.

Employment levels and status affect social security in obvious ways. High levels of remunerative employment obviate the need for certain types of social security. The content, delivery and financing of social security are influenced by the proportion of the labour force in different work categories. The latter also have an impact on the form of worker and enterprise organization and mode of negotiations. Employment levels and remuneration affect the content of collective bargaining. They also

Figure 1. Interdependence between rights at work, employment, social security and social dialogue

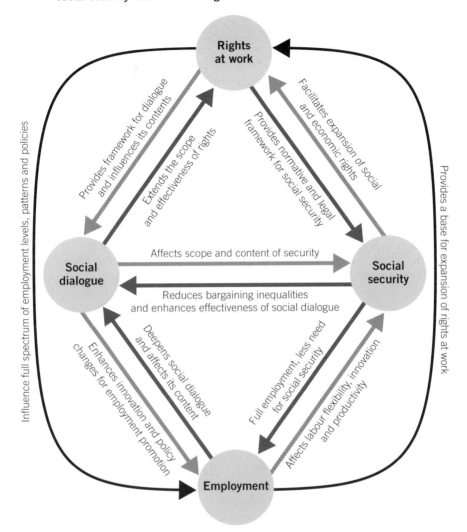

affect the ability of workers to negotiate on a range of issues pertaining to rights at work.

The links between social protection and the other components of decent work are self-evident. The coverage and benefit levels of social security affect employment through their impact on labour supply, investment levels, productivity and worker response to change and innovation. They also influence the bargaining power of workers in social dialogue and their ability to secure other rights at work.

These interdependencies are brought out graphically in figure 1.

Complementarities or conflicts

While there is general agreement on the interdependence between elements of decent work, there are sharp differences of views on their nature and direction. Broadly speaking, two distinctive schools of thought have tended to hold opposing views. With some oversimplification, these might be described as neo-classical and institutional schools. The former holds that state and other interventions in the free functioning of market forces, unless designed to correct market failures, lead to inefficiencies in resource allocation and hence to slower growth, wage and employment expansion and material progress for workers and enterprises. The institutionalists, on the other hand, maintain that apart from correcting market failures, interventions that establish rights at work, collective bargaining, tripartite consultations, minimum wages and social security, contribute to political and social stability, reduced economic inequalities and higher productivity, innovation and risk-taking.

In concrete terms, adherents of the neo-classical school argue, for instance, that interventions such as minimum wages, social security financed through taxation or levies on enterprises, and collective bargaining have an adverse impact on growth, employment and wages because of disincentive effects on investment, savings, innovation and risk-taking. Some of these measures such as unemployment benefits and welfare payments also tend to exacerbate unemployment.

The institutionalists contend that state interventions tend to mitigate economic fluctuations and help maintain economic activity and employment at high levels. Minimum wages and social protection serve to improve worker productivity through improved nutrition, better health and greater security. Trade unions, collective bargaining and tripartite consultations provide a mechanism for worker participation and information sharing, thus increasing mutual trust, sense of responsibility and motivation for better work. All this should lead to fewer conflicts, higher productivity and better quality of work. Income security during periods of unemployment enhances workers' receptiveness to technological change and acts as an incentive to the acquisition of new skills.

In the context of developing countries, both the preceding arguments are somewhat modified to take into account their economic and social differences. Many economists argue, for instance, that the setting up of minimum wages and the operation of trade unions and collective bargaining have particularly negative economic and social effects because they apply only to a small minority of the labour force. They distort the economies, accentuate inequalities among the working people and hold back investment and job creation. The establishment of social security schemes under these conditions has a similar negative impact, according to them, further eroding the competitive position of developing countries in an increasingly integrated global economy.

Institutional economists, on the other hand, argue that precisely because of extreme underdevelopment and mass poverty, the state has to play a more important role in relieving destitution, overcoming structural barriers to growth and building institutions, including trade unions and market systems, and encouraging enterpreneurship and innovation. This requires a more active state role in regulating monopolies, promoting nascent industries, encouraging social institutions and providing security for the vulnerable groups.

The contrasting positions taken by the two schools of thought have not been fully resolved by empirical research. Those in favour of free markets, including flexible labour markets, have pointed to the superior economic performance of countries with fewer state interventions and labour standards such as Australia, Chile, Hong Kong (China), New Zealand and the United States. They also hold up the impressive economic performance of the South East and East Asian countries, and of China, Vietnam and now India, as examples of economic reforms spurring rapid growth, employment generation and poverty reduction.

Other scholars draw the opposite conclusion from the same data set. They attribute the superior economic performance of most Asian countries to a carefully thought-out policy of active state intervention in a variety of areas. They further point to the excellent social and economic performance of countries such as Austria, Ireland, the Netherlands, and the Nordic group. Their success has resulted from combining free market policies with extensive social security and active labour market policies, supported by institutional cooperation between strong trade unions, employers' organizations and the public authorities. These researchers also point to the relatively poor performance of most African and Latin American countries since they initiated free market policies in the 1980s.

More specific research, investigating for example the impact of minimum wages, of collective bargaining systems and of core labour standards on investment, growth, employment and poverty reduction, has yielded mixed results. It is difficult to draw any clear-cut conclusions. Evidently a great deal depends upon the nature and extent of state interventions and labour standards, the manner in which they are introduced and the social, economic and institutional features of the countries concerned. There is, however, widespread agreement that respect for fundamental civil, political and social and economic rights, including core labour standards, is essential for human dignity and indispensable for political stability and sustainable and equitable development. The essence of the decent work approach is precisely to overcome potential trade-offs and constraints through institutional innovation, raising the capabilities of the working people and promoting social dialogue among the major social and economic groups and between them and the state authorities.

5. Indicators and patterns of decent work performance

The discussion so far has focused on the conceptual and analytical aspects of decent work. But what has been the pattern of decent work performance among countries and over time? Are there any distinctive patterns of decent work performance displayed by different countries? This section addresses these issues.

Indicators for evaluating performance

Decent work performance is measured by indicators relating to its different components. Indicators provide information on the extent to which a specified objective or outcome has been achieved. However, it is rarely possible to devise an indicator that measures "perfectly" a given objective or outcome. Because of conceptual and data limitations, indicators can at best give an approximate estimate of performance in a given domain.

Ideally, indicators should provide a direct measure of the specified objective. For instance, if the objective is a healthy population, the indicator should give information on the number or proportion of people who are sick. As this information is seldom available, recourse may be had to indirect measures such as life expectancy. Often it is difficult to give a precise meaning to a general objective. For instance, one of the attributes of decent work is remunerative employment, but the term "remunerative" must first be defined before a suitable indicator to measure it can be developed. Often it is more difficult to obtain a direct measure, so an indirect measure may have to be used. For instance, the nutritional status of children may be measured directly by intakes of various food nutrients, or indirectly (and more easily and cheaply) through weight or height for age. The accuracy and comparability of data are other issues that must be considered when selecting and using indicators.

There is rarely one single indicator of the desired outcome, and a combination of several may give a more accurate measure of a specified objective. Thus, the degree of gender discrimination in employment may be captured by wage differentials, opportunities for training, prospects for promotion and gender division of skills and responsibilities. Moreover, the indicators may be either quantitative or qualitative: for instance, quantitative indicators of social security may relate to the proportion of people receiving different types of benefits, while qualitative indicators concern the quality and effectiveness of services. Thus, in order to obtain an accurate picture it may be necessary to combine several indicators into an overall indicator or index.

Some analysts have proposed a three-fold classification of indicators: input indicators (policy variables), process indicators (institutional variables), and outcome indicators (data on the effectiveness of those policies and institutions). The different types of indicator are then combined into an overall index of the different components of decent work and of decent work as a whole.

The construction of an index raises questions about the weight to be given to different indicators, and also the formula to be used for combining qualitative and quantitative indicators. Similar but more acute problems arise when synthetic measures are derived by combining indicators from different domains. The Human Development Index developed by the United Nations Development Programme is an example of such a synthetic indicator combining indicators of health, education and income.

Decent work indicators

Any attempt to develop decent work indicators involves a decision on the choice of categories for decent work. The simplest approach – followed here – is to treat the four components of decent work as separate categories with sub-categories added as appropriate. A different approach used by some analysts is to classify decent work into eleven measurement categories: employment opportunities, acceptable work, adequate earnings and productive work, decent hours, stability and security of work, balancing work and family life, fair treatment in employment, safe work environment, social protection, social dialogue and workplace relations, and the economic and social context of decent work.

Another attempt at constructing indicators views decent work from the perspective of security. Indicators are developed for seven types of security – labour market, employment, job, work, skill reproduction, income and representational. Decent work is then measured at three levels – the macro (national), meso (enterprise) and micro (individual). The indicators developed under these two approaches have been included, when appropriate, in the list below which follows the original four-fold categorization of decent work. Some of them overlap, offering alternative measures. No attempt is made here to evaluate the suitability of these indicators for different country situations, including the availability and quality of data. Some of the items in the selected reading list given at the end of the paper deal at length with these issues.

The rights at work component may refer to all rights, including those covered in other decent work components – employment, security and social dialogue. But it is more convenient to discuss here the core rights that have been incorporated in the Declaration on the Fundamental Principles and Rights at Work. As seen earlier, these refer to child labour, forced labour, discrimination in employment and freedom of association and collective bargaining.

For child labour, the proposed indicators include the proportion of working children in different age categories (if possible by number of hours worked), the school enrolment rates of children, children not in school by employment status and children in hazardous work. For forced labour, there are no readily available indicators. A picture of the extent and gravity of the forced labour problem in a given country may, however, be built from the reports prepared by various organizations such as the ILO Committees on Labour Standards and on Freedom of Association, the ICFTU, Amnesty International, Freedom House and other human rights bodies. All such reports in the end depend upon information collected nationally through a variety of means such as interviews, testimonies, surveys and in-depth research in specific localities.

Discrimination at work may be based on race, colour, sex, language, political opinion or social origin. Indicators on discrimination may be illustrated with reference to gender. These comprise the ratification and enforcement of ILO Conventions on discrimination and equal remuneration; the female labour force participation rate or employment-to-female working age population ratio; the unemployment rate; differences in earnings (and other benefits); occupational segregation by sex; and female share of employment in managerial and high level administrative posts. While information on gender indicators is available for many countries, there is a great scarcity of data on ethnic, racial or linguistic minorities. This makes it difficult to develop any worthwhile indicators on discrimination against them in the labour market.

Indicators on freedom of association comprise ratification and enforcement of ILO Conventions on freedom of association and collective bargaining; the proportion of workers in trade unions or similar organizations; information on freedom of association contained in country reports by ILO and other international bodies and human rights organizations.

The **employment** component of decent work comprises opportunities, remuneration and conditions of work. The indicators relating to opportunities include the ratification and observance of relevant Conventions; labour force participation rate; employment-to-working age population ratio; the unemployment rate; youth unemployment rate; share of wage employment in non-agricultural labour force; excessive working hours; time-related underemployment rate; and job insecurity. Adequacy of remuneration may be measured by percentage of workforce earning less than the minimum wage or than one-half of the median rate; and proportion of workforce living in poverty. Indicators on conditions of work include observance of relevant Conventions; fatal occupational injury; incidence of sickness among workers; and labour force inspection.

Indicators on **social security** include ratification and implementation of relevant Conventions; proportion of workers covered against main contingencies and receiving benefits in respect of sickness, unemployment, old age, maternity, disability etc; adequacy of benefits received under these heads; public social security expenditure as proportion of GDP; public expenditure on needs-based cash income support as proportion of GDP; and levels of deprivation in specific areas such as nutrition, health, education and poverty among vulnerable groups.

Indicators on **social dialogue** include ratification and observance of ILO Conventions on freedom of association and collective bargaining; proportion of workers covered by collective bargaining agreements; participation in workplace decision-making; and participation by workers, employers and civil society organizations in national policy-making bodies.

Patterns of decent work performance

The indicators given above may be used for constructing indices of performance for individual categories or for decent work in its entirety. In both cases, it is necessary to specify a methodology for giving values and weights to indicators to arrive at indices for individual categories or for decent work as a whole.

It is clear that different patterns and results of performance may be obtained depending upon the indicators and the valuation methodology used. The different attempts that have been made to measure decent work performance use different indicators and valuation systems, and they do not cover the same number of countries. It is therefore not surprising that they do not yield exactly similar results. On other hand, there is a good deal of overlap in their results. Often the same groups of countries come at the top and at the bottom of the performance tables. The methodology used and the results yielded by the various attempts to measure decent work performance may be consulted in the list of publications provided below.

Without listing the countries by patterns of performance, it may nevertheless be useful to make some general remarks on the results yielded by these studies. First, there appears to be a relatively high correlation between decent work performance and income per capita. Higher income countries perform better than lower income countries on decent work, but there are exceptions to this. Some countries with low incomes score high marks on decent work performance and vice versa. Among the high income countries, those pursuing social democratic policies appear consistently to top decent work league tables.

Similar results are obtained from regressions between decent work and the Human Development Index (HDI). This index was developed by UNDP and combines measures of longevity, education and income per head. As with per capita income, there are countries with low HDI and high decent work performance and vice versa. According to one study at least, the differences in performance with regard to different decent work categories are smaller in high than in low income countries.

Selected reading list

Anker, Richard; Chernyshev, Igor; Egger, Philippe; Mehran, Farhad; Ritter, Joseph, A. 2002. *Measuring decent work with statistical indicators*, Working Paper No. 2, Policy Integration Department, ILO, Geneva.

Baccaro, Lucio. 2001. *Civil society, NGOs, and decent work policies: Sorting out the issues*, Discussion Paper No. 127, International Institute of Labour Studies, ILO, Geneva.

Dore, Ronald. 2004. *New forms and meanings of work in an increasingly globalized world*, International Institute of Labour Studies, ILO, Geneva.

Egger, Philippe; Sengenberger, Werner (eds.) 2003. *Decent work in Denmark: Employment, social efficiency and economic security*, International Labour Office, Geneva.

Ghai, Dharam. 2002. *Decent work: Concepts, models and indicators*, Discussion Paper No. 139, International Institute of Labour Studies, ILO, Geneva.

Godfrey, Martin. 2003. *Employment dimensions of decent work: Trade-offs and complementarities*, Discussion Paper No. 148, International Institute of Labour Studies, ILO, Geneva.

Hepple, Bob. 2003. *Rights at work*, Discussion Paper No. 147, International Institute of Labour Studies, ILO, Geneva.

ILO. 1998. International Labour Review, Volume 137, Number 2, Special Issue: *Labour rights, human rights*, Geneva.

ILO. 1999. *Decent work*, Report of the Director General, Geneva.

ILO. 2000. *Your voice at work*, Geneva.

ILO. 2001a. *Reducing the decent work deficit*, Report of the Director-General, Geneva.

ILO. 2001b. *Social security: Issues, challenges and prospects*, Geneva.

ILO. 2002a. *A future without child labour*, Geneva.

ILO. 2002b. *Decent work and the informal economy*, Geneva.

ILO. 2003. International Labour Review, Volume 142, Number 2, Special Issue: *Measuring decent work*, Geneva.

ILO. 2004 a. *Organizing for social justice*, Geneva.

ILO. 2004 b. *A fair globalization: Creating opportunities for all*, World Commission on the Social Dimension of Globalization, Geneva.

ILO. 2004 c. *Economic security for a better world*, Geneva.

Jose, A.V. (ed.) 2002. *Organized labour in the 21ˢᵗ century*, Geneva.

Kucera, David. 2001. *The effects of core workers' rights on labour costs and foreign direct investment: Evaluating the "conventional wisdom"*, Discussion Paper No. 130, International Institute of Labour Studies, ILO, Geneva.

Kuruvilla, Sarosh. 2003. *Social dialogue for decent work*, Discussion Paper No. 149, International Institute of Labour Studies, ILO, Geneva.

Majid, Nomaan. 2001a. *The size of the working poor population in developing countries*, Employment Paper 2001/16, Employment Sector, ILO, Geneva.

Majid, Nomaan. 2001b. *Economic growth, social policy and decent work*, Employment Paper 2001/9, Employment Sector, ILO, Geneva.

Peccoud, Dominique. (ed.) 2004. *Philosophical and spiritual perspectives on decent work*, ILO, Geneva.

Saith, Ashwani. 2004. *Social protection, decent work and development*, Discussion Paper No. 152, International Institute of Labour Studies, ILO, Geneva.

Chapter II
Rights at work

Bob Hepple

Executive summary

1. Introduction

This paper aims to develop a framework for thinking about rights at work, particularly in response to the argument that rights, such as those articulated in ILO Conventions, are of little relevance to the needs and conditions of most developing countries.

2. Concepts

a) Rights and goals

The rights of working people are based on ideas of social justice. Even if not legally enforceable, moral rights are claims to be treated with the dignity that befits a human being. Personal rights *(droits subjectifs)* – such as the right of association and freedom of speech – are negative rights in the sense of protecting the autonomy of the individual from coercive interference. On the other hand most social rights – such as the right to work, the right to social security and health care – require positive action by the state, and have to be progressively realized.

b) Rights and obligations

Another approach is to consider the agencies which are obliged to provide workers' rights (e.g. the state, employers). This makes rights specific, and allows us to determine who is to grant and who is to benefit from the right in question. So the rights and obligations of employers and workers (the "wage-work" bargain) are mutual. When discussing social rights we should carefully distinguish between those which are simply goals or aspirations and those which are effective because a correlative obligation exists.

c) Substantive and procedural rights

Substantive rights determine the conditions of labour (e.g. wages, hours). Procedural rights shape the processes by which substantive rights are created and enforced. In contemporary labour law, the emphasis is on procedural rights because it is widely believed that desired outcomes are best achieved by enabling employers and workers to make and enforce substantive rules, and that the role of the state is to ensure that certain minimum safeguards exist.

d) Principles and standards

Rights are derived from principles, such those set out in ILO instruments. The latter are usually referred to as international labour standards. These are considered to be universal but their application has to be flexible, so as to take account of different levels of development. A variety of flexibility clauses can be found in ILO Conventions.

3. Historical and comparative models of rights at work

The achievement of rights at work in each country is the outcome of complex, protracted struggles between different social groups. It is in changing power relationships that we can find the key to understanding the nature and extent of rights at work. The four models or ideal types described below will help clarify the different approaches to rights in various historical contexts.

a) The liberal state: Toleration and protection

Liberal constitutional states that emerged in Europe in the nineteenth century promoted ideas such as the freedom of contract and formal equality of employer and employee. Trade unions and collective bargaining came to be tolerated or even recognized. Protective legislation was enacted for vulnerable groups such as children and women, but this was generally not couched in the language of rights.

b) The social democratic welfare state: Equality, security and other workers' rights

This model emerged, for example in the German Weimar Republic (1919-33), and in the Mexican Constitution (1917). This gave constitutional protection to workers' rights and recognized collective solidarity as a means of protecting the individual. The aim was to achieve a fair balance between employers and workers. The idea of rights changed the character of protective legislation: it was no longer seen as the gift of an enlightened ruling class but as the right of the working people. However, some democratic states, especially the United Kingdom until the 1960s and other countries following the common law model, placed the emphasis on freedom of contract and voluntary collective bargaining rather than on individual rights. After the Second World War, ideas of social citizenship and social justice influenced the ILO and regional organizations such as the Council of Europe. A recent comprehensive statement of rights is found in the EU Charter of Fundamental Rights (2000). Another important feature of welfare states was the notion that in return for worker subordination to the commands of management, there would be a guarantee of security and participation.

c) The neo-liberal state: Deregulation

The post-war consensus has broken down since the 1970s. It is now generally necessary to justify regulatory interventions in the labour market, and there is a heavy burden of proof on those wishing to maintain workers' rights. Freedom of contract and of property are seen as the best way of raising standards of living and levels of employment.

d) The development model: Rights-based regulation

Critics of deregulation have put forward alternative versions of regulatory theory with a view to improving economic performance. This new model accepts that special regulation of employment, including a core of basic workers' rights, may be necessary to correct market failures and to forestall unacceptable market outcomes. Labour market institutions which encourage high trust and partnership are seen as leading to superior economic performance.

4. Key questions

a) Can rights at work be reconciled with competitiveness?

It is frequently argued that liberalization of trade and investment throws labour and welfare systems into competition with each other. This is put forward as a justification for limiting employment rights and their enforcement. There are several objections to this line of argument: (1) firms are not likely to relocate to countries with lower nominal labour costs if those lower costs simply reflect lower labour productivity; (2) if labour costs do not reflect relative productivity in a particular country, relocation would increase demand for labour and wage levels would rise; (3) low labour cost strategies trap countries into a downward spiral of repeated cost-cutting rather than giving them an incentive to increase investment in technology and skill creation.

b) What is the relationship between workers' rights and human rights?

Some workers' rights, such as freedom of association, freedom from forced and child labour and non-discrimination, are regarded as basic human rights. But, for a number of reasons, movements for workers' rights and human rights have followed parallel tracks. In particular, there is disagreement as to whether social and labour rights are human rights at all; NGOs have tended to focus on human rights while trade unions have concentrated on economic issues; and there is scepticism about the value of human rights which individualize interests that ultimately depend on collective solidarity. Since human rights cannot exist without social justice, it is argued that they should be formulated in a way that fits into a general framework of social justice.

c) How can workers' rights contribute to the alleviation of unemployment, poverty and inequality?

A conception of workers' rights limited to the classical model of subordinated workers and their employers does not embrace the wider interests of the unemployed, the working poor and independent producers in the formal and informal economies of developing countries. Poverty should be seen, as Sen argues, as the deprivation of basic capabilities. In pursuing the goal of equal capabilities we need to consider not only income but also opportunities to pursue a career of one's own, freedom of association, and the right to participate in economic, social and political life.

d) How should rights at work be progressively realized?

The starting point for countries that wish to realize certain social and labour rights is to distinguish three levels of obligation: (1) the obligation to *respect* a right; (2) the obligation to *protect* a right; and (3) the obligation to *fulfil a* right. The first is negative and is relatively cost-free, so it can be implemented immediately. The second means that the state must prevent violations by third parties (e.g. employers) either by establishing obligations of conduct or obligations of result. This may require some allocation of resources. The third obligation is a positive one and requires real resources, but these may come from sources other than the state – for example technical cooperation, partnerships with international organizations and so on. Action plans to realize the rights, within available resources, need to be conceptualized, implemented and monitored. (See the exercise after section 5.)

5. Policy options for implementing rights at work

a) The pillars of a new institutional structure for rights at work

The classical models of employment rights are plainly untenable in the developed countries and even more so in the developing countries. New directions may be found in a synthesis of traditional models with the modern approach of rights-based regulation as well as human rights theory. Such a synthesis needs to be based on at least four pillars: (1) dialogue between the many different orders that shape power relations (international, regional, national, corporate and local); (2) a new conception of the law of work embracing both employed and independent labour and not privileging certain forms of paid work; (3) the unification of public and private law so as to recognize emerging forms of collective representation as the custodian of individual rights; and (4) ending the traditional divergence between labour rights and human rights, utilizing ILO Conventions as the basis for a new culture of social rights.

b) Soft law or hard law?

Rights at work increasingly take the form of non-binding recommendations, corporate codes of conduct and guidelines (soft law). These instruments may help effective enforcement by amplifying legally binding standards and by recommending voluntary action that goes beyond minimum requirements. However, they have a negative effect when they are used as an alternative to binding instruments. Experience shows that codes do not succeed unless backed by sanctions. Regulation needs to be responsive to the different behaviour of various organizations, and must allow for a progressive escalation of sanctions to deter even the most persistent violator.

c) Public or private enforcement?

The growth of individual legal rights has led to an explosion of litigation in many countries. Alternative dispute resolution procedures, such as mediation and arbitration, are generally cheaper, speedier and more informal than court-based litigation. It is necessary to ensure that such alternative procedures are not simply used by corporate management to increase control and to deny rights, rather than to promote the public policy objectives of legal rights. The best way of doing this is to build low cost, speed, informality and conciliation into public law systems of rights enforcement.

d) How should restrictions on collective solidarity be redefined?

Transnational industrial action is subject to severe legal restrictions, even outright prohibition, in most countries. It is argued that where the decision-making power of enterprises crosses national boundaries, workers should be able to express solidarity beyond those borders. In particular, national laws should allow sympathy action, as a last resort, where there is a common interest between the workers involved in the primary and secondary actions.

1. Introduction

The purpose of this paper is to develop a framework for thinking about rights at work.

The ILO's model of *decent work* is to "promote opportunities for women and men to obtain decent and productive work, in conditions of freedom, equity, security and human dignity" (ILO, 1999). This has four elements: employment, social security, social dialogue and rights at work.

The attainment of rights at work, like the other objectives, is influenced by many aspects of economic, social and institutional structure (Ghai, 2002). Indeed, it is often argued that the concept of rights at work, as derived from ILO standards, is based on the classical employer-employee model in industrialized market economies, and that this has little relevance to the needs and conditions of most developing countries. The great majority of those countries share characteristics in which the language and culture of rights seem out of place. These characteristics are "widespread absolute poverty, extensive under- or unemployment, limited industrialization and dualistic economic structures" (Ghai, 2002, p. 6). There is a fear that the implementation of rights at work will put developing countries at a competitive disadvantage in international trade and in attracting foreign direct investment. This fear is reinforced by the ideology of neo-liberalism and deregulation: the belief that the state should have a minimal role and that "free" and flexible labour markets, supported only by private law rather than public intervention, are the best or only way to ensure economic development and, in the long run, improved conditions of work.

In order to clarify thinking on these matters, the paper starts with a discussion of the basic concepts of rights, goals, obligations, principles and standards. Secondly, four historical and comparative models of rights at work are critically assessed. These models are: (a) protection and toleration in the liberal state; (b) equality, security and other rights in the social democratic welfare state; (c) market regulation in the neo-liberal state; and (d) rights-based regulation in the emerging development model. Thirdly, the paper considers a number of controversial questions: (a) can rights at work be reconciled with competitiveness? (b) what is the relationship between workers' rights and human rights? (c) how can these rights contribute to the alleviation of poverty and inequality? and (d) how can these rights be progressively realized? In the final section, there is a discussion of policy options for realizing rights at work. This starts with a general review of the pillars of a new institutional structure for rights at work, and then considers some specific issues: soft or hard law? public or private enforcement? and how should restrictions on collective solidarity be defined?

2. Concepts

a) *Rights and goals*

What do we mean when we say that all working people have *rights*? The word "right" is ambiguous. First, there is a sense in which to have a right is to have a claim which can be enforced in a court of law, that is a *legal right*. To say that I have a right not to be dismissed without good cause, or a right to be paid in full the wages agreed with my employer is to assert a claim that forms part of positive law. If it cannot be enforced it is not a legal right.

A second sense of the word "right", which is different from a legal right, is that of a *moral right*. If I say that I have a right to decent work, or to fair pay, this does not mean that I am able to enforce that right. On the contrary, if I assert a moral right to decent work or fair pay it is likely that I do not think I enjoy these rights. We are most acutely aware of a moral right when it is not being conceded. *Moral rights* generally precede their recognition as *legal rights*. This does not mean that they cannot be realized without legislation. Voluntary arrangements and a general social consensus may support such moral rights without legal intervention. Legal rights become necessary when moral rights are not being observed. (In section 3 below there is a discussion of the processes by which rights have become recognized).

The rights of working people are based in ideas of social ethics, of what is considered to be good or just. We can find examples of what the international community believes to be good in documents such as the UN Declaration of Human Rights, the International Covenants on Civil and Political Rights (ICCPR), and on Economic, Social and Cultural Rights (ICESCR), and in the Conventions and Recommendations of the ILO. The Constitutions of many countries set out the basic rights of citizens. Although these are not infrequently a mere façade (as they were in the USSR Constitution), the iteration and formulation of moral rights in these documents gives them considerable political legitimacy. But the mere fact that rights are asserted in this way does not in itself amount to an ethical justification for them.

In ancient Greek philosophy, rights were justified on two main grounds. First, some rights, such as to equal freedom of speech, derived from an individual's status as citizen of a city-state. Secondly, rights were justified as deriving from the order of nature or from the nature of man, rather than from society or from history. These "natural rights" belonged to all free men at all times – slaves and women, however, were not included. Every free man everywhere was entitled to his "natural rights" by virtue of being a rational human being. In the European Age of Enlightenment the idea of natural rights was revived as a powerful argument against the divine right of kings and political authoritarianism. A political regime was regarded as legitimate only if it was based on these natural rights. Natural rights were said to derive from natural law, that is what is universally and immutably regarded as "good". What is "good" could be discovered by human reason. Natural law was regarded as a "higher" law than any law made by political authorities. Since natural rights, derived from this higher law, were inherent in the human condition, there was a smooth transition in the second half of the twentieth century from this to the phraseology of *human rights*.

The continuity from natural rights to human rights has had some important consequences. First, lists of rights have expanded as economic, social and political circumstances have changed. Starting in the eighteenth century with "life, liberty and property", by the mid-twentieth century the UN Declaration of Human Rights itemized 30 human rights, and there has been an explosion of rights in the second half of the twentieth century as economic, social, cultural, labour and environmental rights have been added. Secondly, natural rights are seen as assertions of *individual*

autonomy. Their function is to protect the individual from arbitrary interference by the state or other coercive bodies. For this reason traditional
rights are expressed as *negative rights*. For example, the right to life did not
involve commitment to a universal public health service or a safe environment. The inclusion of social, economic and labour rights among the list
of human rights has been one of the most controversial areas of debate.
This is largely because they require positive action by the state and other
bodies to provide resources for their realization, on a far greater scale than
is needed to secure observance of negative rights. For example, the right
to work might require the state to provide work and training or at least to
take measures to ensure full employment.

A third consequence of the thinking based on natural rights is that
a right is recognized only if it is demanded by *justice*. Unlike a legal right,
which is a right because it can be enforced, a natural right is justified by
natural law (see above). It is precisely this reliance on natural law which
has led to attacks on the idea of moral rights from both right and left.
Conservative thinkers like Edmund Burke and David Hume denied that
natural rights could be derived from natural law and disliked the "rights
of man" because this idea led those "destined to travel in the obscure
walk of laborious life" [i.e. the common people] to believe that they were
entitled to things which they could not possibly have. Liberal thinkers like
the Utilitarian Jeremy Bentham, too, were scornful: "from real law comes
real rights; but from imaginary law, from 'law of nature', comes imaginary
rights...Natural rights is simple nonsense, rhetorical nonsense, nonsense
upon stilts" (Bentham, 1843). Bentham was a radical. He objected to natural rights because they took the place of positive legislation from which
legally enforceable rights are derived. By the end of the nineteenth century,
philosophers and jurists generally came to agree that rights are based on
utility, and that they are historically shaped by cultural and environmental
factors unique to particular communities.

Although the idea of natural rights is no longer popular, the idea
of human rights took root with the rise and fall of Nazi Germany and
was renewed by dissidents in the communist states and by those struggling against colonialism and apartheid. The UN Declaration of Human
Rights recognized two sets of rights: civil and political rights; and economic, social, and cultural rights. There are abiding disagreements about
whether economic, social and cultural rights are "rights" at all (see section
4.b below).

To sum up, we can say that there are two conceptions of "rights". First
is the Western conception of *personal rights (droits subjectifs)*. This focuses
on the individual's autonomy and protection from coercive interference.
It is concerned with rights such as freedom of association and freedom
of speech. The second twentieth century conception is concerned with

fundamental social objectives and leads to the enumeration of rights such as the right to work, the right to social security, the right to adequate food, the right to health care, and the right to education. Although the lists of both personal rights and social rights are fairly systematic, they are not a complete statement of what is universally good or just, and they do not in themselves tell us which rights are to be given priority over others. For example, is the right of the unemployed to work greater than the right of those in employment? Labelling a particular right as "fundamental" simply begs the question as to why one right is more important than another. The only feasible way to uphold social rights therefore, is to recognize that they are not absolute, but have to be progressively realized.

b) *Rights and obligations*

There is another approach to rights, and that is to link them with co-related obligations. Any human right must have its counterpart in some obligation. The right to work is meaningless unless it is linked to an obligation on the part of the state to provide work. The right to equal opportunities is just loose talk if there is no obligation on anyone to ensure that it is fulfilled. Effective rights depend not on the claims of individuals, but on the existence of others who consider themselves in some way obliged to provide those rights. Several advantages are claimed for this approach (O'Neill, 1996, 2002). The first is that it overcomes one of the main objections to rights, that is their indeterminacy and high level of abstraction. By linking rights with obligations we can determine who is to give and who is to receive. The obligation must be described with reasonable certainty if it is to be acted upon. It may be a negative obligation, to desist from doing something, or it may be positive, to actively do something. But it has to be specific if it is to be secured; it must be what Immanuel Kant called a "perfect obligation". Secondly, a right without an obligation cannot be enforced. Only a right which springs from an obligation is capable of being effective. Thirdly, the obligations approach focuses on the *relationships* between right-holders and bearers of obligations, rather than simply on those who claim rights. So it is less individualistic than simply talking about rights. Obligations are usually mutual: for example, an employer owes a duty to pay wages in return for the worker's duty to perform the agreed work. We speak of a "wage-work bargain". Employers and workers have rights *and* obligations. We may owe an obligation to the whole world, for example, not to make anyone perform forced labour; or obligations may be owed to individuals to carry out our promises to them; or they may be owed to a specific class of people, such as our obligation to take reasonable care towards our neighbours or our work colleagues.

This insistence on a linkage between rights and obligations is not universally accepted. Amartya Sen (2000, p. 124) writes:

> Why demand the absolute necessity of a co-specified perfect obligation for a potential right to qualify as a real right? Certainly a perfect obligation would help a great deal towards the realisation of rights, but why cannot there be *un*realised rights?

According to this view a right may exist even though it cannot be realized because there is no specified person or agency to provide it. The fact that a right cannot be realized does not mean that it does not exist. This may appear to be simply a matter of language. But most lawyers and some distinguished philosophers believe that the close analogy between moral rights and legal rights is necessary if the ethical concerns of the human rights movement are not to be brought into contempt (O'Neill, 2002). The practical conclusion seems to be that when talking about social rights we should be careful to distinguish between those for which a correlative obligation exists, and those which are simply aspirations. We can measure the *extent* to which those aspirations or goals have been realized, even though they cannot be enforced.

c) *Substantive and procedural rights*

In broad terms *substantive rights at work* are those which determine the actual conditions of labour, such as minimum wages and maximum working time, and the right to equal treatment. *Procedural rights* are those which shape the procedures by which substantive rights are determined, such as the right to collective bargaining, the rights of workers' representatives, and the right to equal opportunities. One of the features of contemporary labour law is the emphasis on procedural rights which aim to encourage autonomous processes, in particular by supporting mechanisms for workers' representation and participation in corporate governance, rather than imposing particular substantive outcomes (Barnard and Deakin, 2002). This emphasis on procedural rights stems from the view that regulatory interventions are most likely to be successful when they seek to achieve their aims not by direct prescription but by enabling social actors (such as employers and workers) to make and enforce their own substantive rules. The objective is to encourage autonomous processes, in particular by supporting mechanisms for workers' participation.

d) Principles and standards

Rights are derived from principles. So the Constitution of the ILO sets out a number of principles of social justice, such as the principle of freedom of association, and the principle of equal remuneration for work of equal value. These principles are elaborated in Conventions and Recommendations, which also enunciate specific rights to give effect to the principles.

There is some lack of clarity in this respect between principles and *standards* (Murray, 2001, p. 11). The latter term is generally applied to the principles to be found in ILO Conventions and Recommendations, which are called *international labour standards*. The phrase *minimum standards* is applied to ILO standards which permit of higher standards, without any connotation that the standard is set at a low level. ILO standards are characterized by two features. First, they are universal and are intended to be applied in all member States that ratify the Convention. In the case of the Conventions set out in the ILO Declaration of Fundamental Principles and Rights at Work, the standards must be applied by all member States even if the Convention itself has not been ratified.

Secondly, the price of this universality is *flexibility*. If standards have to be universal, and therefore applicable to states whose level of development and legal approaches differ considerably from one another, the only realistic approach is to develop standards with sufficient flexibility so that they can be adapted to the most diverse of countries (Valticos and von Potobsky, 1994, paras. 96-105). A variety of flexibility clauses can be found in ILO Conventions, for example:

–   An option as to which obligations are accepted.

–   An option to specify at the time of ratification the level at which standards will be applied (e.g. as to minimum age, holidays with pay, etc.).

–   An option to describe the scope of the persons or undertakings or industries to be covered (e.g. in relation to hours of work, wages and maternity pay).

–   Allowing specific exceptions (e.g. allowing countries whose economy and medical facilities are insufficiently developed to have recourse to temporary exceptions in relation to health and social security).

–   Using promotional language stating the policy to be pursued without specifying any particular rights, and providing guidelines in a Recommendation as to how the objective might be progressively realized (e.g. equal remuneration for women and men).

–   Allowing flexibility as to the method of application, for example through collective bargaining or national legislation, or a combination of these methods.

3. Historical and comparative models of rights at work

One of the best ways to understand the relevance and application of rights at work in different countries and at different times is by the comparison of deductive "models" or "ideal types". Models of this kind, freed from specific national features, help to illuminate the common tendencies and divergences in different countries, but they are not a substitute for close analysis of the actual circumstances in each country or locality at a particular time. Rights at work have not developed as a series of evolutionary stages, or as a "necessary" or "natural" response to capitalist industrialization. The achievement of these rights in each country was the outcome of complex, protracted and bitterly contested struggles (Hepple, 1986, p. 4). The comparativist has to examine the specific features of historical change in each country in order to explain differences in the extent to which rights were recognized. For example, why was the workbook or "pass" system a feature of labour markets in some countries but not others? Why was the 8-hour day achieved in some places by collective bargaining and in others by national legislation? Why is "protection" treated as a gift from the state in some periods and as a "right" in others?

In seeking answers to questions such as these one has to examine how particular rights came to be introduced into each country. Rights at work are the outcome of struggle between different social groups – monarchy, bureaucracy and middle class; bourgeoisie and aristocracy; bourgeoisie and working class; townspeople and country folk – and of the competing ideologies of conservatives, liberals and socialists, and of religious and secular groups. The rights which any particular group obtains are "not just a matter of what they choose or want but what they can force or persuade other groups to let them have" (Abrams, 1982, p. 15). The crucial element in the making of rights at work is *power*. Many of the demands by labour movements and reformers were unsuccessful because they were unacceptable to those with greater economic and political power. It is in power relationships, which are rooted in social structure, that we may find a key to the achievement and denial of rights at work.

a) The liberal state: Toleration and protection

In pre-industrial societies the worker is a member of a closed society and a closed economy with little freedom of movement. In Western Europe this covered broadly the period before the French Revolution of 1789. The employment relationship was within the family or guild controlled by the head of the household or the master. Master and servant or apprentice, employer and labourer, had mutual obligations. So a master had to provide professional training to an apprentice and to protect him, while the apprentice had to swear obedience and loyalty to the master. Public authorities regulated the rules of the guilds.

Under the early factory system, the factory owners enjoyed almost absolute rights or prerogatives within their own domain. They could also rely on penal master and servant laws to enforce their rights or prerogatives, for example by imprisoning workers who breached their contracts, or who combined into trade unions or went on strike. The workbook (*livret* or "pass") system restricted the worker's freedom, especially on termination of employment.

The liberal constitutional states which emerged in Europe in the nineteenth century actively promoted liberal doctrines, purporting to leave the economy alone (*laissez-faire*). This was, of course, a form of intervention in the sense that it gave uncontrolled support to the power of property in the form of capital. Under the influence of liberal contractual ideas, the formal equality of employer and employee was proclaimed. The pre-industrial remnants of penal master and servant laws and laws against combinations were removed. Trade unions and collective bargaining were tolerated and sometimes gained legal recognition. The social problems resulting from industrialization, including the degradation of children and women, urban poverty, unemployment and strikes, became political questions. The enfranchisement of (male) workers increased the pressure for state action to ameliorate these problems. Protective legislation was enacted for workers who were regarded as particularly vulnerable, starting with children and women, and later for other groups of workers. This was generally described in terms of "protection" rather than in the language of rights. The subjects included the length of the working day, the fencing of dangerous machinery, minimum wages and other basic working conditions.

b) The social democratic welfare state: Equality, security, and other workers' rights

The challenges to the liberal model of toleration and protection came from two directions. One was from the Marxian socialists and communists whose primary aim was not to establish "rights" under a capitalist order. Their real objective was the assumption of political power by the working class so as to end the system of wage labour itself. In the Soviet Union this took on the distinctive Leninist form of the "dictatorship of the proletariat" (in reality the dictatorship of the Party). The centralized state took control of the economy and trade unions degenerated into "conveyor belts" between the "vanguard" Party and the workers. The protection, welfare and job security of individual workers was seen as the reward for loyalty and strict observance of labour discipline. "Evasion of socially useful work", declared Article 60 of the Soviet Constitution, "is incompatible with the principles of socialist society."

The other challenge was from the social democrats whose aim was to redress the inequality between the suppliers and the purchasers of labour power. Labour "rights" were demanded for subordinate or dependent labour. This idea comes from Gierke, Weber and Durkheim and it stands in contrast to liberal and neo-liberal theories which ignore the inequitable distribution of wealth and power in society. The social democratic model of rights was tried in the German Weimar Republic (1919-33). It also appeared in some other countries such as the Mexican Constitution of 1917. The aim of the social democrats was – in Kahn-Freund's words (1981, pp. 190-191) – "to legalise the class system in a class-divided society and to make it a component of the legal system." They did this by giving constitutional protection to workers' rights and enabling the works councils to act as custodians of individual protection. It was in the quest for some kind of substantive and not merely formal equality between employer and worker in a pluralist society that they put their faith. The fragile collectivist system of the Weimar Republic came crashing down in the economic crisis of 1929-33. The huge rise in unemployment which virtually destroyed the new state system of unemployment insurance, and the effective abolition of collective bargaining by presidential decrees, was followed by the victory of the National Socialists over a divided labour movement.

The theory of balanced industrial pluralism was still the dominant theory of labour law in the 1970s when Kahn-Freund (1976, p. 8; 1981, p. 18) wrote: "the main object of labour law has always been, and we venture to say, will always be, to be a countervailing force to counteract the inequality of bargaining power which is inherent and must be inherent in the employment relationship." Labour law was seen as providing institutions and processes, mainly collective, which created a fair balance between employers and workers. The focus was on subordinated workers within the employment relationship and not on wider aspects of the labour market. Labour law was regarded as serving primarily a social, and not an economic function. "Rights" were a useful tool to end the distinction drawn in liberal societies between the "private" sphere of economic life – what Adam Smith called civil society – and the "public" sphere of what was directly controlled by the state. This was conceptualized in Continental European countries in the distinction between private law and public law. In the liberal state protective legislation for groups such as women and children could be justified on the ground that these groups lacked capacity to contract as equals. The idea of "rights" changed the character of the legislation from a gift granted by an enlightened ruling class into a right of the workers. These new rights – such as the right to work – were different from the rights of the individual proclaimed in the French Revolution and in most liberal constitutions. They were claims on the state to provide work and economic security and to recognize the collective interests of workers through the rights to organize, to bargain collectively and to strike.

However, not all democratic states answered the problem of inequality in the employment relationship by the creation of "rights". For example, in the United Kingdom "Labourism" rather than any ideology of social rights was the dominant influence. The British approach was to defend social and organizational "rights" won through industrial struggle, using the law on a pragmatic basis only when voluntary means were inadequate. Instead of social revolution or social democratic constitutionalism, the ideology shared by the majority of employers and trade unions was a "very special, very British" variant of pluralism (Clegg, 1975). This, in its classic formulation by the "Oxford School", is in essence an ideology of "enlightened management". The focus was on equalizing the position of employers and collective organizations of workers "while leaving room for the continuing effects of market forces". By the 1970s voluntary collective bargaining between employers and trade unions had come to cover about 85 per cent of the workforce. Individual employment rights granted by legislation were mainly relevant in the absence of collective bargaining. However, from the 1960s onwards there was an increasing volume of legislation conferring rights on individual employees. Some of this fulfilled the function of what Wedderburn (1965) called a "floor of rights", that is a basis upon which collective bargaining could improve (e.g. unfair dismissal and redundancy compensation). Other legislation dealing with subjects outside the limited sphere of collective bargaining (e.g. race and sex discrimination) introduced the notion of fundamental human rights in the employment relationship. The decline of collective bargaining and trade union density since the 1980s in the United Kingdom have greatly enhanced the importance of individual rights.

In the United States, too, the approach was market-centred rather than rights-centred (Estlund, 2002). The ideal of free labour after the abolition of slavery became enmeshed with the idea of freedom of contract. Following the Supreme Court's decision in the *Lochner* case (1905),[1] almost every kind of legislation establishing employment rights was struck down as an unconstitutional interference with the right of employers and of workers to buy and sell their labour on such terms as they saw fit. The only guaranteed right was the liberty to contract without state protective legislation. However, in 1937 a new majority of the Supreme Court

---

[1] *Lochner v New York* 148 U.S. 45 (1905), which struck down a state law limiting the hours of work of bakers.

largely repudiated the constitutional liberty to contract. The Court upheld the National Labor Relations Act (NLRA) which prohibited discrimination against union activists and established a legal framework for union representation and collective bargaining. The Court also upheld the Fair Labor Standards Act which prescribed minimum wages and maximum working hours. What is striking is that these decisions were grounded in the federal government's power to regulate inter-state commerce, rather than on fundamental rights at work. Two major shifts occurred after 1960. The first was civil rights legislation against discrimination on grounds of race, gender, age and disability. The second was the development, largely by courts on a state-by-state basis, of individual legal rights, derived from the common law, on matters such as discharge from employment and the right to privacy.

With the coming of welfare regimes after 1945 protective legislation changed its character. New social rights were supported by theories of "social citizenship". Citizenship was seen as a source of social cohesion. Citizens enjoyed political rights (to participate in the exercise of political power), and civil rights (to make contracts, to speak and to associate). These political and civil rights provided the means to secure social rights (to welfare and security on the basis of equality with others). Social rights were regarded as a component of the concept of citizenship. At the end of the Second World War, the ILO's Declaration of Philadelphia (1944) espoused the language of rights. It proclaimed the principle that "all human beings, irrespective of race, creed or sex, have the right to pursue their material well-being and their spiritual development in conditions of freedom and dignity, of economic security, and of equal opportunity." Social rights were also set out in regional treaties such as the European Social Charter (1961, revised 1996), and in the International Covenant on Economic, Social and Cultural Rights [ICESCR] of 16 December 1966. This includes the right to work, the right of freedom of association for trade union purposes, the right to social security, the rights of the family, the right to adequate food, the right to health, and the right to education.

In the European Union an attempt has been made to set out all fundamental rights in a single integrated document, the Charter of Fundamental Rights of the European Union of 7 December 2000 [summarized in Box 1].

Another feature of the welfare states was a change in the nature of the wage-work bargain. In Supiot's words "under the model of the welfare state, the work relationship became the site on which a fundamental trade-off between economic dependence and social protection took place. While it was, of course, the case that the employee was subjected to the power of another, it was understood that in return there was a guarantee of the basic conditions for participation in society" (Supiot et al., 1999b, p. 8).

Box 1. Charter of fundamental rights of the European Union

Summary

Chapter I. Dignity
Art. 1.   Human dignity
Art. 2.   Right to life
Art. 3.   Right to integrity of the person
Art. 4.   Prohibition of torture and inhuman or degrading treatment
Art. 5.   Prohibition of slavery and forced labour

Chapter II. Freedoms
Art. 6.   Right to liberty and security
Art. 7.   Respect for private and family life
Art. 8.   Protection of personal data
Art. 9.   Right to marry and to found a family
Art. 10.   Freedom of thought, conscience and religion
Art. 11.   Freedom of expression and information
Art. 12.   Freedom of assembly and of association
Art. 13.   Freedom of the arts and sciences
Art. 14.   Right to education
Art. 15.   Freedom to choose an occupation and right to engage in work
Art. 16.   Freedom to conduct a business
Art. 17.   Right to property
Art. 18.   Right to asylum
Art. 19.   Protection in the event of removal, expulsion or extradition

Chapter III. Equality
Art. 20.   Equality before the law
Art. 21.   Non-discrimination
Art. 22.   Cultural, religious and linguistic diversity
Art. 23.   Equality between men and women
Art. 24.   The rights of the child
Art. 25.   The rights of the elderly
Art. 26.   Integration of persons with disabilities

This corresponds to the so-called "Fordist" model in which large industrial enterprises engage in mass production based on narrow specialization of tasks and skills and in a pyramidal organization of work. The worker is subject to the commands and organization of a hierarchy of management. In return the worker is promised a secure livelihood and a measure of job security. Social legislation in the fields of workers' compensation for accidents, social insurance and employment protection is enacted.

c) *The neo-liberal state: Deregulation*

The post-war consensus based on the notion of equality between employer and worker and support for collective representation has broken down since the 1970s. In place of the traditional ideologies, the focus has been on varieties of regulatory theories. These all take the market system as their foundation. They assume that individuals are rational beings motivated solely by self-interest. Through the mechanism of the market, individuals are able to satisfy their preferences of which they are the best judges, in this way increasing their wealth. Values are measured by what people are willing to give up, their lost opportunities. So for example, a woman who seeks part-time work loses the opportunity to be paid at the same rate as a man doing full-time work because of her "preference" for time to look after her children. The employer's "taste" for discrimination is balanced against the cost to the woman. She is assumed to be a person of indeterminate gender or social background, but a calculating person able freely to choose her economic relations. Her preferences, such as caring for her children, are valued only in the process of exchange. Her right as a human being to equal treatment and respect is not seen as a social value in itself: the only value recognized by this theory of markets is self-interest.

In regulatory theories, law is a means of intervening in the market order. Collins remarks that "the regulatory agenda for the traditional field of labour law commences with a disarmingly naïve question: Why regulate the employment relation?" Or, put another way, "why should we exclude ordinary market principles such as the general law of contract and property from employment relations in favour of special rules?" (Collins, 2000, p. 4). There is a "heavy burden of proof" on advocates of employment rights "to establish the superiority of regulation over ordinary market rules," and "the special regulation must be demonstrated to be efficient in the sense that its costs do not outweigh the potential benefits or improvements." The question, and the burden of proof required to justify labour regulation, ignore the existing inequitable distribution of wealth and power. They treat the market and the private law of contract and property as a state of nature into which legal institutions intrude. They do not recognize that labour markets are themselves social institutions structured by law and that these laws can be made to reflect a different set of social values from those drawn solely from economic self-interest. Moreover, the cost-benefit calculations tend to ignore the costs of protecting the so-called negative rights of property and contract enjoyed by employers. "The assignment, interpretation and protection of property rights of the owners of a business are not cost-free but are delivered as a cost to taxpayers, workers and consumers. Employment rights are part of an ancillary exchange by which government and employers recompense or give recognition to workers for the inequality of outcomes of the employment relationship" (Hepple and Morris, 2002, p. 249).

Not surprisingly, in view of the presumption in favour of private law rules, regulatory theory has been used to justify deregulation of the employment relationship. By "deregulation" in this context is meant leaving employment relations to ordinary market principles as underpinned by the private law of obligations. Hayek argued that trade unions used labour law to cartelize the market, so in the British context they had to be stripped of their "special privileges" which protected them from the operation of the ordinary law of obligations (Hayek, 1980, pp. 89-90). In relation to individual rights – such as against unfair dismissal, and against discrimination – Epstein (1984, 1995) claims that such special legislation interferes with efficient incentive structures provided by private law contracts. The arguments for decollectivization helped to shape the policies of many governments in the 1980s, but most of those governments never went as far as supporters of the Chicago School would have liked in deregulating individual employment rights. While legislation such as that on minimum pay and working time was repealed, and welfare rights were dismantled, the individual right not to be unfairly dismissed was generally not removed, and rights to equal pay and equal treatment between women and men were expanded. Even neo-liberal governments, intent on individualizing the labour market, saw the need for laws which regulated termination of the contract, and guaranteed certain fundamental rights such as those against discrimination.

The main critique of deregulatory theory in the context of labour law is that the economic model of freedom of individual choice and action is in practice illusory. Free markets are presumed to achieve allocative efficiency because the parties will trade with each other until they cannot further improve their position. This wrongly equates efficiency or cost-effectiveness with wealth-maximization; and it makes claims about the links between labour regulation and job creation which are not evidence-based. Criticisms such as these led, in the 1990s, to alternative versions of regulatory theory being applied to labour law, with a view to improving economic performance. These are of particular importance to developing countries.

d) The development model: Rights-based regulation

The new model accepts that special regulation of the employment relation may be justified on two grounds. First, there may be market failure. This occurs when there is a significant deviation between the ideal outcomes which would result from perfect competition and the actual operation of the labour market. Secondly, regulation may be needed to correct unacceptable distributive outcomes. These justifications may sometimes conflict or they may overlap.

One version of market regulation (here called rights-based) sees employment rights as beneficial and necessary to economic development. According to this version, workers come into the labour market with different levels of education and training, as well as differences in gender, class and race, and markets tend to generate differentials in wages and conditions which bear no relationship to the value added by individual workers. The labour of some is over-valued while that of others is under-valued. Under-valued labour leads to productive inefficiency, hampers innovation and leads to short-term strategies and destructive competition. Only regulation (e.g. a minimum wage, equal pay for women and men, etc.) can correct this market failure.

Secondly, this version of market regulation rests on the redistributive purposes of labour rights. While the deregulators would say that competitive market outcomes are always the just distribution, because they are dictated by individual choice, rights-based regulation tends to favour a transfer of resources to enable those who wish to enter the labour market to do so, for example by providing better education, training and child care. Unlike the deregulators who see wealth maximization (or allocative efficiency) as the primary goal, the rights-based model regards this as only a partial criterion of distributive justice. Accordingly, in this model certain claims or entitlements, sometimes labelled "fundamental rights", are treated as priorities among the distributive objectives of labour rights. However, there remains a presumption against regulation unless it can be shown that the regulation will not harm those whom it was designed to help. So, if an increase in rights relating to the termination of employment would lead employers to hire or fire fewer workers, this needs to be balanced against the benefits of being more careful in selecting and training workers and monitoring their standards of performance. The question of redistribution is also linked to that of externalities: the self-interested market decisions of the parties to a contract may affect others adversely. For example, redundancies may cause costs to taxpayers who fund the social security system. The regulatory mechanism may therefore seek to transfer all or part of the social costs to the parties to the employment relation.

Thirdly, some advocates of the rights-based version of market regulation argue that labour market institutions which encourage "high trust" or "cooperative" workplace "partnership" lead to superior economic performance. This is the common argument for legal provision for better information, consultation and other forms of workers' participation in the enterprise, and for the improvement of corporate governance (Deakin and Wilkinson, 2000, pp. 56-61).

4. Key questions

a) Can rights at work be reconciled with competitiveness?

One variant of regulatory theory puts the "competitivity" of the enterprise and the "flexibility" of work practices at the centre of the stage. This argument is familiar in the context of federal and transnational labour regulation. It is said that the liberalization of trade and investment within a regional economic area or internationally, by removing barriers on the movement of goods, services and capital, throws the labour and welfare systems of the states concerned into competition with each other. This leads to a process of market selection by which states adopt the most efficient form of regulation. Countries with low labour costs will attract investment; this in turn leads to greater demand for labour, higher wages and improved working and living conditions. On the other hand, it is said, regional or international labour regulations hamper this natural operation of the market and so lead to a loss in general welfare.

In the European Union this kind of argument has been used against the harmonization of employment laws or the setting of universal minimum standards. At national level, regulatory competition theory is increasingly used as a justification for limiting employment rights and their enforcement. A recent example is the British Employment Act 2002 which limits access to employment tribunals. A justification put forward by the government was that this would "strengthen U.K. competitiveness" by creating the "right regulatory framework" with minimum standards "to protect the most vulnerable workers" (Hepple and Morris, 2002, p. 246). Similar arguments have been used in France, Germany, Italy and Spain to justify recent reforms of employment rights. A theory of the employment relationship which concentrates on the competitivity of the employer and not on the welfare of the human being at work is readily used by the state "to limit even access to enforcement procedures both to avoid costs for the employer and to protect its public funds" (Wedderburn, 2002, p. 27).

There are several objections to the competitivity arguments. First, firms are not likely to relocate to another state with lower nominal labour costs if those lower costs simply reflect lower productivity of workers in that state. Empirical evidence shows just the reverse (OECD, 1996, 2000). Transnational companies tend to favour investing in countries where the skills of the labour force are high. Secondly, if labour costs do not reflect relative productivity in particular states and if firms do relocate to those states, the result would be to create increased demand for labour with the likelihood of raising wage levels. This would soon cancel out the advantages of relocation which is simply based on low labour costs. Thirdly, firms which adopt low labour-cost strategies are likely to be trapped in a downward spiral of repeated cost-cutting rather than investment in technology and skill creation. This is a recipe for commercial failure.

b) What is the relationship between workers' rights[2] and human rights?

Labour movements in the nineteenth and twentieth centuries sought civil and political rights to enable them to use political power against the abuse of economic power in the labour market. They also pressed for government recognition of social rights such as the right to work, to education, to adequate food and housing, to health care and social security. Claims against employers have often been asserted as "rights" to decent conditions of work, to fair pay and job security, and the right to participate in trade unions and to engage in collective bargaining. Rights have been seen as a means of redressing the unequal bargaining power between employer and worker. There was traditionally a strong emphasis on freedom of association as a core human right.

Yet it is true to say that the international human rights movement has paid relatively little attention to workers' rights. "The human rights movement and the labour movement run on tracks that are sometimes parallel and rarely meet" (Leary, 1996, p. 22). This is surprising because lists of human rights include many rights relevant to work, such as the right to form and join trade unions, the right to free choice of employment, rights which prohibit forced labour and child labour, and which forbid arbitrary discrimination. The extent of workers' rights in a country is a sign of the status of human rights in general: repressive regimes outlaw independent trade unions, arrest and torture trade unionists.

There are many reasons for the parallel tracks of workers' rights and human rights. The first is the abiding disagreement as to whether social and labour rights are human rights at all. At one extreme, there are those who contrast legal rights with socially accepted principles of justice. They argue that treating the latter as "rights" does not make sense (e.g. Cranston, 1973). One cannot have a right to something which is impossible to deliver, such as holidays with pay for everyone. Social rights generally require positive actions by the state and others. To provide a meaningful

---

[2] In this section the phrase "workers' rights" is used rather than "rights at work" because the latter may include the rights of corporate employers (e.g. the right to associate), trade unions, etc. The term "human rights" is used here in the sense of rights attaching to natural persons.

"right to work" or a "right to social security" requires resources which a poor state does not have. Nor are all these rights, (for example to paid leave) universal moral rights. Although they are desirable social goals, it is said that to call them "human rights" is to devalue the importance of civil and political rights.

Against this extreme position, Amartya Sen (2000, pp. 123-124) has argued that rights-based reasoning and goal-based programming are not necessarily antithetical. He suggests that it is only if we make the fulfilment of each right a matter of absolute adherence (with no room for give and take and no possibility of acceptable trade-offs), as some libertarians do, that there is a real conflict. He suggests that it is possible to formulate rights in a way which allows them to be integrated within the same overall framework as objectives and goals, such as those encapsulated in the ILO's notion of decent work. For example, the rights of those at work can be considered along with – and not instead of – the interests of the unemployed. There is no "right" to protection from starvation, but Sen points out that legal rights of ownership and contract can go hand-in-hand with some people failing to get enough food to survive. For this reason it is natural to promote the right to work and the right to social security in order to provide a minimum guarantee of survival. The legal right to own property has to be balanced against rights such as these.

A second reason for the different trajectories of workers' rights and human rights has been the tendency, until fairly recently, of human rights organizations to give priority to civil and political rights, while trade unions have focused on local and economic issues. At international level, the Conventions of the ILO were not originally conceived as statements of human rights. The ILO's official compilation of Conventions and Recommendations includes only three sets of instruments under the heading of "basic human rights". These relate to freedom of association, forced labour and equality of opportunity and treatment. The ILO's 1998 Declaration of Fundamental Principles and Rights at Work added the elimination of child labour to these categories. The vast bulk of ILO instruments are not classified as human rights (see Box 2).

There is a third reason why the categorization of workers' rights as human rights has met with scepticism. A distinctive feature of rights discourse in the employment context in recent decades has been the *individualization* of these claims. Whether one follows Rawls' "first principle" that "each person is to have an equal right to the most extensive total system of equal basic liberties compatible with a similar system for all" (Rawls, 1973, pp. 11-15) or Dworkin's right of all to equal treatment and respect, (Dworkin, 1977, chap. 6), it is the *individual* and not the collective that is to be protected. So Article 11 of the European Convention on Human Rights and Fundamental Freedoms protects the freedom of association

Box 2. International Labour Conventions and Recommendations

Subject matter

I.   Basic human rights
II.   Employment
III. Social policy
IV. Labour administration
V.   Labour relations
VI. Conditions of work
VII Social security
VIII. Employment of women
IX. Employment of children and young persons
X.   Older workers
XI. Migrant workers
XII. Indigenous workers and tribal populations
XIII. Workers in non-metropolitan countries
XIV. Particular occupation sectors

and the right to join trade unions as an *individual* right, and is not directed at the inequality of the employment relationship (Hepple, 1998, pp. 72-76). Although rights such as the right to work are nowadays not infrequently included in the constitutions of democratic societies, it is rare for such rights to be justifiable or legally enforceable.

It has to be recognized that there are serious limitations on the use of such *individual* rights as a basis for the modernization of labour law. First, most social and labour rights – other than a few core values such as the freedom from slavery, forced and child labour, freedom of association and freedom from discrimination (enshrined in the ILO Declaration, 1998) – are not universal or unqualified. Rights to decent working conditions and fair pay depend upon the level of socio-economic development in a particular country and they generally presuppose economic growth and expanding social welfare. Secondly, there is a contradiction between the inequality of class in the marketplace and the democratic element of citizenship and equal rights in the political sphere. Experience in many countries shows that social rights can be devalued by political action because industrial citizenship does not match political citizenship. Thirdly, there is a conflict between civil rights (such as the freedom to contract) which generally favour the operation of markets, and some social rights which may come into conflict with those markets. For example, the freedom to contract implies the freedom to refuse to contract with another person on grounds of race or gender. This conflicts with the freedom against discrimination on these grounds. Fourthly, social rights lack effective procedures and mechanisms for their enforcement. Indeed, increasing reliance on "soft law" (such as voluntary corporate codes), the tendency to privatize enforcement through management-controlled dispute resolution procedures rather than public tribunals, and restrictions on collective solidarity, all reduce much talk of rights to a rhetorical device – in Jeremy Bentham's famous phrase "so much bawling on paper" (Bentham, 1843, p. 23).

To sum up: the language of human rights is widely used today rather than "social justice". But human rights cannot exist without social justice. For this reason rights should be formulated in a way which allows them to be integrated within the same overall framework as the goals of social justice. This can be done by defining rights not simply as negative means of defence against the state, but also as positive means to achieve meaningful participation in society. For example, a constitutional right to equal treatment must be understood not merely as a formalistic defence right, but as a right to equal opportunities. A right to education and to vocational training has to be understood as requiring the provision of educational and training services.

c) How can workers' rights contribute to the alleviation of unemployment, poverty and inequality?

A conception of workers' rights that is essentially limited to the classic model of subordinated workers and their employers does not embrace the wider universe of the unemployed, the semi-employed, the working poor and the small independent producers in both the formal and informal economies. A central task of labour law in developing countries in the era of globalization must be to facilitate equality of capabilities.

In the developing countries, it is not possible to obtain a meaningful picture of unemployment because of the large proportion of the working population who are not in paid employment. So in addition to unemployment, we must look at poverty and inequality. These concepts are often used together but they are distinct. Poverty refers to those who fall below a certain minimum standard. It can be measured first on an absolute basis, referring to people whose income is insufficient to cover basic needs; or it may be defined on a relative basis by referring to those people whose income does not allow them to function properly in their particular social environment. Amartya Sen (1999) argues persuasively that poverty should be seen as a deprivation of basic capabilities, rather than merely as low income. Even where there is some form of social security for those who are unemployed, loss of work can have "far-reaching debilitating effects on individual freedom, initiative, and skills". It contributes to "social exclusion" by reducing self-reliance and self-confidence, as well as harming psychological and physical health.

Relative poverty within the world's richer countries is put into the shade by the gap between rich and poor countries. The average income in the richest twenty countries is 37 times the average in the poorest twenty, a gap that has doubled in the past forty years. The increasing prosperity of an élite in the developed countries has "gone hand-in-hand with mass poverty and the widening of already obscene inequalities between rich and poor" (Oxfam, 2002, p. 5). According to the World Bank, in 1998 almost half the world's population were living on less than $2 a day and a fifth on less than $1 a day, the same figure as in the mid-1980s (World Bank, 2001, p. 3). Human development indicators, such as infant mortality, undernourishment, adult illiteracy and access to clean water, reveal extremely high levels of deprivation in South Asia and sub-Saharan Africa. "The wealth that flows from liberalised trade is not pouring down to the poorest, contrary to the claims of the enthusiasts for globalisation" (World Bank, 2001, p. 65).

The concept of equality is elusive. "Equality of what?" This may refer to equality of income or resources, or it may be what Sen calls the "equality of capabilities", such as education and training, human rights and democratic freedoms. There is, of course, an overlap because lack of income may make it impossible to acquire capabilities and lack of capabilities affects the capacity to earn a living. "Equality for whom?" Some groups, such as women, disabled people and ethnic minorities are at a particular disadvantage and are victims of discrimination in respect of both income and capabilities. There is also general inequality of incomes. If our concern is with equality of capabilities, then our measures of inequality will relate not simply to income, but more broadly to opportunities to pursue an occupation or career of one's own choosing, to freedom of association including the right to form and join trade unions, and to participate in economic and political decision-making that affects one's life, as well as other rights.

Attempts are currently being made to resolve the paradox of a world in which those protected by labour law are "more equal" than those who fall outside its traditional scope. One approach is to extend the coverage of labour law to those dependent workers who have lost, or never had, its protection. This involves treating part-time workers, those on fixed-term contracts and those supplied by employment agencies or labour suppliers in the same way as directly employed workers on indefinite contracts. Other, much bolder proposals seek a new conception of work, not restricted to dependent labour that embraces both employed and self-employed paid labour. Even the privileging of paid work above "family" work is criticized by feminist scholars as being incompatible with gender equality (Conaghan, 2002). Yet others argue that "labour law will become increasingly stultified and marginalized" within the framework of labour markets unless it engages intensively with the redistributive functions of welfare law (Williams, 2002).

Another currently popular approach is to relocate labour law within the sphere of labour market regulation. In particular, active labour market policies to reduce unemployment and to improve "flexibility" and "competitivity" are often seen as central aspects of labour law. There is a danger, however, that such strategies for creating more work may be achieved at the cost of such traditional labour law values as employment protection. The European Employment Strategy, for example, has been criticized for failing to ensure that the goal of more jobs goes hand-in-hand with the goal of labour law to provide "decent" work (Ball, 2001). Any such strategy needs to be linked with the promotion of rights at work and social protection, and must guard against simply creating a large number of temporary and casual jobs.

To sum up: while active labour market policies are certainly important to the reduction of unemployment, poverty and inequality it does not follow that they will in themselves produce "decent work", or more broadly "equality of capabilities". They must be accompanied by the promotion of rights at work.

d) How should rights at work be progressively realized?

Article 2.1 of the ICESCR permits State parties to

Take steps, individually and through international assistance and co-operation, especially economic and technical, to the maximum of its available resources, with the view to achieving progressively the full realisation of the rights recognised in the present Covenant by all appropriate means, including particularly the adoption of legislative measures.

This approach to social rights places the emphasis on determining whether there are certain minimum or core obligations which must be observed, on finding ways to balance resource constraints against the achievement of these obligations, and on monitoring progress towards realization. A similar approach may be relevant to the implementation of workers' rights contained in the ILO Declaration and ILO Conventions. The *minimum or core content* of a right is usually defined as an essential element without which it loses its significance (Chapman and Russell, 2002, p. 9). *Core rights* are characterized as the "floor of rights" below which standards should not fall. There is a danger that a "floor" will be regarded as a "ceiling". States may seek to do only the minimum that is necessary to fulfil their obligations under the ILO Declaration or in respect of ratified Conventions. The minimum must therefore be seen as a starting point not a final destination.

It has been suggested that at least a partial way out of this dilemma is to talk about *minimum state obligations* (Chapman and Russell, 2002, p. 9). This focuses on what the state must do immediately in order to realize the right. First it has to tackle the fundamental element of the right. This approach recognizes that poorer countries simply do not have the resources to realize a right fully from the start. This consideration does not justify non-ratification and non-implementation, as it aims to facilitate progressive implementation. If this approach is followed, one may distinguish three levels of obligation: (1) the obligation to respect a right; (2) the obligation to protect a right; and (3) the obligation to fulfil a right. The first is negative: the state must not interfere with the right, and it must respect the right itself. For example, ILO Convention No. 87, Art. 3(2) provides that "the public authorities shall refrain from any interference which would restrict this right [freedom of association] or impede the lawful exercise thereof." Article 8(2) of the Convention elaborates this: "the law of the land shall not be so applied as to impair the guarantees provided for in this Convention." These minimum obligations – in respect of administrative and legislative action – are cost-free. They do not demand resources, and so they are capable of immediate application.

The second obligation, to protect rights, means that the state must prevent violations by third parties. For example, Convention No. 87 requires State parties "to take all necessary and appropriate measures to ensure that workers and employers may exercise freely the right to organise." This is not cost-free because it entails administrative measures (including an inspection regime), judicial and other means to ensure that third parties do not violate the right. Since these are essential features of any form of state, it can be said that, despite their costs, the obligation to protect is part of minimum state obligations. However, there are degrees of compliance. In this connection it is useful to distinguish *obligations of conduct* from *obligations of result*. The former require action aimed at realizing a goal; the latter sets targets which must be met in order to meet substantive goals. In the context of the right to work, for example, a state's minimum obligation is to implement strategies and policies aimed at achieving high levels of employment. Particular outcomes, such as high rates of unemployment, should trigger state action.

The third obligation, to fulfil, raises the most difficult questions about available resources. Unlike the obligation to respect, which is a negative obligation, the obligation to fulfil is a positive one, and it requires real resources. However, these resources need not come from the state itself. The state can require employers and workers or others to pay. For example, the obligation under Convention No. 98 on ratifying states to enable workers' organizations to engage in collective bargaining requires positive legal provisions, including the protection of rights to bargain collectively (ILO, 2000). The costs of implementing this can, however, be shared between employers and trade unions. Another example would be action plans to eliminate child labour which can rely on technical cooperation, partnerships with international organizations and private initiatives coordinated by governments (ILO, 2002).

This approach to progressive realization, based on core minimum obligations, has already been utilized in some countries. For example, in South Africa, the Constitutional Court has interpreted the constitutional right of access to adequate housing to require the state to devise and implement a comprehensive programme to progressively realize this right, including measures to provide relief to those in desperate need of shelter, subject to available resources.[3] The Court has also interpreted the right of access to health care services and the rights of children to require the state to remove restrictions on the provision of anti-retroviral drugs, and to permit their use, when medically indicated, in order to prevent mother-to-child transmission of HIV/AIDS.[4] This has been done by having regard to the needs of the most vulnerable group that is entitled to the protection of the right in question. A reasonable housing programme requires making provision for those most in need; a reasonable health programme requires making drugs available to those most at risk from HIV/AIDS. This is an approach that may help other countries to conceptualize and implement core obligations in relation to rights at work (see Box 3).

5. Policy options for implementing rights at work

a) The pillars of a new institutional structure for rights at work

The potential of rights at work can be realized only if old modes of thinking about them are abandoned. The traditional theories and the categories of legal thinking – such as "employee" and "contract of employment" – were shaped in industrialized nation states where the typical subjects of the law were Fordist manufacturing companies employing full-time male workers in life-time jobs on standardized contracts often regulated by

---

[3] Government of South Africa v Grootboom 2001 (1) SA 46 (CC).
[4] Minister of Health v Treatment Action Group 2002 (5) SA 721 (CC).

Box 3. Constitution of the Republic of South Africa

23. Labour relations

(1) Everyone has the right to fair labour practices.

(2) Every worker has the right: (a) to form and join a trade union; (b) to participate in the activities and programmes of a trade union; and (c) to strike.

(3) Every employer has the right: (a) to form and join an employers' organisation; and (b) to participate in the activities and programmes of an employers' organisation.

(4) Every trade union and every employers' organisation has the right: (a) to determine its own administration, programmes and activities; (b) to organise; and (c) to form a federation.

26. Housing

(1) Everyone has the right to have access to adequate housing.

(2) The state must take reasonable legislative and other measures, within the available resources, to achieve the progressive realisation of this right.

(3) No one may be evicted from their home, or have their home demolished, without an order of court made after considering all the relevant circumstances. No legislation may permit arbitrary evictions.

27. Health care, food, water and social security

(1) Everyone has the right to have access to: (a) health care services, including reproductive health care; (b) sufficient food and water; and (c) social security, including if they are unable to support themselves and their dependants, appropriate social assistance.

(2) The state must also take reasonable legislative and other measures, within its available resources, to achieve the progressive realisation of each of these rights.

(3) No one may be refused emergency medical treatment.

---

collective agreements with trade unions. In the twenty-first century that classical model of labour law is plainly untenable even in the post-industrial countries. In those countries union density and collective bargaining coverage have dramatically declined, and the contract of employment has lost much of its analytical value as paid work is increasingly performed outside conventional employment relationships. The feminization of the workforce is now an irreversible fact, with profound consequences for the division between "work" and "family", between paid and unpaid work, and between "jobs" and "careers".

The classical models are even less relevant in the developing countries. The most important changes are those resulting from modern globalization – the liberalization of trade and investment, the domination of transnational companies (TNCs), the growth of a worldwide network society, and increasing global competition. A major consequence of this is the reduced power of nation states to regulate labour within their own borders or migration across frontiers, the growth of complex multivalent legal orders with murky boundaries between supranational, transnational, national and workplace legal norms, and the prevalence of "soft" law such as corporate codes of conduct. The classical models are also inappropriate because of the differences in employment structure. Not only is there a large informal sector in developing countries, but even in the formal sector many workers tend to be independent and self-employed.

Some advocates of rights at work are still hidebound by the classical models. But there are others who are attempting to develop new theoretical frameworks and legal concepts to comprehend the changing world of work. The deregulatory school of thought on the Right would abandon labour law altogether and dissolve its subject matter back into the realm of the general law of obligations and property. Those supporting a social democratic "Third Way", seek to invoke regulatory theory in the context of individualized labour markets, human resource techniques such as information and consultation, "flexible" work rules and "family-friendly" policies. Within this broad field of regulatory theory there are many different perspectives, some of which focus on rights-based universal minimum standards, and others which emphasize the need for competitiveness and flexibility in the face of global competition.

An alternative response focuses on the welfare and human rights of workers, rather than on market success or failure. The values underlying this approach are avowedly egalitarian and democratic. Karl Klare has correctly observed that the law regulating work cannot be fitted into a single over-arching paradigm (Klare, 2002). Moreover, a transformative project of egalitarian redistribution and democratic participation needs more than negative ideological criticism of regulatory theory. Instead we need to reconstruct rights at work to safeguard the individual in the changing world of work.

New directions may be found in a synthesis of traditional models with the modern approach of rights-based regulation as well as human rights theory. Such a synthesis needs to be based on at least four pillars.

The first is dialogue between the many different legal orders that shape power relations. The dialogue between these orders may lead, in Kilpatrick's words in relation to gender equality, either to "emancipation through law" when new opportunities are created for groups struggling for equality, or by contrast, "emasculation by law" when the result undermines more favourable treatment under another legal order (Kilpatrick, 2002). This dialogue is an integral part of the process of social and political change. An example of how this can work is the freedom of association dispute at the BJ&B factory in the Dominican Republic (see Box 4).

Box 4. Freedom of association: A case study

In the Dominican Republic, the BJ&B factory, owned by a Korean parent company, produces Nike, Reebok and Adidas products. In October 2001, a group of 20 workers employed at the factory filed a petition under Dominican law for the recognition of their union. (The Dominican Republic has ratified 35 ILO Conventions including those on freedom of association and the right to organize). In the course of the next two months all these workers were dismissed or resigned in circumstances that led to the allegation that they had been victimized for trade union activity. Over a five-year period there had been other allegations of forced overtime, physical and verbal abuse of workers and lack of proper grievance procedures. The Labour Code of the Dominican Republic leaves considerable discretion to management with respect to dismissal without cause, and this coupled with managerial practices at BJ&B led to unfair actions and the restriction of the right to organize. Nike and the other brands filed a complaint against their contractor with the Fair Labor Association based in Washington DC. The FLA investigated the complaint, with the support of the Dominican Department of Labour, put on a training course on freedom of association for all 1600 workers (in small groups) with supervisors, and negotiated the return to work of the dismissed trade unionists. The brands involved put pressure on the head office of BJ&B's Korean parent company to observe the brands' corporate codes which include freedom of association. Despite a threat from that company to relocate the facility in Bangladesh, as at October 2002 it was still operating in the Dominican Republic. The union has now secured support from a majority of workers and is seeking negotiations for a collective bargaining agreement. The company's lawyers are trying to use the letter of Dominican law to avoid this.[1] This is a case where a combination of ILO standards and a corporate code, coupled with the active involvement of a human rights group collaborating with the government and local workers, is in the process of holding the contractor to a higher standard than could be enforced under national labour law.

[1] Information supplied by Auret van Heerden, Fair Labor Association, Washington DC.(http//www/fairlabor.org).

The second pillar is a new conception of the law of work, not restricted to dependent or subordinated labour, that embraces both employed and "self-employed" paid labour. Moreover the privileging of paid work above "family" work is also incompatible with gender equality. Rights at work will also become increasingly stultified and marginalized within the framework of labour markets unless they are linked to the redistributive functions of social protection (see Saith, Chapter IV).

The third pillar is the unification of "public" and "private" law in this field – a still unfulfilled ambition of the early twentieth century founders of the subject. This goes beyond removing technical distinctions; it involves treating the private law of property and contract as a form of regulation that sustains inequality. The twentieth century belief was that collective bargaining could compensate for this bias in the common law; a modern approach to the subject of "countervailing workers' power" needs to foster the idea of *institutional* participation, but much remains to be said on the forms of such participation (see Kuruvilla, forthcoming 2003). These emerging collective forms are the ultimate custodians of individual rights.

The fourth pillar is a notion of "social rights" which ends the traditional dichotomy between labour rights and human rights. We must not underestimate the familiar objections to the constitutionalization of social rights (lack of positive right to a particular allocation of resources, vagueness, and undermining of the separation of powers), nor the weakening of the social dimension by judicial protection of the individual. However international human rights law, and ILO Conventions, provide a basis for a new culture of social rights. The creation and enforcement of these rights enables the law "to act relatively autonomously to restrain public and private power for the benefit of at least some of the people for some of the time" (Hepple, 2002, p. 16).

b) Soft law or hard law?

Rights at work are sometimes expressed in binding legal instruments, with enforcement mechanisms, but increasingly they take the form of non-binding recommendations, codes of practice and guidelines. The former are usually referred to as "hard law" and the latter as "soft law".

In public international labour law, ratified ILO Conventions are the best-known example of hard law. They create legally binding obligations on member States, subject to international supervision. ILO Recommendations cannot create international legal obligations and so are usually described as "soft law". But the distinction with Conventions is to a large extent more a matter of theory than practice. Recommendations have some significant features in common with Conventions: they are drawn up by the same lengthy and careful tripartite procedures, and are subject to the same follow-up procedures as Conventions, apart from those designed to monitor the application of ratified Conventions. After studying a selection of Recommendations that entail varying degrees of difficulty in implementation, Francis Maupain concluded that ILO Recommendations, like unratified Conventions, "can exercise a real influence on national law and practice, with the degree of influence varying widely depending on the subject matter" (Maupain, 2000, p. 383). What is much more difficult to assess, however, is the extent of "compliance" in the strict sense. Maupain suggests that some other terminology may be more appropriate "to describe what the limited evidence suggests, that in many cases there is a selective impact of some of the normative provisions of the instrument, but not necessarily of the instrument as an integrated whole" (Maupain, 2000, p. 393).

Another example of soft international law is the ILO's disappointing Tripartite Declaration of Principles Concerning Multinational Enterprises and Social Policy (1977), which bears a close resemblance to the OECD's Guidelines for Multinational Enterprises (1976). As in the case of the OECD guidelines, compliance is voluntary. Neither is legally enforceable, and they cannot be invoked before national courts or tribunals. The ILO Tripartite Declaration has been ineffective because of the absence of sanctions to secure compliance with its standards, even by countries which adopt them (Murray, 1998).

A final example of soft law at international level is the rapid proliferation of corporate codes of conduct issued by transnational corporations (TNCs). These codes have in common the fact that they are *voluntary* written commitments to observe certain standards in the conduct of business, usually including labour and employment rights. The choice of particular labour issues is highly selective and they are usually made unilaterally without the involvement of trade unions. They are ineffectively implemented, with inadequate (if any) monitoring, a lack of training and incentives for local managers to comply, and an absence of sanctions. Most codes make no reference to the consequences of non-compliance; a few mention "working with suppliers or business partners to make improvements", but termination of a contract or business relationship for non-compliance is a rarity (Hepple, 1999).

There are many reasons for the popularity of soft law. One, which may actually help effective enforcement, is to amplify broad legally binding standards and sometimes to recommend voluntary action which goes beyond strict requirements. ILO Recommendations are an example, as are some national and local codes of practice, issued under statutory powers and capable of being used as an aid to interpretation and enforcement. A second reason is far less acceptable. This treats codes as exclusive alternatives to binding instruments. This approach is profoundly mistaken. First, national experiences indicate that in practice voluntary codes do not succeed unless backed up by legal sanctions. Secondly, the antithesis between soft law and hard law is a false one. One form of regulation (voluntarism) is not an alternative to another (legal enforcement). The point is that a voluntary approach may work in influencing the behaviour of some organizations (e.g. a leading-edge company selling mainly to ethnic minorities will readily want to project an equality policy), but not others who for economic or social reasons are resistant to change. The theory of "responsive regulation" persuasively suggests that regulation needs to be responsive to the different behaviour of various organizations. Although regulators start with attempts to persuade those subject to them to cooperate, they may need to rely on progressively more deterrent sanctions until there is compliance. In order to work, there must be a gradual escalation of sanctions and, at the top, sufficiently strong sanctions to deter even the most persistent offender. When a low sanction fails, more severe ones need to be available. The theory is supported by much empirical evidence (Hepple, Coussey, Choudhury, 2000).

c) Public or private enforcement?

Rights at work developed in part as a response to the distinction between the "private" sphere of economic life – what Adam Smith called "civil society" – and the "public" sphere of all that was controlled and administered by the state. This was conceptualized in Continental Europe in the distinction between private and public law. The challenge came from those who were subjected to the domination of private power in the economic sphere but were gradually securing the rights of political and social citizenship. Protective labour legislation changed its character from the gift of the liberal state into the "rights" of workers. Independent state inspectorates (starting with the British factory inspectors) played an important role. As the idea spread of integrating workers into liberal society, so safety delegates, workers delegates and "mixed" labour courts (starting with the French *conseils de prud'hommes*), emerged in Europe as participants in a system of publicly accountable enforcement of workers' rights. On the other hand, in the United States, private arbitration of labour disputes under collective agreements has been favoured.

The growth of individual legal rights, under statutes and through developments in the common law, has led to an explosion of litigation in many countries. This has prompted the growing popularity of alternative private dispute resolution procedures, such as mediation and arbitration. The main advantages of these procedures are that they are generally cheaper, speedier and more informal than court-based litigation. The main disadvantage is that they usually require the employer and worker to waive their statutory rights. This may be done by way of a pre-dispute mandatory arbitration clause, in which the parties give up their rights to go to court; or it may be post-dispute, i.e. after a specific dispute has arisen. The rights which may be lost in this way include the right to a public hearing (publicity may be an important element where a union seeks to use individual rights as an organizational tool); the right to compel the attendance of witnesses and to cross-examine them; the right to compel production of relevant documents; and the right to published and full reasons for a decision. In some cases arbitration substitutes the unfettered discretion of the arbitrator for the application of pre-existing legal rules. Instead of a judicial process applying laws enacted through the democratic process, private arbitration may simply be used by management to further corporate objectives and to increase control, rather than to promote the public policy objectives of legal rights (Hepple, 2002, pp. 250-252).

An alternative approach is to build the low cost, speed and informality of conciliation, mediation and arbitration into public law systems of rights enforcement. A public law system is able to address the inequality of resources of the parties in a system of individual rights. This can be done by guaranteeing the right of workers to be assisted by workers' representatives, and to obtain legal advice. State mechanisms for conciliation and mediation can play a major role in resolving disputes over rights.

d) How should restrictions on collective solidarity be redefined?

"The dilemma which globalisation poses for labour law is that the more comprehensive and effective legislation or collective bargaining is, the more likely it is that [multinational corporations] will wish to relocate" (Hepple, 1997). The threat of "strikes" by capital are greatly facilitated by the new mobility of international capital, and by the legal guarantees of free movement of capital, goods and services. The freedom of movement of individual workers is no counterpart to these freedoms. Morgan and Blanpain (1977) argued 25 years ago, that "if the decision-making power of the enterprise crosses national boundaries, as can be the case with multinational enterprises, employees should equally be able to express solidarity beyond national boundaries." Yet, transnational industrial action is subject to severe legal restrictions, sometimes outright prohibition, in almost every country, and these restrictions have increased over the past two decades. A recent survey (Germanotta, 2002) indicates that among OECD member States only Belgium appears to leave national and international solidarity action unregulated. Outright prohibition is a feature of UK law, a legacy of market individualism which has been left undisturbed under the New Labour government. In most other OECD countries solidarity action is permissible only if certain strict conditions are satisfied.

The ILO's response to this has been equivocal and contested. Although the Director-General has spoken strongly about the need for the ILO to contribute to the empowerment of workers, the ILO's Governing Body has not moved beyond inconclusive discussions. The 1998 ILO Declaration, with its reassertion of freedom of association and collective bargaining as fundamental rights, does provide a framework for new ILO initiatives. The crucial issue is the extent to which the ILO's supervisory bodies, in particular the Committee of Experts on the Application of Conventions and Recommendations (CE) and the Committee on Freedom of Association (CFA), are willing to recognize that solidarity action, particularly across national boundaries, is encompassed by the freedom of association. The right to strike, including the right to solidarity action, is not expressly recognized in ILO Convention No. 87 on Freedom of Association, but the CE has derived the right to strike from Articles 3 and 10 of the Convention. In relation to solidarity action, the CE and CFA have generally taken the position that "a general prohibition on sympathy strikes could lead to abuse, and workers should be able to take such action, providing the initial strike they are supporting is itself lawful." The applications of these standards have been ambiguous. In relation to the United Kingdom, the CE has recently reiterated that "workers should be able to participate in sympathy strikes provided the initial strike they are supporting is itself lawful." In 1989, the CE said that "where a boycott relates directly to the social and economic interests of the workers involved in either or both the original dispute and the secondary action, and where the original dispute and the secondary action are not unlawful in themselves, then that boycott should be regarded as a legitimate exercise of the right to strike."

The main problem with the CE's approach is that it makes lawful sympathy or secondary action dependent upon the lawfulness of the primary dispute. If the law applied is that of the country in which the primary dispute occurs, this limitation may make it impossible to take solidarity action with workers in a country where strikes are prohibited or severely restricted. Testing the legality of the primary dispute by the law of the country in which the sympathy action occurs is also beset with difficulties because of the different institutional arrangements and collective bargaining procedures in each country. Application of the law of the country in which the sympathy action occurs would involve artificial modifications of unfamiliar systems. It would, therefore, make sense for national legislation to apply simply a test of "common interest" between the workers involved in the primary and secondary actions.

Exercise: Indicators of progressive realization of rights

In his Report to the International Labour Conference in 2001, the Director-General of the ILO drew attention to the "gap between the world we work in, and the hopes that people have for a better life." This exercise is concerned with the *rights gap*. This gap arises when a country is willing to adhere to certain rights but is unable to do so because of legal or practical difficulties or lack of available resources.

The purpose of the exercise is to enable you: (1) to determine the minimum or core obligations which must be observed; (2) to find ways to balance these against real or imagined constraints; and (3) to monitor progress towards realization.

We shall take three sets of ILO Conventions as examples. These are (1) Convention Nos. 87 (freedom of association and protection of the right to organize) and 98 (right to organize and to bargain collectively); (2) Conventions Nos. 29 and 105 (forced or compulsory labour); (3) Conventions Nos. 138 and 182 (child labour) The texts and ratifications can be found in the readings below, or on the ILO website. These texts should be examined using the criteria discussed in section 4 above.

First Indicator – *Willingness to adhere.* Has the state ratified the Convention? Has the Convention been ratified by other states (a) in the same region, and (b) at a similar stage of development?

Second Indicator – *Obligations to respect a right.* Identify which rights in the Convention are capable of immediate application without cost or at low cost. Have these been implemented in practice in the country concerned?

Third Indicator - *Obligations to protect a right.* Identify those rights in respect of which the state must prevent violation by third parties. Then break down these rights into (a) obligations of conduct and (b) obligations of result. What *net* costs would implementation of these rights involve? To what extent have these rights been implemented in the country concerned?

Fourth Indicator – *Obligations to fulfil a right.* Identify those rights in respect of which real resources are required. Who could provide these resources (e.g. state, employers, workers' organizations, etc.)? What technical and/or financial assistance might be obtained from other sources? To what extent have these rights been implemented in the country concerned?

On the basis of these indicators, you should draw up an action plan for the progressive realization of these rights in the country in question.

Reading: Chapman and Russell, 2002; ILO, 2000, 2001, 2002.

Bibliography

Abrams, P. : *Historical sociology* (Shepton Mallett, Open Books, 1982).

Ball, S.: "The European employment strategy: The will but not the way", in *Industrial Law Journal*, 2001, Vol. 30, pp. 353-374.

Barnard, C.; Deakin, S.: "Corporate governance, European governance and social rights", in B. Hepple (ed.): *Social and labour rights in a global context: International and comparative perspectives* (Cambridge, Cambridge University Press, 2002), pp. 122-150.

Bentham, J.: "Anarchical fallacies", in J. Bowring (ed.): *Collected works of Jeremy Bentham* (London, 1843).

Chapman, A.; Russell, S.: "Introduction", in A. Chapman and S. Russell (eds.): *Core obligations: Building a framework for economic, social and cultural rights* (Antwerp, Intersentia, 2002).

Clegg, H.A.: "Pluralism in industrial relations", in *British Journal of Industrial Relations*, 1975, Vol. 13, p. 309.

Collins, H.: ch. 1 in H. Collins, P. Davies and R. Rideout (eds.): *Legal regulation of the employment relation* (London, Kluwer Law International, 2000).

Conaghan, J.: "Women, work and family: A British revolution?", in K. Klare (ed.): *Labour law in an era of globalisation* (Oxford, Oxford University Press, 2002), pp. 53-74.

Cordova, E.: "Some reflections on the overproduction of international labour standards", in *Comparative Labor Law Journal*, 1993, Vol. 14, pp. 138-162.

Cranston, M.: *What are human rights?* (London, Bodley Head, 1973).

Deakin, S.; Wilkinson, F.W.: "Labour law and economic theory", in H. Collins, P. Davies and R. Rideout (eds.): *Legal regulation of the employment relation* (London, Kluwer Law International, 2000).

Dworkin, R.: *Taking rights seriously* (London, Duckworth, 1977).

Epstein, R.: "In defense of contract at will", in *University of Chicago Law Review*, 1984, Vol. 51, p. 947.

—: *Forbidden grounds* (Cambridge, Mass., Harvard University Press, 1995).

Estlund, C.: "An American perspective on fundamental labour rights", in B. Hepple (ed.): *Social and labour rights in a global context: International and comparative perspectives* (Cambridge, Cambridge University Press, 2002), pp. 192-214.

Germanotta, P.: *Promoting worker solidarity action: A critique of international labour law* (London, Institute of Employment Rights, 2002).

Ghai, D.: *Decent work: Concepts, models and indicators*, Discussion Paper 139/2002 (Geneva, International Institute for Labour Studies, 2002).

Hayek, F.A.: *Law, legislation and liberty* (London, Routledge, 1980), Vol. 3.

Hepple, B.: "Introduction", in *The making of labour law in Europe* (London, Mansell, 1986), pp. 1-30.

—: "New approaches to international labour law", in *Industrial Law Journal*, 1997, Vol. 26, pp. 353-366.

—: ch. 7 in B. Markesinis (ed.): *The impact of the Human Rights Act on English law* (Oxford, Clarendon, 1998).

—: "A race to the top? International investment guidelines and corporate codes of conduct", in *Comparative Labor Law and Policy Journal*, 1999, Vol. 20, pp. 347-363.

—: *Labour law, inequality and global trade* (Amsterdam, Hugo Sinzheimer Institute, 2002).

—: Coussey, M.; Choudhury, T.: *Equality: A new framework. Report of the independent review of the enforcement of UK anti-discrimination legislation* (Oxford, Hart, 2000).

—: Morris, G.: "The Employment Act 2002 and the crisis of individual employment rights", in *Industrial Law Journal*, 2002, Vol. 31, pp. 245-269.

International Labour Organization: *Decent work: Report of the Director-General* (Geneva, ILO, 1999).

—: *Your voice at work* (Geneva, ILO, 2000).

—: *Stopping forced labour* (Geneva, ILO, 2001).

—: *A future without child labour* (Geneva, ILO, 2002).

Kahn-Freund, O: *Labour and the law* (London, Stevens, 1976).

—: in J. Clark and R. Lewis (eds.): *Labour law and politics in the Weimar Republic* (Oxford, Blackwell, 1981).

—: in P. Davies and M. Freedland: *Labour and the law* (London, Stevens, 3rd ed., 1983).

Kilpatrick, C.: "Emancipation through law, or the emasculation of law? The nation-state, the EU and gender equality at work", in K. Klare (ed.): *Labour law in an era of globalisation* (Oxford, Oxford University Press, 2002).

Klare, K. (ed.): *Labour law in an era of globalisation* (Oxford, Oxford University Press, 2002).

Kuruvilla, S.: *Indicators of social dialogue: National social dialogue data sheets*, (Discussion Paper, Geneva, IILS, 2003).

Landy, E.A.: *The effectiveness of international supervision: Thirty years of ILO experience* (London, Stevens, 1966).

Leary, V.: "The paradox of workers' rights as human rights", in L.A. Compa and S.F. Diamond (eds.): *Human rights, labor rights and international trade* (Philadelphia, University of Pennsylvania Press, 1996), pp. 22-47.

Maupain, F.: "International Labour Organization Recommendations and similar instruments", in D. Shelton (ed.): *Commitment and compliance: The role of non-binding norms in the international legal system* (Oxford, Oxford University Press, 2000).

Morgan, A.: Blanpain, R.: *The industrial relations and employment impacts of multinational enterprises: An enquiry into the issues* (Paris, OECD, 1977).

Murray, J.: "Corporate codes of conduct and labour standards" in R. Kyloh (ed.) *Mastering the challenge of globalization* (1998).

—: *Transnational labour regulation: The ILO and EC compared* (The Hague, Kluwer Law International, 2001).

O'Neill, O.: *Towards justice and virtue: A constructive account of practical reasoning* (Cambridge, Cambridge University Press, 1996).

—: *Autonomy and trust in bioethics* (Cambridge, Cambridge University Press, 2002).

Organisation for Economic Co-operation and Development: *Trade, employment and labour standards* (Paris, OECD, 1996, 2000).

Oxfam: *Rigged rules and double standards: Trade, globalisation and the fight against poverty* (Oxford, Oxfam, 2002).

Rawls, J.: *A theory of justice* (Oxford, Clarendon, 1973).

Saith, A.: *Conceptualising social protection*, (Discussion Paper, Geneva, IILS, 2003).

Sen, A.: *Development as freedom* (Oxford, Oxford University Press, 1999).

—: "Work and rights", in *International Labour Review*, 2000, Vol. 139, pp. 119-128.

Supiot, A.: "The transformation of work and the future of labour law in Europe: A multi-disciplinary perspective", in *International Labour Review*, 1999a, Vol. 138, pp. 31-35.

— et al.: *Au-delà de l'emploi: Transformations du travail et l'avenir du droit du travail en Europe. Rapport pour la CE* (Paris, Flammarion, 1999b).

Valticos, N.; von Potobsky, G.: "International labour law", in *International encyclopedia for labour law and industrial relations* (Deventer, Kluwer, 1994).

Veneziani, B.: "The evolution of the contract of employment", in B. Hepple (ed.): *The making of labour law in Europe* (London, Mansell, 1986), pp. 31-72.

Wedderburn, K.W.: *The worker and the law* (Harmondsworth, Penguin, 1965), 2nd ed., 1971; 3rd ed., 1986.

—: "Common law, labour law, global law", in B. Hepple (ed.): *Social and labour rights in a global context:*

International and comparative perspectives (Cambridge, Cambridge University Press, 2002), pp. 19-54.

Williams, L.: "Beyond labour law's parochialism: A re-envisioning of the discourse of redistribution", in K. Klare (ed.): *Labour law in an era of globalisation* (Oxford, Oxford University Press, 2002), pp. 93-114.

World Bank: *World development report 2000/1: Attacking poverty* (Washington, DC, World Bank, 2001).

Chapter III
Employment dimensions of decent work: Trade-offs and complementarities

Martin Godfrey

Executive summary

Decent work has many dimensions. Anker et al. (2002) derive six from the Director-General's original statement that ILO should promote 'opportunities for women and men to obtain decent and productive work, in conditions of freedom, equity, security and human dignity' (ILO, 1999):

(a) opportunities for all to find any kind of work, including self-employment, family work, and wage employment in both the informal and formal sectors;

(b) freedom of choice of employment, i.e. excluding forced, bonded and slave labour and unacceptable forms of child labour;

(c) productive work, providing adequate incomes and ensuring competitiveness;

(d) equity in work, including absence of discrimination in access to and at work;

(e) security at work, as far as health, pensions and livelihoods are concerned; and

(f) dignity at work, not only in the respect that is extended to workers, but also in their freedom to join organizations which represent their interests and to voice concerns and participate in decision making about working conditions.

All these dimensions (of which the first four will be mainly discussed in this paper) are precisely definable and, to a varying extent, measurable but, as objectives, they are not necessarily mutually compatible. The discussion about the practicalities of decent work policy essentially comes down to possible trade-offs and complementarities between its dimensions.

Before getting into questions of policy, this paper reviews these dimensions in more detail and spells out some of the possible conflicts between them. Two schools of thought – 'distortionists' and 'institutionalists' – are then distinguished, and their views on the impact of labour market regulations, and hence on the possibilities of trade-offs and complementarities between the various decent-work dimensions, are summarized. Since this is ultimately an empirical and not an ideological question, a review of the evidence follows, with mixed implications for the controversy. A six-category typology is then developed, with Ghai's (2002) classical, transition and development models further distinguished according to the degree of flexibility in the economy. Next, the range of indicators of the employment dimensions of decent work is reviewed, and the possibility of developing a single index, analogous to the Human Development Index, is explored. A framework for policy formulation is then proposed, with a focus on increasing the demand for labour and the 'integrability' of the most disadvantaged workers or labour-market 'outsiders'. Next, in the longest sections of the paper, the policy options and prospects for promoting decent work (through increasing both labour demand and integrability) in the six types of labour market in our typology – flexible and inflexible x industrialized, transitional and developing – are reviewed in some detail. Finally, conclusions and recommendations for policy are outlined.

1.1 Dimensions of decent work

Decent work has many dimensions. Anker et al. (2002) derive six from the Director-General's original statement that ILO should promote 'opportunities for women and men to obtain decent and productive work, in conditions of freedom, equity, security and human dignity' (ILO, 1999):

(a) opportunities for all to find any kind of work, including self-employment, family work, and wage employment in both the informal and formal sectors;

(b) freedom of choice of employment, i.e. excluding forced, bonded and slave labour and unacceptable forms of child labour;

(c) productive work, providing adequate incomes and ensuring competitiveness;

(d) equity in work, including absence of discrimination in access to and at work;

(e) security at work, as far as health, pensions and livelihoods are concerned; and

(f) dignity at work, not only in the respect that is extended to workers, but also in their freedom to join organizations which represent their interests and to voice concerns and participate in decision making about working conditions.

Some would still argue that the first objective of decent work – minimizing the unemployment rate – should be given top priority, at least in industrialized countries. Sen (1997, p. 160) lists ten types of damage inflicted on Europe by massive unemployment.

(a) *Loss of current output and fiscal burden.* Unemployment "cuts down national output and…. increases the share of output that has to be devoted to income transfers".

(b) *Loss of freedom and social exclusion.* The unemployed are excluded not only from economic benefits, such as social insurance and pension and medical entitlements, but also from social activities, such as participation in community life.

(c) *Skill loss and long-run damage.* People who are out of work 'unlearn' by 'not doing'. And loss of confidence and sense of control can have a long-term effect on competence.

(d) *Psychological harm.* Unemployment, especially if prolonged, can "play havoc with the lives of the jobless, and cause intense suffering and mental agony": a country's suicide rate often varies directly with its unemployment rate.

(e) *Ill health and mortality.* Unemployment is often associated with a higher incidence of illness and resulting mortality.

(f) *Motivational loss.* Motivational decline and resignation, typically connected with long-term unemployment, are detrimental to the search for future employment, weakening the distinction between those who are in and those who are outside the labour force.

(g) *Loss of human relations and family life.* Unemployment can disrupt social relations and increase tensions within the family.

(h) *Racial and gender inequality.* Ethnic minorities are often disproportionately affected by unemployment, which also feeds the politics of intolerance and racism and hardens gender divisions.

(i) *Loss of social values and responsibility.* The material deprivation of the job-less and their feelings of alienation boost crime and threaten social cohesion.

(j) *Organizational inflexibility and technical conservatism.* A high unemployment rate increases workers' resistance to economic reorganization involving job losses.

"These costs", suggests Sen, "diminish the lives of all, but are particularly harsh on the minority – a large minority – of families severely afflicted by persistent unemployment and its far-reaching damages.... Increasing employment cannot but be at the very top of the list of things to do. It is amazing that so much unemployment is so easily tolerated in contemporary Europe."

The costs of unemployment are undeniable but, as Sen would of course recognize, its minimization cannot be the only objective of employment policy in industrialized countries. Britton (1997, p. 313) points out that full employment defined only in these terms "could be a nightmare. It could amount to a return to the conditions of the nineteenth century. It could mean that workers become so impoverished that they are obliged to accept work which is exhausting, soul-destroying or unsafe. It could mean the direction of labour and the loss of personal freedom."[1] He argues that full employment as an objective must be accompanied by an acceptable "distribution of income, the preservation of decent employment conditions and the right to choose whether to work or not".

Also, in countries without effective unemployment benefit systems, particularly developing countries, an employment policy which gives top priority to minimizing the unemployment rate is usually misconceived. In many such countries the highest unemployment rates are found among the more educated young in urban areas, who can rely on family support to finance an extended job search.[2] Those who are least favourably placed in a national labour market of this kind may not be unemployed: they may be working long hours for extremely low pay, doing unpaid work in a family farm or struggling to survive on a city street.

Equity, security and dignity at work are other dimensions of decent work identified by Anker et al., 2002. They are usually associated with social security arrangements, health and safety regulations, freedom of association, avoidance of discrimination, etc., but some argue that we should go beyond this – work should also be 'meaningful' to workers. Meaningful work must be freely chosen, but also satisfying and compatible with prevailing culture

---

[1] E.g., see Rama (1999) on Sri Lanka.

[2] Britton is not implying that this is the only route to reducing the unemployment rate, merely that it is a logical possibility.

and norms. Bruton and Fairris (1999, p. 21) suggest that the abrupt shift to modern factory work in countries that have adopted export-led growth strategies may cause problems in this respect. They contrast the experience of Japan and Taiwan (China), with that of Thailand and Malaysia. In Taiwan (China), the development of small firms in rural areas helped to maintain the links between work and other activity. In Japan the workforce and the workplace were part of a 'network of innovation' that made use of knowledge from abroad without destroying the link between work and the prevailing social framework. In Malaysia and Thailand, on the other hand, foreign investors have imported an approach to work that is often "incompatible with existing institutions, practices and routines, and ideas of what is legitimate": as a result, workers in free trade zones have "little involvement with their work and little commitment to the company".

The degradation of labour in modern factory work[3] has come to be seen not so much as an inevitable consequence of capitalist relations of production but rather as a consequence of the system of mass production perfected by Henry Ford in the 1920s and 1930s and generalized in industrialized countries in the 1940s to 1960s. Fordist mass production, to which the moving assembly line was central, carried division of labour to its extreme. "The assembler …. had only one task – to put two nuts on two bolts or perhaps attach one wheel to each car. He didn't order parts, procure his tools, repair his equipment, inspect for quality, or even understand what workers on either side of him were doing …. Special repairmen repaired tools. Housekeepers periodically cleaned the work area. Special inspectors checked quality, and defective work, once discovered, was rectified in a rework area after the end of the line …. The role of the assembly worker had the lowest status in the factory" (Womack et al., 1990, p. 31).[4]

In the last 20 years the Fordist model has given way in industrialized countries to new models of the labour process – flexible specialization, lean production, just in time (JIT), total quality management (TQM) etc. – which (in the interests of higher productivity) give the production worker a responsible and creative role in checking quality, preparing and maintaining machines, monitoring systems, improving methods, and solving problems. This requires a new kind of worker – highly literate, numerate and, above all, flexible – and a team-based rather than individual approach to work (Ozaki, 1996). These models have recently begun to spread to developing countries, often in clusters of small firms along Italian lines (Humphrey 1995, 1997; Schmitz and Nadvi, 1999; Gulyani, 2001), but the

---

[3] Degradation of labour is of course relative: as in many developing countries today (see below), Fordist factory work is often preferred to the available alternative.

[4] See Thompson (2003) for a clear introductory discussion of Fordism, post-Fordism and the flexible system of production.

extent of their potential impact is not yet clear. From the point of view of decent work, they draw attention to another trade-off. For workers in new-model enterprises they represent a huge improvement on the Fordist model – a shift towards more meaningful and more satisfying work. But the shift is accompanied by a big fall in demand for unskilled workers, declining union membership, an increase in precarious and 'atypical' forms of work, and in some countries stagnant or falling real wages.

Thus the promotion of decent work is clearly a complicated endeavour. Objective a, minimization of unemployment, could in principle be achieved by policies which depress wages or limit the freedom of choice of the unemployed about the types of work they would accept, conflicting with objectives b and c. Incomes and security at work (objectives c and e) could be increased in ways which reduce the number of new employees that could be absorbed (objective a). The meaningfulness of work (objective f) could be promoted for a few at the expense of the incomes and conditions of the many (objective c). There might also be trade-offs between current and future gains and losses. It is possible, however, that there are complementarities rather than, or as well as, trade-offs between some of these dimensions.

1.2 Distortionists v. institutionalists

As is often the case in economics, there are two schools of thought on the issue of complementarities and trade-offs between decent-work dimensions – the 'distortionists' and the 'institutionalists' (Freeman, 1993). The litmus test of allegiance to either school is one's view on labour market regulation.

Distortionists (i.e. most neo-classical labour economists) argue that minimum wage and employment security regulations discourage hiring and favour insiders with good jobs against outsiders with bad jobs or no jobs at all. Their hypothesis about minimum wages is that setting them above the market clearing level, given a downward sloping demand curve for labour and an upward sloping supply curve in a competitive market, reduces employment and increases unemployment. If, as in most developing countries, it is not possible to extend coverage of minimum wage regulations to the whole labour market, dualism or segmentation of that market is institutionalized. Employment in the protected sector falls. The supply of labour to that sector increases. Employment outside the protected sector and unemployment also increase.

The parallel hypothesis about employment security regulations is that they increase the incentive to adopt capital-intensive techniques, because they make it more difficult and costly to dismiss unsatisfactory workers, and more difficult to increase labour productivity and restrain or reduce labour cost per unit of output. They also reduce the flexibility that enterprises need to adjust to changing market conditions. When business falls off, it is difficult and costly for them to dismiss workers. When business picks up, they will be cautious about hiring new workers. This school also points to the negative side-effects of all kinds of labour market regulations. For instance, employers will try to bypass them by hiring casual or temporary workers, by keeping their establishments below the critical size and by putting out work to women and children in households.

Institutionalists take the opposite view about the likely impact of such regulations. On minimum wages, they point out that the assumption of competition in the labour market may not hold and that firms' market power may enable them to set wages below market levels – in which case, setting a minimum wage may lead to a rise in employment (O'Higgins, 2001, p. 80). They also use the 'efficiency wage' argument that there is a positive relationship between wages and productivity, in which case the demand for labour may increase in response to a wage increase. This may be a matter of high-wage employers being able to select more effective workers for a given task; or to obtain greater 'commitment' from their workers, with lower turnover and absenteeism; or, in the poorest countries, to enjoy higher productivity due to the better health and nutritional standard of their workers (Leibenstein, 1957). In any of these cases it would pay employers to offer higher wages than would be necessary to attract the minimum number of workers required.

Similarly, they would argue that employment security regulations may yield increases in productivity by: improving workers' commitment to the enterprise and thus raising work motivation and productivity (with an effect similar to that of the efficiency wage); reducing labour turnover and thus increasing on-the-job learning; encouraging workers to accept productivity-raising rationalization and modernization measures, as well as occupational and work-environment changes; inducing greater acceptance of disciplinary measures; and encouraging managers to find ways of increasing efficiency and competitiveness other than laying off workers (Standing, 1989, p. 42).

The differing views of these two schools about the impact of labour market regulations have implications for the possibility of conflict between the various decent-work dimensions. Distortionists would warn that there is indeed a danger of conflict between (i) improving wages and other conditions of work and (ii) increasing employment. They believe that assuring high wages and labour standards for some can harm others. Institutionalists would probably see no necessary conflict between these two sets of objectives. Ultimately, though, this is an empirical and not an ideological question, and has to be answered by a review of the evidence.

1.3 Evidence on distortionism v. institutionalism

As far as minimum wages are concerned, much depends on their level in relation to the average wage and on their incidence rate. During the 1990s minimum wage levels tended to decline, both in real terms and as a percentage of the average wage; this probably reduced their incidence and their impact on employment. A lively debate has ensued in the United States, following a challenge to the distortionist view by Card and Krueger (1995), who found an increase in employment in the fast food industry following an increase in the minimum wage. A review by the OECD (1998) of nine member countries found that there is a significant negative effect on the employment of teenagers, a 10 per cent increase in the minimum wage being associated with a fall in their employment of 2-4 per cent. This impact decreases as the age of workers increases, and effectively disappears for the prime-age group. Overall, the effect on employment is negative, but modestly so.

In many transition countries, "the minimum wage has fallen well below the subsistence minimum, thus losing its social and economic function" (Nesporova, 2002, p. 34). In a sample of 30 developing countries, mainly in Latin America and Africa, Saget (2001) finds no significant effect of minimum wages on employment, which she attributes to the extent of non-compliance and the fall in the real minimum wage in the period covered (from the 1970s to the late 1990s). However, (interestingly for the debate about trade-offs and complementarities) she does find that increases in the real average manufacturing wage in these countries have a significant negative impact on the level of employment.

On the basis of data from 27 member countries, the OECD (1999) found that stricter employment protection legislation raises employment for prime-age men, but lowers it for youths and women, with the overall effect being a net reduction. But these are simple bivariate associations. When multivariate techniques are used to control for other factors, these associations tend to be weaker or entirely absent. Betcherman et al. (2001) comment on these and other results for industrialized countries that "the actual importance of employment protection arrangements might be less than many economists would assume". However, in transition countries their impact has been described as "somewhat limited but not insignificant" (Nesporova, 2002, p. 31). And in Latin America, researchers (using an ingenious job security index which attempts to measure the expected future cost, at the time of hiring, of dismissing the worker for economic reasons) have found clearer evidence of negative employment effects: "an increase in expected dismissal costs equivalent to one month of pay is associated with a 1.8 percentage points decline in employment rates" (Heckman and Pagé, 2000, p. 20).

These results have mixed implications for the question of trade-offs and complementarities between decent-work dimensions. Minimum wages only seem to have a negative impact (and then just a modest one) on employment in countries where their level in relation to the average wage and their incidence rate are both high, and even there some positive effects have been identified. However, a faster rate of increase in wages than in productivity (as may have been the case in the developing countries in Saget's sample) can have negative implications for employment. The evidence for a negative effect of employment security regulations on employment is more convincing, particularly in Latin America. While these potential trade-offs should be borne in mind, a more hopeful message is that the emphasis should always be on increasing productivity – the key to converting a zero-sum into a positive-sum game. This will be explored further in the discussion of policy later in the paper.

1.4 Typology

Differences in economic structure affect the way in which the objective of decent work can be approached. Ghai (2002) uses three criteria – income per head, share of wage employment in total employment, and share of total government and social security expenditure in GDP – to distinguish three broad models of decent work: classical; transition; and developing. As table I shows, there are differences within each category in some of these respects. While income per head does not differ much between classical-model industrialized countries (the US level is not much more than twice that of Portugal), wide differences have emerged within the transition (e.g. between the Czech Republic and Tajikistan) and development categories: indeed, some 'developing' countries, such as the Republic of Korea, with a GDP per head as high as that of Portugal, are overdue for reclassification. Although the proportion of wage-earners in total employment has diminished in transition countries, it is still comparable with that in western market economies. Within the development category, however, a huge gap has emerged between countries which have been more (e.g. East Asia) and less successful (e.g. Sub-Saharan Africa) in boosting wage employment. Industrialized and transition countries are converging as far as the share of government and social security expenditure are concerned, but with big variations: government expenditure in Russia, for instance, now accounts for a lower percentage of GDP than in most Western European countries, and many transition countries spend a lower proportion on social security than any OECD member country except Japan. Government expenditure varies widely as a proportion of GDP in developing countries, but only a few Latin American countries spend more than a small part of it on social security. An important component of social security for the labour market

(affecting the meaning of unemployment statistics) is an effective unemployment benefit system: in general, most industrialized and a few transition countries have effective systems, while developing countries do not.

Table 1. Three models of decent work

	Income per head	Share of wage employment In total employment	Share of total government & social security expenditure in GDP
Classical	High, with modest inter-country differences	High	High, with fairly wide range
Transition	Middle-income, but wide inter-country differences	Still high, but lower than pre-transition	Much lower than before, but still relatively high
Development	Very wide range, from middle-income to impoverished	Very wide range	With a few exceptions, low or negligible

Source: Ghai, 2002, tables I, II and III.

Several other dimensions suggest themselves as possible additions to
Ghai's useful typology. For example, countries differ in their factor endowments, the extent of their integration with the global economy, whether
they export or import labour, and in the relationship between rates of
change in productivity and in real value-added per worker. However, the
most interesting additional dimension, to which some of those in table 1
are related, is the nature of the labour market.

Freeman (2002) has recently described two competing visions of the
future world of work – the Live to Work (LTW) and the Work to Live
(WTL) vision. The LTW model has four characteristics:

(a) Everyone works, including most women.

(b) There is limited social protection.

(c) There is great inequality, and hence big rewards for success and big
penalties for failure.

(d) Labour unions are weak.

Freeman comments (p. 155) that "at its best, this is the world of
shared capitalism, where employees have a real stake in their company and
everyone contributes and benefits from success.... At its worst, this is an
insecure rat race, where employees work long hours for fear of losing their
job, and hope of winning the big promotion or salary increase".

The WTL model also has four characteristics:

(a) Hours worked are limited, and holidays are long.

(b) There is national wage-setting and extensive social protection.

(c) Unemployment durations are long, because employees have job security and low mobility.

(d) Labour unions are strong.

"At its best" says Freeman (p. 156), "this is a world where security generates risk-taking and where leisure generates stronger families, limited hours produce deep insights and labour-saving innovation. At its worst, ... the employed guard their positions against newcomers, which makes entrepreneurship costly, and .... the young remain in their parents' homes for years while they wait for the good job". Freeman has in mind the contrast between the LTW United States and WTL Europe, but a distinction between more and less flexible labour markets can be applied to all three categories of table 1.

In the case of transition countries, the distinction is mainly between countries where progress with overall economic reform (connected with a move away from pre-transition labour market rigidity) has been quite fast and those where it has been slower: the more successful economies are actually trying to move towards the Western European WTL model, but in the process their labour markets have become more flexible than those of the less successful, where rigidities such as residence permits and unreconstructed state enterprises are still important.[5] In developing countries, the distinction is between (i) countries where the public sector is an important employer and governments are heavily involved in labour market regulation and (ii) countries where the share of the public sector in total wage employment is quite low and there is little government regulation of the labour market: labour markets would tend to be more segmented in (i) than in (ii).[6] This suggests a six-category distinction as in table 2, with some provisional allocations to each category. This typology will be discussed further in the sections on policy below.

Table 2. A six-category typology

	More flexible	Less flexible
Classical	USA, UK	Other W. Europe
Transition	Central Europe, the Baltics	CIS
Development	E. & S.E. Asia	South Asia, Latin America, North Africa & Middle East

[5] See Nesporova (2002) and Cazes and Nesporova (2001) for discussions of the complicated situation with labour market flexibility in the transition countries.

[6] Labour market regulations and strong labour unions are not the only sources of segmentation, which can reflect discrimination by employers and differences in the extent to which they recognize a wage-productivity relationship.

1.5 Indicators

The general move away from decent work in industrialized countries in recent decades could be characterized as a move away from what Kornai many years ago called 'resource-constrained' labour markets (in which, as he put it, workers were 'playing on their home ground') to 'demand-constrained' labour markets (in which employers are playing at home) (Kornai, 1980). In a demand-constrained labour market the participation rate is low, so that there is always a large potential reserve of labour, only part of which appears in the unemployment statistics. Specific labour shortages are not eliminated (there are always some vacancies) but there is chronic unemployment in that the rate considerably exceeds the minimum caused by friction. Many of those 'used to employment' are unemployed. It is, thus, a buyer's labour market in which the employers are on top and in which job-seekers have to wait or accept 'forced substitution' in taking a job below their talent and training, and pressures for wage increases are weak.

In such a buyer's market changes have taken place in the way that employers use labour. Within firms in industrialized countries labour markets have become increasingly segmented. Employers have reorganized their personnel systems into fixed (primary or core) and variable (secondary or peripheral) components. Most firms contain both primary forms of employment (stable, career-oriented, male-dominated, and benefiting from the labour-process improvements described earlier) and secondary forms (high turnover, with little career progression, involving little training). Peripheral groups, which are growing more numerous in relation to the core, include part-time and job-sharing employees, those on short-term contracts, probationers, public-subsidy trainees, etc. Extensive use is also made of external groups, such as agency temporaries, outsourcing, subcontracting and self-employment. This process increases the vulnerability of the growing number of secondary workers, restricts their career and training prospects and adversely affects their conditions of employment. The challenge is to find indicators which can measure these dimensions in industrialized countries and keep track of analogous processes in transition and developing countries.

In thinking about indicators, it is important to insist that decent work as a concept must be firmly located in the labour market. Promoting decent work is an excellent way of alleviating poverty in a situation in which most of the poor have nothing to sell but their labour, and some human development indicators may reflect the adequacy of remuneration of some household members. But poverty is still distinguishable from 'indecent work'. A household with a high average income from profits, interest, rent or transfer payments may include individuals who are unemployed or working for low pay. And a person with a good job may be a member of a poor household in which no-one else has an income. It is less confusing to locate the employment problem firmly in the labour market and to subject the poverty problem to separate analysis. This means that poverty data not related to work should not be used as indicators of decent work – for instance, the Human Development Indicators in Ghai's tables VII or IX, or the 'working poor' estimates based on membership of poor households rather than the earnings of individuals from work (table VIII). Data that are directly related to the experience of people at work are also preferable to input data: for example, it would be more useful to know what proportion of people are covered by various social security provisions than simply to know what percentage of GDP corresponds to public social security expenditure (table X).

The traditional labour market indicators unfortunately tell us little about decent work. For instance, the **unemployment rate** is problematic as a measure because the extent to which a job-seeker can afford to refrain completely from work will vary. In industrialized countries this will depend partly on the generosity of the unemployment benefit system, as it affects both the level of benefit and access to it. Many governments have found that they can reduce the numbers on their unemployment register by tightening up on benefit. In developing countries, in the absence of an unemployment benefit system, most of those who are seeking work have to find some way of keeping themselves alive which places them outside the ranks of the unemployed on the standard definition. The extent to which those without work look for it will also vary between countries and time periods. There is no point in looking for waged work if no such work is available in that area or at that time. Thus in depressed areas or bad times there may be a hidden reserve of discouraged workers outside the labour force.[7] Should work become available the number seeking it would increase dramatically.

For similar reasons, the **labour force participation rate** and **employment-to-population ratio** can be suspect measures in developing countries. Where unemployment is an almost impossible condition to maintain, employment is largely supply-determined, and indicators that contain either measure are relatively insensitive to changes in market conditions.

The **time-related underemployment rate**, in the form that it is usually used in developing countries, also raises problems. It is supposed to cover those who are working for fewer than the 'normal' number of hours in the reference period and doing so involuntarily. The second part of the definition is often disregarded and all those working for less than, say, 35 hours a week are counted as 'visibly underemployed'. This yields huge

---

[7] It could be argued that, in most developing countries, while few can afford to be unemployed, few can afford to be discouraged workers either.

estimates of the underemployment rate in many developing countries. In any case, counting the number of hours worked misses the point. In rural areas agriculture usually involves relatively few hours of work per week, except in peak seasons. In urban areas many of the self-employed work very long hours, often waiting or looking for customers. In both cases the point is not so much the hours of work as the very low returns to labour.

A much more robust labour-force series in such circumstances is **wage employment**, and it is worth collecting and analysing information about this, even when, as in many developing countries, it represents a relatively small proportion of total employment (see table 1 above). This focus on wage earners in such countries is not intended to imply that the majority of the labour force who are self-employed or unpaid family workers are unimportant: on the contrary, they are the ones who suffer much of the pain related to the labour market. The contention is merely that, as a guide to changes in the labour market as a whole, wage employment is a better indicator.

In industrialized countries, within wage employment it would be useful to distinguish between primary and secondary forms of employment: statistics on part-time and temporary employment are available for many OECD countries, though not quite in the detail that would be ideal for this purpose (OECD, 2002, chapter 3 and statistical annex). Three categories of **part-time** work can be distinguished:[8] (i) short-time employment, when a firm temporarily reduces workers' hours during a recession; (ii) secondary part-time jobs, with low pay and fringe benefits, lack of social protection, lack of career opportunities and high turnover, chosen involuntarily; and (iii) 'retention' part-time jobs, chosen voluntarily by people who want to work part-time. Available statistics do not distinguish between these categories, lumping together all forms of part-time employment (which is particularly prevalent among women). **Temporary** jobs are another category of 'atypical' or precarious employment, which employers use to facilitate lay-offs and reduce social insurance contributions: data for EU member countries show an only slightly higher incidence among women than among men. The total number in these two types of 'flexible' work increased in all countries of the European Union for which data are available, except Denmark, Greece, Luxembourg and Portugal, between 1985 and 1995 (de Grip et al., 1997). Whether these two types of 'atypical' work should be classified as 'indecent' depends primarily on whether they are chosen voluntarily, which existing statistics are unable to clarify.

One of the most disappointing aspects of labour market statistics around the world is the weakness of data about **earnings** from work. As far as the earnings of the self-employed are concerned, this partly reflects the difficulty of isolating the returns to labour and the problem of ensuring

---

[8] From Tilly (1991), quoted by de Grip et al. (1997).

a comparable and representative sample over time. However, data on **wages** are also thin. Some household labour force surveys have questions about wages of individual household members. The *ILO October Inquiry on Statistics on Occupational Wages and Hours of Work* has collected occupational wage data since 1921: these have serious problems (Anker et al., 2002, p. 31) but are a guide to trends in wage rates and earnings in selected representative occupations (ILO KILM 2001/2: tables 16a and 16b). For manufacturing, UNIDO compiles data on average wages from national sources (KILM table 15), and the US Bureau of Labor Statistics[9] collects data for selected countries on direct pay of production workers, including: pay for time worked (basic time and piece rates plus overtime premiums, shift differentials, other premiums and bonuses paid each pay period, and cost-of-living adjustments); pay for time not worked (such as for vacations and holidays); seasonal or irregular bonuses and other special payments; selected social allowances; and the cost of payments in kind. *Improvement in wage statistics is the most urgent priority for the development of decent work indicators*, but meanwhile creative use has to be made of the data available. Both of the suggestions made by Anker et al. (p. 26) – percentage of the employed below half of the median or an absolute minimum, whichever is greater, by status in employment, and average earnings in selected occupations – are worth pursuing.

As for **non-wage aspects of the quality of employment**, the Bureau of Labor Statistics (BLS) measure of hourly compensation costs for manufacturing production workers includes, as well as direct pay, employers' contributions to funds for the benefit of workers. Such funds include those providing deferred income, insurance or current social benefits (retirement and disability pensions, health insurance, income guarantee insurance and sick leave, life and accident insurance, occupational injury and illness compensation, unemployment insurance, and family allowances).[10] Unfortunately for our purpose, the BLS measure also includes in a few countries taxes or subsidies on payrolls even if they do not finance programmes which directly benefit workers. In some countries, also, social benefits are financed out of general government revenue rather than from funds partly financed by employers.

All indicators can and should be disaggregated for further analysis by **gender** and **age group** and, if possible, by **education** level – since the incidence of indecent work is undoubtedly greatest among the less

---

[9] At ftp://ftp.bls.gov/pub/special.requests/ForeignLabor/supptab.txt

[10] But not employer expenditures on training or subsidies to plant facilities and services such as canteens and medical clinics. These expenditures are part of the ILO definition of total labour costs but are omitted from the BLS definition of compensation costs because of lack of data. In countries for which data are available they account for no more than 4 per cent of total labour costs. Training may also be reflected in the supply price of labour – those who have been trained should earn higher wages.

educated. Special indicators will also be needed for special purposes: for instance, Anker et al. make a good case for the percentage of **children in wage employment** as a useful initial indicator of the incidence of unacceptable work.

1.6 Towards a single index?

Would it be possible to develop a single index of at least the employment dimensions of decent work, analogous to the Human Development Index? Any such indicator must pass two tests: it must be as simple as possible, easily understood by non-specialists, and it must be based on data that are easily retrievable without too much of a time lag. The following 'index of labour morale', which combines data on wage trends with data on wage employment is suggested as a starting point (although a way of integrating some of the non-wage aspects of quality of employment would still have to be found).

The wage series used is that on compensation of production workers in manufacturing, compiled since 1975 from 29 countries by the US Bureau of Labor Statistics (BLS). Even on its own, the table on trends in hourly direct pay in US dollars, shown here for three selected countries (table 3), is one of the best illustrations available of the impact of globalization on the world labour market.

Table 3. Hourly direct pay in US$, production workers in manufacturing, United States, Republic of Korea and Sri Lanka, 1975-2001

	1975	1980	1990	1995	1998	1999	2000	2001
US	5.30	7.98	11.80	13.47	14.72	15.16	15.63	16.14
Korea, Rep. of	0.29	0.87	3.25	6.13	4.16	5.17	5.97	5.47
Sri Lanka	0.25	0.20	0.30	0.41	0.40	0.40	0.41	...

Source: US Bureau of Labor Statistics ftp://ftp.bls.gov/pub/special.requests/ForeignLabor/supptab.txt

The Republic of Korea and Sri Lanka started at around the same point in 1975 (with wages about one-twentieth of those in the United States) but, in the century's last quarter, wages in the Republic of Korea raced ahead: by 1996 they were almost half the US level. Since then, they fell temporarily as a result of the Asian crisis, but bounced back and in 2000 were almost 15 times the level in Sri Lanka – where an earlier attempt to join the global economy was thwarted by civil strife.

Since the purchasing power of a pay packet is of more importance to a worker than its value in US dollars, the more useful BLS series for our purpose is an index of real hourly direct pay in national currency, as in table 4.

Table 4. Index of real hourly direct pay in national currency, production workers in manufacturing, Sweden, Japan, United States and Republic of Korea, 1990-1998 (1990 = 100)

	1990	1991	1992	1993	1994	1995	1996	1997	1998
Sweden	100	98	101	98	100	103	109	113	118
Japan	100	103	106	107	109	111	113	114	115
US	100	99	99	98	98	98	98	99	100
Korea, Rep. of	100	114	127	135	143	152	167	168	158

Source: Nominal pay as for table 3, deflated by IMF consumer price index.

The dynamism of the US labour market is not evident from this table: real pay, though rising since 1996, was no higher at the end of the period than it had been at the beginning. Swedish workers did better: having endured stagnation in the first few years of the decade, they enjoyed a steep increase in real pay towards its end. The Japanese crisis does not seem to have been reflected in workers' real pay trends, although the rate of increase slackened towards the end of the period. Korean workers enjoyed the fruits of democracy in the form of large wage increases until the Asian crisis hit them in 1997.

Trends in real wages tell part of the story but only part. They are likely to be a good indicator of how wage-earners feel, but they do not indicate how easy or difficult it is to get a wage job, nor what conditions are like for those labour force participants (in many developing countries the majority) who are not wage earners. For a fuller picture we need to look at another variable also – the percentage of the labour force represented by wage employees – a key indicator of the development of a labour market, as already emphasized. A rise in this percentage is a good sign for those who are in the wage jobs: *it is also likely to be a good sign for those who are still looking for work or trying to earn a living in self-employment – more wage earners means fewer competitors and more customers.* Table 5 shows how this indicator has changed in our four selected countries.

Table 5. Wage employment as a proportion of the labour force, Sweden, Japan, United States and Republic of Korea, 1990-1998 (%)

	1990	1991	1992	1993	1994	1995	1996	1997	1998
Sweden	88	87	84	81	80	81	81	81	84
Japan	76	77	78	79	79	79	79	79	80
US	86	86	85	85	86	86	87	87	88
Korea, Rep. of	59	60	60	59	61	61	62	61	57

Source: ILO, KILM database.

The US labour market looks much more dynamic on this criterion: since 1993, as unemployment has fallen, wage employment (already very high as a proportion) has grown consistently faster than the labour force. Sweden has gone in the opposite direction over the period as a whole, but it was a case of collapse (along with that of the welfare state) and recovery rather than consistent decline. Japan has been steadily building towards a Northern European level for this indicator. And for the Republic of Korea, on a similar upward path until 1996 (when its percentage was higher than Spain's), the impact of the Asian crisis is again clear.

The proposed indicator is a combination of these two – specifically, an index of real wages multiplied by the percentage of the labour force in wage employment – itself expressed as an index to show comparative progress over time. As figure 1 shows, the rate of progress in this "index of labour morale" differed markedly between the four countries.

Over the period as a whole (and in spite of the dip towards its end) there is no doubt that, from the point of view of labour, the Korean labour market showed the greatest improvement: the extent to which it was a sellers' market, with workers 'playing at home', increased markedly. The steady progress in Japan, though with some easing off towards the end, is also notable. The trend in the US index, on the other hand, is remarkably flat: to some extent, this reflects the difficulty of increasing the proportion of workers in wage employment when it is already approaching 90 per cent of the labour force; nevertheless, it chiefly reflects the lack of any substantial rise in real wages. Certainly, since 1993 the morale of Swedish workers must have been increasing faster than that of their US counterparts.

Figure 1. Index of labour morale, Sweden, Japan, United States and Republic of Korea, 1990-1998

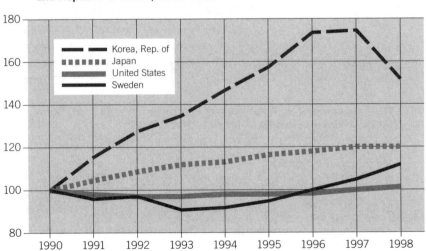

Segmentation of a labour market (more likely in the 'less flexible' categories of country in table 2 above) does not necessarily invalidate this index: if the earners whose wage is used in the index enjoy a wage increase higher than market forces can bear, this will tend to slow the rate of growth of wage employment and so be reflected in the index. It would be useful in industrialized countries to distinguish between primary and secondary jobs: while most primary jobs will be waged, not all wage-earning jobs are primary. However, employment statistics are insufficiently subtle for this purpose and it would, in any case, be a pity to sacrifice the simplicity of the index as proposed and the accessibility of the data (though speed of retrieval needs to be increased).

2.1 A framework for policy formulation

The decent work approach introduces a concern with the quality as well as the quantity of employment; this concern can be best understood if related to the demand for labour. A change in the demand for labour can have three effects:

(a) It can lead to a change in the quantity of employment. This used to be the sole focus of analysis – especially in the emphasis on employment elasticity (the rate of growth of employment associated with a one per cent increase in output). This was particularly misleading in developing countries, where, as already discussed, most labour force participants cannot afford to be unemployed and thus 'employment' is largely supply-determined and of extremely varied quality: in such circumstances employment elasticities tend to vary inversely with output growth (rising in a slump and falling in a boom), with significant but unmeasured consequences for employment quality.

(b) It can lead to a change in remuneration, one aspect of the quality of employment.

(c) It can lead to a change in conditions of work, the other aspect of quality of employment.

An analysis of the impact of a change in demand for labour ideally has to take in all three dimensions noted above.

Figure 2 illustrates how this works in the case of wage-earners. The X axis measures the number of people, the Y axis total benefits of work – both wages and those non-wage benefits which impose a cost on the employer. The supply price of labour has two components, wage and non-wage benefits: so S_{w+nw} is the labour supply curve in relation to total benefits, S_w is the

Figure 2. Effect of an increase in the demand for labour on quantity and quality of employment

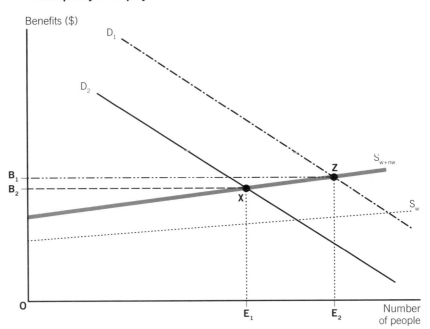

labour supply curve in relation to wage only. As a result of an increase in productivity, the demand curve shifts from D_1 to D_2. The number employed increases from OE_1 to OE_2. This is where the analysis used to stop. Average total benefit per worker (partly wage, partly non-wage) increases from OB_1 to OB_2. Total returns to labour (the 'size of the cake' which defines decent-work possibilities) increase from OB_1XE_1 to OB_2ZE_2.

Focusing on the demand for labour rather than merely on the numbers employed also enables us to reject the false conflict set up by employment-elasticity analysis between increasing productivity and increasing employment. It led employment planners to talk about the threat posed to jobs by 'too fast' growth in productivity,[11] whereas the process is entirely opposite. *Increasing productivity is at the centre of a decent work strategy.* Elementary economic theory tells us that outward shifts in marginal and average productivity curves are reflected in increases in demand for labour. More practically, the scope for improving the earnings and conditions of the working poor increases with the size of the 'cake' available to labour as

---

[11] Even the current ILO *Global Employment Trends* (ILO, 2003) is guilty of this approach: 'in the USA, productivity gains in recent years are impressive, but with slower growth in demand, now risk causing a further jobs shakeout.'

a whole, which depends on productivity. And in global market places the capacity to compete depends on keeping unit labour cost (labour cost per worker divided by productivity) under control: the most successful expansion of employment in exports of manufactured goods occurs not in countries where wages are falling but in those where productivity is rising faster than wages.

Increasing the overall demand for labour is only part of a strategy to promote decent work. As Osmani (2002) points out, it is also necessary to increase the 'integrability' of the most disadvantaged workers or labour-market outsiders (the working poor rather than the unemployed in many developing countries), to enable them to take advantage of any increase in labour demand. This involves dealing with market failures, including those affecting the labour market (due to a lack of widely available accurate information), the credit market (which discriminates against those without assets), and those arising from the high transaction costs of living in remote areas. It involves making a judgement on the net effect in a particular country of the labour market regulations discussed earlier: if their main effect is to limit the integrability of the most vulnerable outsiders, they may need to be redesigned. It involves improving the skills of the excluded, to enable them to integrate into expanding sectors. And it involves action to ensure that the integrability of women, ethnic minorities and people with disabilities is not hampered by discrimination against them.

2.2 Policy options and prospects

What are the policy options and prospects for promotion of decent work in the six types of labour market depicted in table 2 above – flexible and inflexible x industrialized, transitional and developing?

2.2.1 Industrialized countries

In industrialized countries, the struggle between Freeman's Live to Work (LTW) and Work to Live (WTL) models will presumably continue. In his view (p. 157), the outcome of the struggle will depend on: their relative ability to provide full employment; their relative performance in periods of full employment; their relative performance in periods of high unemployment; and their relative implications for technological advance and productivity increase. He judges that the LTW model still has the edge in achieving full employment, particularly in the favourable environment it provides for growth of jobs in the services sector and among women, but possible threats to investment levels from high foreign and personal debt have to be borne in mind. The flexibility of the LTW model gives it an advantage in periods of full employment: for instance, the time worked by older workers is more easily increased and welfare problems can be eliminated in such periods at no expense to the government. On the other hand, the WTL model, with its mechanisms to deal with unemployment and poverty and to stabilize aggregate spending, performs better when times are bad. Finally, the LTW model may be more favourable to the rapid adoption of new technologies, but there are enough counter examples to cast some doubt on this.

In any case, at least until recently, there were signs that the two models were beginning to converge. As summarized by Cichon (1997, p. 29), the traditional European model was based on "high productivity and relatively high wages, high unemployment and decent levels of social transfers", while the US model was based on "lower productivity and lower wages, low unemployment and low transfers". In the United States, unemployment was lower than ever between 1995 and 2000, and transfers were still low, but productivity and wages began to rise (see figure 1 above). In Europe, (although the IMF warns about the need for further labour market reform) a reduction in the role of government and the social partners, cuts in public-sector employment, deregulation, privatization, lean organization, etc. have reduced the contrast with the US model. Auer (2000) points to the success of four of the continent's smaller economies: Austria, Denmark, Ireland and the Netherlands have, in their different ways, reduced unemployment rates or maintained them at low levels, lowered the incidence of youth and long-term unemployment, increased employment rates, and reduced gender gaps. However, he concludes that the four European success stories have been due, not to throwing the baby out with the bathwater but, rather, to the countries retaining but adapting their institutions. In particular, "democratic corporatism", very much out of fashion nowadays, is still alive and well in all four countries: "corporatist governance and social dialogue, combining mutual information and discussion of issues at higher levels with the ability to implement reforms on lower levels, facilitates wage moderation and is conducive to policy-making, combining the divergent interests of society and the economy as a whole" (p.90). Thus, in all four countries, although membership has tended to decline, the role of trade unions remains important (box 1).

Both models are faced with a period of extreme uncertainty, as far as prospects for growth in the *demand for labour* is concerned – with the interconnected combination of global insecurity, oil price worries, declining equity markets that are volatile and capable of declining further, increased awareness of corporate malpractice especially in the United States, a housing market bubble in many countries, currency realignments that may become

---

Box 1. Can a resurgence of trade union movements roll back the 'new insecurities' in industrialized countries?

In a presentation to a recent symposium on the Future of Work, Employment and Social Protection, Appelbaum identified the 'four horsemen' of the transformation of work and employment, and the associated new insecurities, as the internationalization of production processes, the decline of the standard employment relationship, the marginalization of care work, and the ubiquity of digital technology.

- The growing economic power of footloose and borderless companies has undermined the ability of governments of industrialized countries to regulate their markets for social purposes and weakened the social protection previously enjoyed by workers.

- Partly as a result of this trend, the employment relationship has become more tenuous (with the growth of the atypical or precarious modes of employment already discussed), as has the commitment of firms and workers to each other.

- The collapse of the 'breadwinner-homemaker' model has not been accompanied in many countries by the development of an adequate system of caring for the children of working women and paid maternity, parental and sick leave.

- And, while new technology has increased productivity and improved the quality of core jobs in a few organizations, it has boosted sub-contracting and the geographic de-integration of production.

But Applebaum finds two reasons for some optimism about the future.

- Not all countries are the same. The extent to which the four trends contribute to the new insecurities depends on the strength in each country of the institutions that represent workers' interests – trade unions, works councils, union confederations, and labour parties – and on the availability of social protection. For instance, 'the difference between the degree of insecurity between non-professional women workers in the US and their Swedish counterparts ... is extraordinary'. And multinational companies seem to be able to live with this.

- The newly insecure are not all from underprivileged backgrounds. Regardless of skill, gender, race or national origin, regular full-time workers everywhere are anxious about their futures. High-powered web designers and software engineers are as likely as low-paid workers to be laid off and to lack health insurance.

Applebaum suggests that 'this is fertile soil for the resurgence of trade union movements that can capture the popular imagination by organizing women and men around themes that resonate across a wide spectrum of occupations, skills and earnings' – and roll back the new insecurities.

Source: Applebaum, 2002.

---

disorderly, the unsustainability of indebtedness in the United States, continued sluggishness in the European and Japanese economies, etc. (IMF, 2002: ILO, 2003). In these deflationary circumstances, even the IMF is arguing for macroeconomic policies in industrial countries that are 'supportive of activity' (p. 13). This includes the possibility of further interest rate cuts in the United States (though 'medium-term fiscal consolidation is a priority' there) and the euro area (especially given the recent appreciation of the euro), and a definite need for aggressive monetary easing to support the reform of banking and the corporate sector in Japan. A straw to be clutched at in all this is the maintenance of high rates of productivity growth in the United States even as the level of economic activity has weakened. If, as seems likely, the diffusion of information technology in Europe follows a similar pattern to that experienced in the United States, a cyclical upturn (if and when it comes) may be accompanied by faster productivity growth (IMF, 2002: box 1.3).

As for increasing the *integrability of labour-market outsiders*, there is unfinished business (OECD, 2002, p. 8). In particular, schemes to 'make work pay' need to be implemented more widely. Such schemes provide in-work benefits and tax credits for low-paid workers and their families, or reduce the cost to employers of hiring such workers, for instance through reduced social security contributions. The range of supporting services also needs to be increased, including help with child-care costs, transport and work facilities for the disabled, and training in job-search and job-readiness skills. On the whole, the OECD approves of the various schemes to 'activate' the unemployed, i.e. a combination of incentives, advice and sanctions to get them off the unemployment register, but points to the need to improve their design, with a view to building careers not just moving people into jobs. The need to adjust hiring, firing and training policies to the phenomenon of an ageing workforce is also emphasized. One lesson learned from the experience of the past 30 years is that policies that discourage labour force participation (e.g. early retirement or loosely administered disability/long-term sickness schemes) are ultimately unsustainable and may end up promoting rather than alleviating social exclusion.

Another lesson is that 'success in the fight against unemployment and social exclusion requires renewed emphasis on a comprehensive lifelong learning strategy' (OECD, 2002, p. 12). To this should be added the need to look carefully at inequities within education systems. Recent international tests [12] enable not only the quality of education but also inequity in the distribution of that quality to be compared between countries. UNICEF (2002b) puts the results of these tests together to measure the degree of 'relative educational disadvantage' – the gap between the lowest and the average scores – in each country. It finds that relative disadvantage

---

[12] The Trends in International Mathematics and Science Study (TIMSS), testing 14-year olds in 1999 (Mullis et al. 2000; Martin et al. 2000), and the OECD Programme for International Student Assessment (PISA), measuring ability of 15-year olds in reading literacy, scientific literacy and mathematical literacy, i.e. the ability to use academic knowledge and skills (OECD, 2001).

is significant in all 24 OECD countries covered by the tests, 'with gaps in test scores between low and average achievers being significantly wider than both the differences in average scores between nations and the differences that can be expected between one year of schooling and the next'. In the bottom quarter (or relegation zone) of a league table based on rankings in the five PISA and TIMSS tests are Switzerland, Greece, the United States, Germany, New Zealand and Belgium.

2.2.2 Transition countries

Among the transition countries, the more and less flexible groups are distinguished mainly by their relative progress with governance and enterprise reforms. In the more flexible group the front-runners in this respect are the four Central European countries (the Czech Republic, Hungary, Slovakia and Poland), closely followed by the Baltics (Estonia, Lithuania and Latvia), Slovenia and Croatia. The laggards in the less flexible group include the CIS (particularly its Central Asian members), South Eastern Europe, and the other former-Yugoslavian countries (European Bank for Reconstruction and Development, 2002).

For both groups, overall economic reform remains the prime means of increasing the *demand for labour*. The first group has moved further along this road than the second. The IMF (2002, p. 48) identifies four key measures for the CIS countries. These are: the effective enforcement of legislation establishing basic market institutions; the liberalization of factor and goods markets; enterprise restructuring; and strengthening the financial sector. One area where further reforms are definitely needed is in the regulation of small enterprises, of which there are a relatively low number in CIS countries (as opposed to the 'shadow-economy' activities described in box 2). A survey in Russia in March-April 2002 revealed a big gap between sensible new laws (a 'deregulation package' targeting registration, licensing, certification and inspections) and effective implementation. It found evidence that 'it is not only hard to establish a small business in Russia, but there are strong regulatory obstacles preventing small firms that do manage to enter the market from growing into medium sized firms' (World Bank, 2002a, p. 17). It also found evidence that in some municipalities administrative interventions are used to block market entry in the interest of incumbent firms. Another survey nine months later was more encouraging, finding that the deregulation package was beginning to work: small firms were more worried about increased competition than about regulations. However, the situation was still not good and the main message of the new survey was the need to press on with implementing the package (Rühl, 2003).

Looking further ahead at the prospects for growth in demand, there are also worries connected with the virtual collapse of educational systems in many transition countries in the second group, where real public education expenditure per school-age child and teachers' salaries are a fraction of their pre-transition levels (UNICEF, 2002a). This is beginning to be reflected in performance in the international tests, already discussed, which measure the ability to use academic knowledge and skills (OECD, 2001) and to raise doubts about the prospects of shifting the comparative advantage of such economies from cheap labour + natural resources to high-technology skills. These prospects are also threatened in natural-resource-rich countries by 'Dutch disease' – the name given since the 1970s to the negative impact of a windfall increase in foreign exchange earnings on the rest of an economy. In an economy with Dutch disease, a booming sector (in Russia's case oil and other mineral exports) attracts resources to itself and bids up their prices, pushing up the value of the national currency to the detriment of other tradable sectors. New ICT-based sectors in the region can only become and remain competitive if their unit labour costs in dollars undercut those of India and others in international markets, which implies a need for realistic exchange rates as well as favourable trends in productivity relative to wages.

In order to increase the *integrability of outsiders*, labour market reforms are still needed. For instance, in Russia, which has recently made more progress in overall economic reform than other CIS countries, the following labour market policy options are under consideration (World Bank, 2002a, p. 91):

- reducing the excessive rigidity of the labour code in relation to hiring and dismissing workers (coupled with improvements in social protection);

- continuing to increase minimum wages, to a level which would reduce poverty among low-wage workers without affecting the incentive to hire;

- developing institutions to allow worker voice, improve work conditions, enforce contracts and resolve disputes, including true worker and employer representation in their respective organizations, increased resources and capacity for the federal labour inspectorate, and alternative dispute-resolution mechanisms;

- improving the design of unemployment-benefit and active labour market programmes, to protect workers against poverty, help facilitate restructuring, and move protection out of firms and into the public domain.

In many transition countries, also, a huge gap has opened up between places where declining industries are concentrated and places where new employment is being generated. In Russia, for instance, the share in total

Box 2. The challenge of the shadow economy in transition countries

What a visitor sees on the streets of many towns in transition countries looks inconsistent with official figures on GDP decline and job losses. This is because a large proportion of workers (including many public sector-wage earners and many officially counted as unemployed) are working in a sector which generates a large proportion of income but which is unrecorded by official statistics – the 'shadow economy'. Its other characteristics are that it evades taxes, avoids regulatory requirements and may be engaged in illegal activities. Using an ingenious method based on electricity consumption, economists have estimated the size of the shadow economy in 24 countries in Central and Eastern Europe and Central Asia in 1996-97, and find that it ranges from 11 per cent of official GDP in Lithuania to 180 per cent in Kyrgyzstan: other countries in which it exceeds official GDP are Macedonia, Moldova and Ukraine, while in Armenia, Azerbaijan, Bulgaria, Estonia, Georgia, Russia and Tajikistan it accounts for more than half.

Shadow economies on this scale have an obvious negative impact on tax revenue and hence on the quality of public goods and services. They also make it more difficult for governments to achieve macroeconomic stability, and create many distortions in resource allocation. The existence of a large shadow economy also reflects and reinforces distrust in the ability of the political system to govern and engenders respect for those who get away with evading taxes and laws. As far as decent work is concerned, workers in shadow firms are not protected by labour regulations and may not be eligible for social safety net services. On the other hand, the shadow economy helps maintain activity and employment, which otherwise might be suppressed by rent-seeking and corruption, and may be of particular benefit to less qualified workers who would otherwise be unemployed or near destitute. Through the multiplier, it may have a positive effect on growth in formal sectors and tax receipts, and it provides entrepreneurial experience for some who may later set up respectable small enterprises.

Nevertheless, the consensus is that a full transition of these economies and labour markets must involve shrinking the size of their shadow economies, which regression analysis shows to hinder long-term growth and international competitiveness. Eilat and Zinnes make the following policy recommendations for this purpose:

- exchange rate unification, rather than dual exchange rates or foreign exchange rationing;
- improvement in regulations, to make them less predatory and obstructive;
- civil service reform including salary increases, and adequate funding for regulatory bodies;
- transparency and public participation in regulatory processes;
- bank privatization and capital market development;
- decentralization of public administration and better local public finance;
- rule of law, particularly protection of property rights;
- further liberalization and deregulation of markets;
- tighter budgetary and monetary policies to reduce the rate of inflation;
- government payment for goods and services in cash rather than barter;
- tax reform (based on an accurate judgement as to whether an increase or reduction in rates will increase revenue);
- stricter and more strategic enforcement of penalties for illegal activities.

Source: Eilat and Zinnes, 2002.

income of the top quintile of regions in terms of income per head increased from 38 to 53 per cent between 1994 and 2000, while that of the poorest 40 per cent fell from 18 to 13 per cent. In the first half of 2002, top-quintile regions absorbed 56 per cent of total and 66 per cent of foreign investment, while the poorest 40 per cent received 10 and 2 per cent respectively. Shares of population have not changed much in response to these developments (World Bank 2002b, p. 11), and regional differences in unemployment rates remain striking (World Bank, 2002a, table I.2). Low geographic mobility in Russia and other transition countries reflects significant barriers to labour mobility. Such barriers include: continued use of the *propiska/* residence permit system in some cities, where large bribes have to be paid for such permits, which are needed not only to get a job, but also to send children to school, receive medical treatment, and vote (Karush, 2002); poor functioning of the housing market (affecting front-runners like Hungary as well as CIS countries); and poor communication and transport links (World Bank, 2002a, p. 23).

The integrability of labour-market outsiders is also threatened in the longer run by the problems in the educational system already mentioned. Attention must be paid to reducing drop-out from school, particularly among children from low-income families, in rural areas, and from ethnic minorities. Improving the quality of schooling, especially in the less advantaged schools, is also a priority – in the OECD PISA international tests, already mentioned, children from more privileged socio-economic backgrounds in the four transition countries for which data are available,[13] and children attending more advantaged schools (in terms of average socio-economic background) performed better than others. Performance was more closely related to the quality of schooling than to the socio-economic background of the pupils.

2.2.3 Developing countries

The allocation of developing countries to the more and less flexible categories of the table is fairly easy. **East and South-East Asia** definitely belong to the first group. Labour markets in this region have been relatively free of the kind of regulations and interventions that raise labour costs above their market level, create dualism in the labour market between formal and informal sectors and reduce the mobility of labour. The public sector has accounted for a relatively small share of employment and has not been a wage leader. Minimum wage regulations, where they exist, have

---

[13] The Czech Republic, Hungary, Poland and Russia.

not been such as to affect the level and structure of wages. Employment security regulations have not been strict enough in their implementation to prevent restructuring, social security provisions have been minimal, and trade unions are government-dependent or weak. The fast expansion in demand for labour in these countries has been associated with a relatively equal distribution of its benefits and a high level of investment in education and training.

The countries of **South Asia** have traditionally been in the second group and, although they are changing, the process is slow. The large public enterprise sector has been a drain on the government budget and a negative influence on the efficiency of the private sector. Minimum wages are widespread and high enough to influence the average wage and wage structure in the formal sector. These countries have the most stringent and complex employment protection legislation, but it covers no more than 10 per cent of the workforce. Anant et al. (1999, p. 73) report that employers have responded to it by increasing their reliance on contract labour, subcontracting production to the unorganized sector, and introducing non-wage incentive payments: this legislation is judged to have increased the cost of formal-sector employment, to the detriment of its demand for labour.

Latin America, also, in spite of its 'new economic model' (Reinhardt and Peres 2000, box 3), is still a candidate for membership of the second

---

Box 3. Wages, employment and workers' rights in Latin America

The governments of virtually all Latin American countries during the 1990s reduced trade regulations and capital controls and made some attempt to increase labour market flexibility. According to neoclassical economic theory, workers should have gained from these policy changes, through a reduction in unemployment and increases in employment and wages. In fact, Weeks estimates that labour's gains in the 1990s, when economic growth accelerated, were meagre, and even negative in some countries. Weeks argues that this is due to a decline in the strength of trade unions throughout Latin America, and that workers' rights and the exercise of those rights are central to a more equitable distribution of the gains from growth. In the interests of symmetry between capital and labour, the rights provided for in ILO Conventions (to establish trade unions, not to be subjected to intimidation for joining a trade union, to select representatives by democratic process, and for those representatives to bargain with employers in both private and public sectors) need to be reasserted and their effectiveness needs to be strengthened. In addition to core rights, he argues, measures are required to establish minimum standards in the workplace – both to discourage a competitive process by which standards are reduced to the level of the least regulated country and, through a decrease in accidents and illness, to contribute to an increase in productivity and a reduction in health-care costs.

Source: Weeks, 1999.

group. Traditionally, oligopolistic firms in the modern sector have been faced by strong trade unions and minimum wage and employment protection regulations, with the result that growth in employment has been concentrated in the informal sector. And many countries in **North Africa and the Middle East** have huge public sectors (often effectively the employers of last resort) and regulate their labour markets quite extensively.

What kind of strategy should be followed by developing countries in each of the groups, in order to promote decent work by (i) expanding the demand for labour and (ii) increasing the integrability of disadvantaged workers? Rather than attempting to generalize about such strategy, it may be more useful to discuss two cases – one from each category – in which ILO has recently made a policy-formation input. These are Pakistan, a member of the first, less flexible group (ILO, 2001a), and Cambodia, one of the world's poorest countries, where flexibility verges on anarchy (ILO, 2002).

(a) Expanding the demand for labour in Pakistan and Cambodia

Pakistan's economy is not only relatively inflexible – it is also cash-strapped. The government has been under IMF pressure for several years to reduce its budget deficit. Thus it is necessary to find a way of increasing demand for labour that does not involve subsidies or additional government expenditure. One way of doing this is to get rid of unnecessary regulations. Labour levies and protection laws, though not regarded as major worries by enterprises, raise the costs of entering the formal sector, leading to fragmentation of production and sub-optimal plant sizes (World Bank, 1996). The external trade regime has been liberalized since the 1980s, but import tariffs remain higher than in most countries in the region and restrictions are still in place on the import and export of a number of items (IMF, 2001, table III-2). Small and medium enterprises are held back by 'export' and 'import' taxes imposed by local jurisdictions through which goods pass and by a wide range of zoning and other regulations. Relaxation of restrictions on (and taxation and harassment of) the urban self-employed, particularly in the trade, transport and services sectors would also improve their income opportunities (ILO, 2001b).

As for factor price distortions, another aspect of inflexibility, there has been some improvement since the 1980s. Wage differentials between the formal and informal sectors and between large and small firms remain significant, but productivity has begun to rise faster than wages in large scale manufacturing (ILO, 2001a, figure 10). Nominal and real effective devaluation of the rupee has continued, and the days of negative real interest rates are long over. However, loans have been provided at lower than market rates by state institutions: particularly damaging to the demand for labour have been the loans at low interest rates for tractors and mechanization. In general, trends are in the right direction, but labour demand would be boosted by eliminating the remaining subsidies to capital.

Typical of the South Asian model is the heavy weight of the public sector in Pakistan. In 1996/97 public sector workers represented over 8 per cent of all workers and about 23 per cent of wage employees; and 31 per cent of public-sector employees had degree qualifications compared with 22 per cent of formal private-sector employees. Comparison of public and private sector remuneration is made more difficult by the large range of non-monetary benefits enjoyed by civil servants. However, it is clear that the total remuneration package and other perceived advantages of public service are sufficient to attract a disproportionate number of educated Pakistanis to such employment. This has a debilitating effect on the economy and the labour market, weakening the private sector and making it more difficult to increase the overall demand for labour.

Reforms in these areas, together with a continued drive against corruption, would improve incentives for the expansion of external leading sectors – a leading sector being defined as one which has an 'unexploited or *latent* demand that can be actualized and a sufficiently *large* demand as to cause its satisfaction to have a significant impact on the whole economy' (Currie, 1974, p. 6). A leading sector must also (unlike a 'following' sector) be capable of an *exogenous* increase in growth rate, independent of the current overall rate of growth of the economy. In Pakistan's case the obvious candidates for external leading sectors are exports from such (transformed) industries as textiles and garments, agriculture and food processing, and medical equipment and supplies.

Expansion of these external leading sectors (by definition those where latent demand is most easily found) could be accompanied by the growth of a complementary internal leading sector – house-building, which has a low import component, a high unskilled labour component and strong linkages to other sectors. Huge latent private demand for housing already exists in Pakistan, held back by lack of finance, administrative procedures, insecurity of property rights and excessive construction codes, and demand would be further increased by expanding the external leading sector. Latent private demand for housing (among low- as well as middle- and high-income groups) could be fully actualized, to the benefit of the demand for labour, without subsidies, if these institutional obstacles to the development of a substantial commercial system providing long-term mortgages to people who already have adequate income to repay them, could be removed.

The leading sector strategy could be usefully complemented by changes in the composition of government expenditure. To some extent, this would be a matter of changing the balance between categories – from running enterprises to managing the economy, and from current to development, from defence to non-defence, from salary to non-salary, from non-social to social current expenditure, etc. It would also be useful to increase the labour-demand impact of a given amount of public development expenditure. Choice of techniques in the public investment programme, particularly construction of infrastructure, could be handed over to economists rather than engineers, to the benefit of their labour intensity and the demand for labour.

In overwhelmingly agricultural **Cambodia** only 15 per cent of workers are wage-earners (compared with 38 per cent in Pakistan), and the public sector is relatively small (less than 3 per cent of the country's workforce) and desperately underpaid (Godfrey et al. 2001). Labour-market institutions and regulations are at a very early stage of development. Formally the employees of the few enterprises with more than 20 workers are entitled to injury, sickness and maternity benefits (but not all such enterprises comply) and civil servants are entitled to old-age, invalidity and survivors' benefits (but the levels are miniscule). Minimum wages are set only for the garment industry. Numerous trade unions have been established at national and enterprise level but they are weak, inexperienced and in some cases politicized. In the absence of transparent, fair and expeditious dispute-resolution machinery, the many disputes, over wages, forced overtime, safety and health at the workplace, unjust dismissals, etc., often end unnecessarily in strikes, lockouts and threats by factories to leave the country.

Although these disputes reflect worker dissatisfaction, judgement about the adequacy of wages in the garment industry depends, as always, on the point of comparison (see box 4): at around $60 per month on average, they compare favourably with the alternatives available in Cambodia. A question inserted in October 2000 into a regular survey of garment workers found that 43 per cent of them had been unpaid family workers immediately prior to joining the industry, 16 per cent had been housekeeping or caring for children and 3 per cent had been unemployed – only 13 per cent had been wage-earners, paid family workers or working in their own business. It is not surprising in these circumstances that 50 per cent of those interviewed had paid a 'fee', on average $38, to get their job in a garment factory (Sok et al., 2001, pp. 46-61).

In these circumstances, the main priority for labour relations in the garment industry and the rest of the small private formal sector is to build the capacity of workers' and employers' organizations and to develop machinery for dispute prevention, conciliation, arbitration and adjudication. Through the development of democratic and independent trade unions, Cambodian workers can judge and protect their own interests: this is preferable to relying on pressure on labour standards from foreign governments, trade unions, consumer groups and non-government organiza-

Box 4. Decent or indecent work in *maquiladoras*? Compared with whom? New evidence from Honduras

Are offshore assembly workers being exploited or emancipated? The answer depends on the nature of the comparison that is made. Some analysts apply absolute standards related to basic needs and human rights, but most are 'relativists', comparing the situation of such workers with workers in industrialized countries (inevitably adversely), with workers in the same country in sectors oriented towards the home market (which raises methodological problems), or with unemployed or destitute workers (in Krugman's [1] often quoted phrase, 'bad jobs at bad wages are better than no jobs at all'). A new study [2] by Ver Beek of *maquiladora* workers in the garment industry in Honduras uses an alternative control group – individuals who are applying for employment in the *maquiladora* for the first time, and who are similar in background (age, education, marital status, etc.) and experience to those who are already working there.

In several respects, and in contrast to some earlier research and conventional wisdom, *maquiladora* workers were found to be better off than the control group. They were earning on average two-thirds more than the minimum wage and 55 per cent more than applicants did in their previous jobs – with the improvement in both cases being rather greater for men than for women. Employees were found to provide more financial support to their families, and to be more likely to feel that their household relationships had improved and that they were heads of their household. They were significantly more likely than the control group to have voted in the last election.

On the other hand, *maquiladora* salaries are not high enough to move a Honduran family out of poverty, based on national benchmarks. The proportion of employees reporting health problems affecting their ability to work was significantly higher than for applicants, and most of them thought their problems were work-related. A slightly lower percentage of employees than applicants were or had been working in unionized establishments. And free time among workers was significantly lower than among workers.

There was not much difference between the two groups in the extent of overtime worked (on more occasions by employees but for fewer hours), experience of stress (affecting about half), mistreatment by supervisors (relatively infrequent), and ability to arrange child care and continue their education.

In general, *maquiladora* workers were satisfied with their jobs – 50 per cent very much so, 46 per cent 'somewhat', and only 4 per cent 'not at all'. As the author comments, 'it seems that the principal attraction of *maquiladora* employment is economic, which would explain why hundreds of applicants wait in line each week hoping to get a job in one of the *maquiladoras*'.

[1] Krugman, 1997. [2] The interview survey, in the Department of Cortés covered 270 *maquiladora* workers and 149 first-time applicants in July and August 1998.

Source: Ver Beek, 2001.

tions. This kind of pressure sometimes takes the form of closing markets to Cambodian products (see box 5).

There is a need, also, to identify and encourage sources of dynamism in the labour market, in the interests of continued or accelerated generation of demand for labour. Unfortunately, there is a question mark over

Box 5. Decent or indecent work in globalized production facilities?
Who should set and enforce standards?

As an alternative to top-down regulation based on uniform labour standards and to reliance on voluntary initiatives by corporations, Fung, O'Rourke and Sabel have recently proposed a new approach, which they call Ratcheting Labour Standards (RLS). RLS would use monitoring and public disclosure to create incentives for firms to improve their own and their suppliers' factories, and would create a pool of information about best practices for comparison and diffusion. It would be based on four principles – transparency, competition, continuous improvement, and sanctions.

In practice, it would work as follows. At the top, an RLS council (non-governmental or inter-governmental) would regulate two kinds of entity: firms and monitors. Monitors would be organizations that collect and verify social-performance information and help firms comply with their labour standards. Each firm in an RLS-regulated sector would select a monitor and abide by its protocols. Based on reports from the firms, inspections and occasional independent audits, monitors would rank the social performance of firms under their purview. The RLS council would act as an 'umpire', assuring the accuracy and comparability of information from different monitors and disseminating it. These arrangements, it is hoped, would encourage firms to vie with each other to show that they are better than their competitors. The information generated by this process would be available to consumers, journalists, activists, investors, officials at local, national and international levels, and the firms themselves, and would feed into a wide-ranging debate on global labour standards. Workers in developing countries would make an input into the discussion of appropriate standards, which would be periodically ratcheted up as conditions changed.

Two possible roads to building RLS are envisaged. The first is for one of the non-governmental, multi-stakeholder workplace monitoring programmes to embrace it as an expansion strategy. Alternatively, international organizations (the ILO, the UN, the World Bank) could begin to build RLS: the authors argue that the Bank, in particular,

the prospects of two important sources of dynamism – the garment and tourism industries. In the case of the garment industry the problem is that Cambodia does not have an underlying comparative advantage in a cheap-labour industry of this kind. As the special concessions in world markets which have brought garment factories to Cambodia begin to be eroded, the number of such factories and employees is likely to fall. In the case of tourism, the problem relates not to comparative advantage and competitiveness (which are not a big worry for Cambodia, given its unique assets) but to global tensions. Whether or not it continues, a downturn in arrivals by air since September 2001 is a reminder of this sector's vulnerability to events outside its control.

The starting point in a search for alternative sources of dynamism is recognition of Cambodia's underlying comparative advantage – in natural-resource-based production, initially involving relatively unskilled is being transformed in ways that might make it interested in this task. Officials in regulatory agencies and trade unions could use the information generated by RLS or could even join in as certified monitors.

In response, Standing, while supporting the objectives of RLS, has some worries about its design.

- It could make matters worse, by driving bad practices underground.
- The cost could be excessive in relation to its effect: the same amount of money might be better used to help vulnerable workers to bargain better.
- The principles on which standards are to be based are vague, and need to be spelled out.
- RLS puts excessive emphasis on regulations, monitoring and sanctions ('the smell of the big stick'): incentives to good practice, such as an award scheme, are likely to work better.
- Workers' voices should be at the forefront in selecting monitors, otherwise there is moral hazard in the proposals.
- More attention should be paid to the danger of a ratcheting down of standards in industrialized countries.
- The World Bank should remain a bank, and should not be a standards setter or monitor.

In short, Standing concludes that "incentives to improved practices, combined with public advocacy, have more prospect of success than complex monitoring and sanctions. Above all, though, strengthening the voice of working communities – not putting faith in social auditors – is the most effective way to make substantial progress."

Sources: Fung, O'Rourke and Sabel, 2003; Standing, 2003.

labour, rather than in the non-agricultural labour-intensive activities for which countries like the Philippines and Vietnam, with high skill levels and labour/ land ratios, are suited. The search also needs to start with the question – how does Cambodia's economy differ from others in the region? In what main ways is it an outlier, in particularly difficult circumstances compared with the others? In this respect, two anomalies are particularly striking for the observer of the Cambodian economy in an Asian context: 24 years after the end of the Khmer Rouge regime and ten years after UNTAC, its road system has not been repaired and its economy is consequently fragmented; the proportion of arable land under irrigation is still tiny, both in comparison with other ASEAN countries and in relation to its potential. Emergency programmes in each of these areas would have a greater and quicker impact on demand for labour than any other set of measures.

Between 1992 and 2000 less than 12 per cent of total external assistance went to transport and infrastructure, and only 350 km of primary roads were reconstructed to international standards. As a result, only about a third of the total length of primary roads is passable all the year round, and secondary and tertiary roads are in an even worse state. Cambodia does not have an integrated national economy – many of its inhabitants belong more to the Thai or Vietnamese economies than they do to the Cambodian – and farmers have no incentive to move out of low-productivity subsistence farming into cash crops: poor roads mean that their input prices are high, the prices they get for their crops are low, and commodities take so long to get to market that they are spoiled on the way.

The current shift in emphasis in external aid towards the transport sector should continue. But, at the same time, a comprehensive and prioritized national transport strategy, oriented towards increasing demand for labour, is needed. Wherever possible, labour-based appropriate technology should be used for road-building, repair and maintenance. A new system for routine financing of road maintenance – the most neglected aspect of road programmes in Cambodia – urgently needs to be worked out: and meanwhile an interim, emergency, arrangement for allocating government funds to maintenance needs to be implemented. Progress in reforming public-sector salaries, also, is a necessary condition for success in this and any other approach towards the promotion of decent work in which government is involved.

No large-scale irrigation projects have been implemented in Cambodia in the past 30 years, and most of the medium-scale projects since

Figure 3. Irrigated agricultural area as per cent of total arable land, Cambodia (potential & actual) & other ASEAN countries, 1999

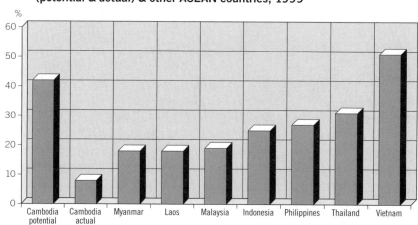

Source: ILO, 2002, figure 24.

1979 have been unsuccessful. Cambodia has the least irrigated economy in the region and its irrigated area could potentially be more than six times larger than it is (figure 3). Lack of good water management and control is at the heart of food insecurity for many of the rural poor and discourages subsistence farmers from borrowing to invest in higher-yield activities.

Investment in roads and irrigation go together. If roads are bad, investment in rehabilitating irrigation systems does not make much sense. But if roads are improved, the social and private profitability of irrigation rehabilitation and development is transformed. Minor repair of existing facilities could, in these circumstances, give an immediate boost to agricultural growth. The planners' emphasis on investment in small-scale, private-sector-led irrigation systems, also, makes it even more necessary for road and irrigation planners to work together: the incentive for farmers to buy and to maintain these small-scale irrigation systems will depend crucially on ease of access to inputs and markets.

(b) Increasing the integrability of labour-market outsiders in Pakistan and Cambodia

In both countries the major obstacle to the integration of outsiders into expanding sectors of the economy is illiteracy. The contrast in adult illiteracy rates, particularly for females, between Pakistan and neighbouring countries otherwise around the same level of development is striking, as table 6 shows.

Table 6. Comparison of GNP per head and adult illiteracy rates, South Asia and China

	Pakistan	Sri Lanka	China	India	Bangla-desh	Nepal
GNP per head (US) 1998	470	820	780	450	370	220
Adult illiteracy rate (% of 15+ population)						
Both sexes	56.0	8.9	17.2	44.3	59.9	60.8
Female	71.1	11.7	25.4	56.5	71.4	78.3
Male	42.0	5.9	9.3	32.9	48.9	43.1

Source: Government of Pakistan, 2001, table 2.

Moreover, functional illiteracy rates in Pakistan and all the countries in table 6 are likely to be much higher than those shown (based merely on respondents' answers' to the question whether they could read or write). For example, Cambodia's illiteracy rate in 1999, based on a similar self-assessment survey, was 36 per cent – higher than in any other South-East

Figure 4. Literacy and illiteracy rates, 15+ age group, by sex, Cambodia, 1999

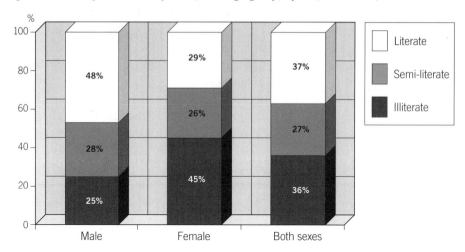

Source: Godfrey et al. 2001, table 2.5.

Asian country except Laos. But, as figure 4 shows, a survey carried out with UNESCO assistance in the same year, in which specially designed tests were administered, found that as many as 63 per cent of Cambodians were functionally illiterate – i.e. either completely illiterate or semi-literate (able to read and write only a few words and numbers, not enough to be of use to them for their everyday life and income generation). As in Pakistan, the situation for women is much worse than for men. Functional illiteracy poses huge problems for a programme of decent work promotion. There is a strong connection between the acquisition of literacy/numeracy and productivity gains in agriculture, and a literate, numerate and trainable workforce is needed for international competitiveness based on productive rather than merely cheap labour.

Improvements in access to and reduction in drop-out from basic education are the most cost-effective way to reduce illiteracy rates over time but, in both countries and the many other developing countries in a similar situation, this is an emergency. A mass campaign aimed at adults is needed, and planners in both countries seem to be thinking along these lines. The key to a successful campaign will be to make it worthwhile to enrol – by reducing the costs of attendance, and by linking it to income generation activities.

In both economies, also, a safety net is needed which will reach labour-market outsiders. In countries such as these a formal-sector-based scheme is of little use for this purpose. Much more relevant is a national guaranteed employment scheme, offering work (building, repairing and maintaining roads, schools, health centres, irrigation infrastructure, etc.) to all who want it – for wages rather than food. If wage rates are set low enough in relation to local market rates, such a scheme is counter-cyclical, self-liquidating and (like a literacy campaign) self-targeting. Appropriately enough for two of the world's poorest economies, this is a safety net that creates and sustains assets: it employs the poor to help the poor.

3.1 Conclusions

The starting point of this paper has been that any discussion about the practicalities of decent work policy essentially comes down to possible trade-offs and complementarities between its dimensions. This question is too often approached in a dogmatic spirit – with 'distortionists' maintaining that assuring high wages and labour standards for some will always harm others, and 'institutionalists' insisting that there is never a conflict between the quality and quantity of employment. In practice, as has been seen, there are potential trade-offs, but they can be offset or postponed by increases in productivity.

The context within which the decent work objective is being approached will differ from country to country. What is possible will depend in part on the category of economy in question, as far as income per head, importance of wage employment and government role is concerned – whether industrialized, transition or developing. It will also depend on the nature of the labour market within each category – whether it is more or less flexible. Thus we have suggested a six-category typology for discussion of policy.

How progress can be measured will also depend on the context. The traditional labour market indicators (unemployment and labour force participation rate and employment-to-population ratio) are particularly unhelpful for this purpose in countries which do not have effective unemployment benefit systems. Wage employment is a more useful proxy for the demand for labour, even in countries where it represents a relatively small proportion of total employment. It would be nice to be able to distinguish between primary and secondary forms of employment, but in practice even in industrialized countries the available statistics are insufficiently subtle for this purpose. Statistics on non-wage aspects of the quality of employment are also problematic, and not comparable between countries. In general, the most urgent and promising direction for developing decent work indicators is to improve statistics on earnings and particularly wages. Disaggregation of all indicators by gender, age group and education level is also important. Our exploration of the possibility of a single national index of at least the employment dimensions of decent work is, it must be admitted, still at the prototype stage: our 'index of labour morale' (see tables 4 and 5, and figure 1) has the virtue of simplicity, but it needs further work.

The focus of the paper's policy discussion has been on the demand for labour. In contrast to the earlier (elasticity-based) fear among employment planners that productivity growth can pose a threat to jobs, this approach puts increasing productivity at the centre of a decent work strategy. At the same time, it is necessary to increase the integrability of labour-market outsiders to enable them to take advantage of any increase in labour demand. How this may work differs between the six categories of country in our typology.

In **industrialized countries**, while the struggle between the more flexible Live-to-Work US model and the less flexible Work-to-Live European model continues (with some signs of convergence between the two models), the prospects for growth in demand for labour are extremely uncertain and macroeconomic policies that are 'supportive of activity' are needed. Unfinished business in the area of increasing the integrability of labour-market outsiders includes: wider implementation of (improved) schemes to 'make work pay'; adjustment of hiring, firing and training practices to the phenomenon of an ageing workforce; renewed emphasis on comprehensive lifelong learning strategies; and greater attention to inequities within education systems.

In **transition countries**, whether flexible or inflexible, the prime means of increasing the demand for labour is further overall economic reform. As well as the establishment of basic market institutions, liberalization of markets, enterprise restructuring, and strengthening of the financial sector, deregulation of the small enterprise sector is an urgent priority for this purpose. Looking further ahead, also, educational systems in many such countries need to be rebuilt after their virtual collapse, if their economies are not to get stuck in low-skill equilibrium. To increase the integrability of outsiders, labour market reforms and reduction in barriers to geographic mobility are still needed, as well as improvements in the quality of education available and in access to it.

Between **developing countries**, as the examples of inflexible Pakistan and flexible Cambodia have shown, ways of increasing demand for labour are likely to vary widely. In Pakistan there is still some way to go with deregulation, eliminating subsidies to capital, reducing the weight of the public sector, and the drive against corruption – all of which would improve incentives for the expansion of external leading sectors. Growth of the complementary internal leading sector of house-building could be encouraged by removing institutional obstacles to the development of a commercial, long-term mortgage system; changes in the composition of government expenditure would also help. In Cambodia, the search for alternative sources of dynamism to revitalize the garment industry (out of line with underlying comparative advantage) and the vulnerability of the tourism industry draws attention to the need for emergency programmes of road building/repair and rehabilitation of irrigation systems, both of which would give a big boost to labour demand.

Programmes needed to increase the integrability of outsiders take a similar form in both types of developing country. Abolition of functional illiteracy, particularly among women, is the priority – through improving access to basic education and reducing drop-outs, but also through emergency adult literacy campaigns. In both cases, also, a national guaranteed employment scheme could provide an appropriate safety net for labour-market outsiders that creates and sustains assets.

Throughout the paper, in the boxes as well as the text, a message that has repeatedly emerged is the importance to a decent work strategy of workers gaining (or in some countries regaining) control of their own destiny. Thus Applebaum (2002) (in box 1) looks to a resurgence of trade union movements in industrialized countries as a way of rolling back the new insecurities associated with the transformation of work and employment over the past few decades. In the 1990s the success of the unfashionable democratic corporatism model in improving the employment situation in four of Europe's smaller economies (Auer, 2000) points in a similar direction. In the same spirit, the World Bank (2002) emphasizes the need to develop institutions in Russia to allow worker voice, improve work conditions, enforce contracts and resolve disputes, including true worker and employer representation in their respective organizations – a recommendation that would be appropriate in many other transition countries.

In developing countries, the lack of much gain for labour from the 'new economic model' in Latin America is attributed by Weeks (1999) (in box 3) to the decline in the strength of trade unions throughout the sub-continent: he calls for a reassertion of the rights provided for in ILO Conventions and of a role for unions in establishing minimum standards in the workplace. In countries like Cambodia, where trade unions are weak, inexperienced and often politicized, the development of democratic and independent workers' organizations is an urgent priority. Such organizations, as Standing (2003) argues more generally (in box 5), provide the most effective route to progress in improving labour standards. Rather than relying on externally imposed monitoring and sanctions systems (such as Ratcheting Labour Standards) or pressure from foreign governments, trade unions, consumer groups and non-government organizations, the workers themselves should be able to make a judgement about their own interests, and should be in a position to protect them.

However, new types of trade union[14] are needed for this purpose – 'swords of justice' rather than merely protectors of vested interest (Hyman, 1999). In order to reverse the decline in their membership, unions need, of course, to pay attention to the special requirements of their traditional constituents, particularly in the protection of their pay and working conditions (while taking care to retain public support for any industrial action). But if they are to advance the wider decent-work objective, they also need to build a new constituency among labour market outsiders. Jose (1999, p. 10) describes some innovative approaches to organizing less skilled workers, women and minority groups in the service industries at a national level, and less skilled workers in small enterprises under the aegis of area-specific organizations in the United States, and suggests that they might provide useful lessons for similar efforts in developing countries. In any case, building a new constituency must be high on the agenda of trade unions in all types of country and certainly a task which the ILO is well placed to assist.

The proper framework for reasserting workers' control over their own destiny and building a new constituency is the ILO Declaration of 1998. Its four core principles are:

(a) freedom of association and the effective recognition of the right to collective bargaining;

(b) the elimination of all forms of forced or compulsory labour;

(c) the effective abolition of child labour; and

(d) the elimination of discrimination in respect of employment and occupation.

As the Declaration points out, merely by joining the ILO, all members have effectively signed up to these four principles.

---

[14] Another paper in this series (see Kuruvilla, chapter V of this volume), on the social dialogue dimensions of decent work, addresses these issues in detail.

References

Anant, T.; Sundaram, K.; Tendulkar, S.: *Employment and labour in South Asia* (New Delhi, ILO South Asia Multidisciplinary Advisory Team, 1999).

Anker, R. et al.: *Measuring decent work with statistical indicators*, Working Paper No. 2 (Geneva, ILO, Policy Integration Department, 2002).

Applebaum, E.: "Transformation of work and employment and new insecurities", in Auer, P; Daniel, C. (eds.): *The future of work, employment and social protection: The search for new securities in a world of growing uncertainties* (Geneva, International Institute for Labour Studies, 2002).

Auer, P.: *Employment revival in Europe: Labour market success in Austria, Denmark, Ireland and the Netherlands* (Geneva, ILO, 2000).

—: Daniel, C. (eds.): *The future of work, employment and social protection: The search for new securities in a world of growing uncertainties* (Geneva, International Institute for Labour Studies, 2002).

Betcherman, G.; Luinstra, A.; Ogawa, M.: *Labour market regulation: International experience in promoting employment and social protection,* World Bank, Social Protection Discussion Paper Series No. 0128 (Washington, D.C., World Bank, 2001).

Britton, A.: "Full employment in the industrialized countries", in *International Labour Review*, 1997, Vol. 136, No. 3.

Bruton, H.; Fairris, D.: "Work and development", in *International Labour Review*, 1999, Vol. 138, No. 1.

Card, D.; Krueger, A.B: *Myth and measurement: The new economics of the minimum wage* (Princeton, New Jersey, Princeton University Press, 1995).

Cazes, S.; Nesporova, A.: "Labour market flexibility in the transition countries: How much is too much?", in *International Labour Review*, 2001, Vol. 140, No. 3.

Cichon, M.: *Are there better ways to cut the cake?*, Issues in Social Protection Discussion Paper 3 (Geneva, ILO, Social Security Department, 1997).

Currie, L.: "The leading sector model of growth in developing countries", in *Journal of Economic Studies (New Series)*, 1974, Vol. 1, No. 1.

de Grip, A.; Hoevenberg, J.; Willems, E.: "Atypical employment in the European Union", in *International Labour Review*, 1997, Vol. 136, No. 1.

Eilat, Y.; Zinnes, C.: "The shadow economy in transition countries: Friend or foe? A policy perspective", in *World Development*, 2002, Vol. 30, No. 7.

European Bank for Reconstruction and Development: *Transition report 2002* (London, 2002).

Freeman, R.B.: *Labour market institutions and policies: Help or hindrance to economic adjustment?* Proceedings of the World Bank Annual Conference on Development Economics, Supplement to the *World Bank Economic Review* and the *World Bank Research Observer* (Washington, D.C., World Bank, 1993).

—: "Working to live or living to work?", in Auer, P.; Daniel, C. (eds.): *The future of work, employment and social protection: The search for new securities in a world of growing uncertainties* (Geneva, International Institute for Labour Studies, 2002).

Fung, A.; O'Rourke, D.; Sabel, C.: "Realizing labour standards: How transparency, competition and sanctions could improve working conditions worldwide", in *Boston Review*, 2002. (http://bostonreview.mit.edu/BR26.1/fung.html).

Ghai, D.: *Decent work: Concepts, models and indicators*, International Institute for Labour Studies Discussion Paper DP/139/2002 (Geneva, International Institute for Labour Studies, 2002).

Godfrey, M. (ed.): *Skill development for international competitiveness* (Cheltenham, Edward Elgar, 1997).

— et al.: "A study of the Cambodian labour market, with reference to poverty reduction, growth and adjustment to crisis", in *Development analysis network: Labour markets in transitional economies in Southeast Asia and Thailand* (Phnom Penh, Cambodia Development Research Institute, 2001).

Government of Pakistan: *Three year poverty reduction programme 2001-04* (Islamabad, Planning Commision, 2001).

Gulyani, S.: "Effects of poor transportation on lean production and industrial clustering: Evidence from the Indian auto industry", in *World Development*, 2001, Vol. 29, No. 7.

Heckman, J.; Pagés, C.: *The cost of job security regulations: Evidence from Latin American labour markets*, NBER Working Paper Series 7773 (Cambridge, Massachusetts, National Bureau of Economic Research, 2000).

Humphrey, J.: "Industrial reorganisation in developing countries: From models to trajectories", in *World Development*, 1995, Vol. 23, No. 1.

—: "Training and motivation in the context of new approaches to manufacturing production: Evidence from Latin America", in Godfrey, M. (ed.): *Skill development for international competitiveness* (Cheltenham, Edward Elgar, 1997).

Hyman, R.: *An emerging agenda for trade unions?* International Institute for Labour Studies Discussion Paper DP/98/1999 (Geneva, International Institute for Labour Studies, 1999).

ILO: *Decent work*, Report of the Director-General (Geneva, 1999).

—: *Employment strategy in support of Pakistan's poverty reduction programme* (ILO, Islamabad, 2001a).

—: *Pakistan: Growth, employment and poverty alleviation – Prospects and policy challenges*, Draft report prepared under the Country Employment Policy Review Programme (Geneva, 2001b).

—: *KILM 2001/2* (Key Indicators of the Labour Market), CD (Geneva).

—: *Generating decent work in an emergency: Poverty reduction in Cambodia* (Bangkok, ILO Regional Office for Asia and the Pacific, 2002).

—: *Global employment trends* (Geneva, 2003).

International Monetary Fund: *Pakistan: Selected issues and statistical appendix*, IMF Country Report No. 01/11(Washington, D.C., IMF, 2001).

—: *World economic outlook 2002* (Washington, D.C., IMF, 2002).

Jose, A.V.: *The future of the labour movement: Some observations on developing countries*, International Institute for Labour Studies Discussion Paper DP/98/1999 (Geneva, International Institute for Labour Studies, 1999).

Karush, S.: "A little booklet that controls all", in *The Russia Journal*, Moscow, 26 Mar. 2002.

Kornai, J.: *Economics of shortage* (Amsterdam, North Holland; New York, Oxford University Press, 1980).

Krugman, P.: "In praise of cheap labour", in *State*, 20 Mar. 1997.

Leibenstein, H.: *Economic backwardness and economic growth* (New York, Wiley, 1957).

Martin, M. et al.: *TIMSS 1999: International science report*, Findings from IEA's repeat of the third international mathematics and science study at the eighth grade (Chestnut Hill, Massachusetts, International Study Center, Lynch School of Education, Boston College, 2000).

Mullis, I.V.S. et al.: *TIMSS 1999: International mathematics report*, Findings from IEA's repeat of the third international mathematics and science study at the eighth grade (Chestnut Hill, Massachusetts, International Study Center, Lynch School of Education, Boston College, 2000).

Nesporova, A.: *Why unemployment remains so high in Central and Eastern Europe*, ILO Employment Paper 2002/43 (Geneva, ILO, 2002).

OECD: *Employment outlook* (Paris, 1998).

—: *Employment outlook* (Paris, 1999).

—: *Knowledge and skills for life: First results from PISA 2000* (Paris, 2001).

—: *Employment outlook* (Paris, 2002).

O'Higgins, N.: *Youth unemployment and employment policy: A global perspective* (Geneva, ILO, 2001).

Osmani, S.R.: *Exploring the employment nexus: Topics in employment and poverty*, Report prepared for the Task Force on the Joint ILO/UNDP Programme on Employment and Poverty (New York, UNDP; Geneva, ILO, 2002).

Ozaki, M.: "Labour relations and work organization in industrialized countries", in *International Labour Review*, 1996, Vol. 135, No. 1.

Rama, M: *The Sri Lankan unemployment problem revisited*, World Bank Working Paper No. 2227 (Washington, D.C., World Bank, 1999).

Reinhardt, N.; Peres, W.: "Latin America's new economic model: Micro responses and economic restructuring", in *World Development*, 2000, Vol. 28, No. 9.

Royal Government of Cambodia: *Report of the assessment of the functional literacy levels of the adult population of Cambodia* (Phnom Penh, Ministry of Education, Youth and Sports, 2000).

Rühl, C.: "Life at the bottom of the sandwich", in *The Moscow Times*, 19 Feb. 2003.

Saget, C.: "Poverty reduction and decent work in developing countries: Do minimum wages help?", in *International Labour Review*, 2001, Vol. 140, No. 3.

Schmitz, H.; Nadvi, K.: "Clustering and industrialisation: Introduction", in *World Development*, 1999, Vol. 27, No. 9.

Sen, A.: "Inequality, unemployment and contemporary Europe", in *International Labour Review*, 1997, Vol. 136, No. 2

—: "Work and rights", in *International Labour Review*, 2000, Vol. 139, No. 2.

Sok, H.; Huot, C.; Boreak, S.: *Cambodia's annual economic review 2001* (Phnom Pehh, Cambodia Development Resource Institute, 2001).

Standing, G.: *Structural adustment and labour market policies: Towards social adustment?* Paper for Workshop on Labour Market Issues and Structural Adjustment (Geneva, ILO 1989).

—: "Human development: A response to 'Realizing Labour Standards', in *Boston Review*, 2003. (http://bostonreview.mit.edu/BR26.1/standing.html).

Thompson, F.: *Fordism, post-Fordism and the flexible system of production*, 2003 (http://willamette.edu/~fthompso/MgmtCon/Fordism&Postfordism.hmtl).

Tilly, C.: "Reasons for the continuing growth of part-time employment", in *Monthly Labour Review*, 1991, Vol. 114, No. 3.

UNICEF: *Social monitor 2002*, The MONEE Project, CEE/CIS/Baltics (Florence, UNICEF, Innocenti Research Centre, 2002a).

—: *A league table of educational disadvantage in rich nations*, Innocenti Report Card Issue No. 4 (Florence, UNICEF, Innocenti Research Centre, 2002b).

Ver Beek, K.A.: "Maquiladoras: Exploitation or emancipation? An overview of the situation of maquiladora workers in Honduras", in *World Development*, 2001, Vol. 29, No. 9.

Weeks, J.: "Wages, employment and workers' rights in Latin America, 1970-98", in *International Labour Review*, 1999, Vol. 138, No. 2.

Womack, J.P.; Jones, D.T.; Roos, D.: *The machine that changed the world* (New York, Macmillan, 1990).

World Bank: *Pakistan: Private sector assessment*, Report No. 14847-PAK (Washington, D.C., 1996).

—: *The Russian labour market: Moving from crisis to recovery* (Washington, D.C., World Bank Human Development Sector Unit, Europe and Central Asia Region, 2002a).

—: *Russian economic report, October 2002* (Moscow, World Bank Russia Office, 2002b).

Exercises

The data for the following exercises are retrieved from the ILO CD-ROM, *Key Indicators of the Labour Market 2001-2002*. Repeat these exercises with a different selection of countries, or carry out your own exercises, using the KILM data to explore other aspects of decent work.

1. Employment status

(a) The following tables show trends in wage employment and labour force in six countries (one from each category in our typology). Construct a table and a chart showing trends in wage employment as a percentage of the labour force in these six countries. What are the implications for decent work of the differences between countries in levels and trends in this percentage?

Table 1.1. Wage employment ('000), selected countries, 1990-1999

	1990	1991	1992	1993	1994	1995	1996	1997	1998	1999
France	19154	19260	19252	19070.3	19121	19352.7	19450	19611	20058	20509
Hungary	3846	3694	3461	3284	3219	3146	3113	3127	3221	3201
Mexico	15936	16877	17489	18102	18749	19397	20760	21730	23251	23763
Korea, Rep. of,	10950	11405	11618	11794	12325	12784	13065	13226	12191	12522
Russia			65386	64190	60404	59786	58976	57194	55192	55966
US	108338	107101	108187	109656	112232	114262	116040	118873	121019	123267

Table 1.2. Labour force ('000), selected countries, 1990-1999

	1990	1991	1992	1993	1994	1995	1996	1997	1998	1999
France	24576	24604.	24825	24978	25136	25278	25589	25581	25755	25982
Hungary	4731	4628	4526	4346	4202	4095	4048	3995	4010	4096
Mexico	23603	30143	31219	32381	33237	34309	35437	37193	38242	38470
Korea, Rep. of,	18540	19115	19498	19879	20395	20852	21242	21662	21455	21634
Russia	77185	75096	73007	71828	70640	69469	68264	67500	66736	69732
US	125840	126346	128105	129202	131057	132302	133946	136295	137674	139369

(b) The following table shows trends in the number of women in wage employment in the same six countries over the same period. Construct a table and a chart showing trends in women's share of wage employment in these six countries. What are the implications for decent work of the differences between countries in levels and trends in this percentage?

Table 1.3. Women in wage employment ('000), selected countries, 1991-1999

	1991	1992	1993	1994	1995	1996	1997	1998	1999
France	8578	8678	8708	8787	8900	8984	9097	9598	9543
Hungary	1719	1658	1580	1533	1468	1453	1447	1509	1519
Mexico	5705	5798	5892	6091	6291	6901	7279	7847	7973
Korea, Rep. of,	4344	4413	4459	4708	4879	5042	5196	4693	4952
Russia		32011	30871	28997	28722	28259	27368	26352	27103
US	49843	50604	51407	52601	53534	54489	55839	56863	58193

2. Real wages

The following tables show trends in nominal wages and consumer prices in five of the six countries. Construct a table and chart showing trends in indices of real wages in manufacturing in these countries (adding Mexico for which an index of real wages in manufacturing is also available).[15] What are the implications for decent work of the differences between countries in levels and trends in this index? How do they modify the message of the results of exercise 1*(a)* above?

---

[15] Data on nominal wages and consumer prices are not available for Mexico, but an index of real wages in manufacturing is available, as follows:

	1991	1992	1993	1994	1995	1996	1997	1998	1999
Mexico	100	109	112	116	100	89	88	91	91

Table 2.1. Index of nominal wages in manufacturing, selected countries, 1991-1999 (1991=100)

	1991	1992	1993	1994	1995	1996	1997	1998	1999
France	100	104	107	109	111	114	117		
Hungary	100	123	153	189	230	281	343	401	445
Korea, Rep. of,	100	116	128	148	163	183	192	186	214
Russia	100	1107	9869	34006	79588	128115	157363	175685	
US	100	103	105	108	111	114	118	121	124

Table 2.2. Consumer price index, selected countries, 1991-1999 (1991=100)

	1991	1992	1993	1994	1995	1996	1997	1998	1999
France	100	102	105	106	108	110	112		
Hungary	100	118	145	172	221	273	323	369	406
Korea, Rep. of,	100	106	111	118	124	130	135	146	147
Russia	100	1629	15869	64688	192521	284429	326484	416814	
US	100	103	106	109	112	115	118	120	122

3. Index of labour morale

Multiply the index of real manufacturing wages (constructed for exercise 2) by the series on percentage of the labour force in wage employment (constructed for exercise 3). Convert the resulting figures into an 'index of labour morale' (1991=100) and show your results in a table and chart.[16] If trends in manufacturing wages are accepted as a rough guide to trends in average wages in each economy, what are the implications for decent work of the differences between countries in levels and trends in this index?

4. Part-time employment

(a) The following tables show trends in total and part-time employment in the six countries. Construct a table and chart showing trends in part-time as a percentage of total employment in these countries. What are the implications for decent work of the differences between countries in levels and trends in this percentage?

---

[16] See tables 4 and 5 and figure 1 in the paper for an attempt to construct such an index, with a different set of countries and a different source of data.

Table 4.1. Total employment ('000), selected countries, 1990-1997

	1990	1991	1992	1993	1994	1995	1996	1997
France	18633	19145	19220	19350	19150	19321	19374	19225
Hungary			4028	3770	3519.5	3269	3220	3222
Mexico						32222	34116	35842
Korea, Rep. of,	18085	18611	18809	19119	19699	20237	20615	20867
US	104875	103722	104668	106104	101833	103360	104232	

Table 4.2. Part-time employment ('000), selected countries, 1990-1997

	1990	1991	1992	1993	1994	1995	1996	1997
France	2264	2306	2405	2583	2669	2752	2772	2868
Hungary			108	109	106.5	104	100	106
Mexico						5336	5050	5657
Korea, Rep. of,	809	867	924	882	904	894	908	1074
US	14494	14891	15077	15280	13730	13760	13754	

(b) The following table shows trends in the number of women in part-time employment in the six countries. Construct a table and chart showing trends in the female share of part-time employment in these countries. What are the implications for decent work of the differences between countries in levels and trends in this percentage?

Table 4.3. Women in part-time employment ('000), selected countries, 1990-1997

	1990	1991	1992	1993	1994	1995	1996	1997
France	1806	1834	1908	2054	2122	2176	2181	2260
Hungary			71	71	71	71	70	76
Mexico						3246	3152	3603
Korea, Rep. of,	474	510	558	536	548	547	577	670
US	9886	10087	10126	10266	9469	9534	9597	

5. Trade-offs? Wages, employment and productivity compared

The following tables show trends in employment and productivity (value added per worker) in manufacturing in four of the six countries. As a result of exercise 2, you should already have a table showing trends in indices of real wages in manufacturing in the same countries. Combine the information from these three tables to construct a table and chart for each of the four countries, showing trends in employment, real wages and real productivity in each country. Compare the country charts with each other. What are the implications of this inter-country comparison for the debate about trade-offs and complementarities between dimensions of decent work?

Table 5.1. Index of employment in manufacturing, selected countries, 1991-1999 (1991=100)

	1991	1992	1993	1994	1995	1996	1997	1998	1999
France	100	97	92	90	90	89	88	88	88
Mexico	100	103	106	107	108	120	130	145	
Korea, Rep. of,	100	97	93	94	95	93	89	78	80
US	100	98	96	98	100	100	101	101	98

Table 5.2. Index of real value added per person in manufacturing, selected countries, 1991-1999 (1991=100)

	1991	1992	1993	1994	1995	1996	1997	1998	1999
France	100	104	104	113	118	119	127	129	132
Mexico	100	106	111	118	119	122	125	120	118
Korea, Rep. of,	100	109	119	131	143	156	175	186	220
US	100	104	107	114	120	123	128	133	141

Chapter IV
Social protection, decent work and development

Ashwani Saith

Summary

This paper analyses the field of social protection within the broader concept of decent work and relates both social protection and decent work to development, emphasizing the interface between them. The linkage with poverty alleviation is discussed.

The ILO's decent work concept and associated policy agenda have marked a major intervention in the discourse on deprivation since the late 1990s. Its four components include economic dimensions, but they also include social aspects which qualify as ends in their own right. This widens the analytical and policy framework considerably and may allow the decent work concept to incorporate the agendas of poverty reduction, human development and social integration. The concept makes it possible to address the full range of development concerns and to question the nature of the structures and processes that reproduce the cycles of poverty and exclusion.

The concept of decent work has to underwrite decent living. Decent living standards involve elements which fall outside the sphere of employment and work, a fact which also widens the agenda: it implies the existence of social mechanisms which successfully transform decent work into decent living. Many basic needs such as health and education cannot automatically be read into the employment or work relation, and the failure of even good incomes to translate into good social services is a familiar reality.

The paper considers the question of a trade-off between decent work and economic growth. An understanding of the synergetic and sequential relationships could inform the phasing of policies addressing various decent work components. Many different views prevail, and there is little consensus on the issue. The paper comments on the interactions between economic growth and employment, between growth and labour rights, and between growth and social protection, and goes on to consider different aspects of social protection and security.

The author points out the dangers of generalization and situates the debate in the framework of three types of national economy - the classical, the transitional and the development model. He then goes on to consider the patterns and processes of socio-economic vulnerability, distinguishing four categories of fluctuations, shocks and crises which affect large sections of a population.

Part three of the paper develops a framework for mapping the extent of social protection coverage for any given population. The framework highlights three elements, one on each axis of a cube. The first of these represents the multiple dimensions of social protection; the second pertains to different social constituencies in the population; the third lists the alternative provisioning systems (potentially) available for addressing the specific dimensions of social protection identified on the first axis. The cubic form of the matrix makes it possible to investigate the modes and forms of cover which are best suited to addressing the insecurities and deficits of specific population groups.

The fourth section of the paper deals with the design of social protection systems, reflecting on macro considerations and micro parameters; it comments on a number of strategic issues. Section five discusses appropriate monitoring indicators and the paper concludes by noting four main tendencies in the policy discourse on poverty reduction and social protection.

In general, the paper argues that the notion of decent work (and social protection, which is one of its four constituents) needs to be considered within a broad development context, rather than in a narrow focus on the workplace or enterprise alone. Hence the agenda for decent work, and for universalizing social protection, must engage with wider processes and policies of development. It is essential to remain aware of the wide structural differences between various types of economies, and to ensure that the search for universality does not generate a false uniformity in concept or policy.

1. Social protection, decent work and development discourse

This paper analyses the field of social protection, viewed within the broader concept of decent work. The analysis relates both social protection and decent work to development. This approach widens the focus from conventional narrowly defined elements of social protection to a broader interpretation which emphasizes the interface between social protection and development. The linkage with poverty alleviation is discussed. Issues concerning potential trade-offs between, or sequencing of, the different components of decent work are also addressed where appropriate.

1.1 Shifting paradigms of deprivation and emancipation: From poverty to social exclusion to decent work

In order to evaluate the significance of the concept of decent work, it is necessary to view it against the backdrop of a string of earlier paradigms of deprivation and emancipation that have sequentially dominated development discourse and policy formulation. It is useful to identify especially the contributions that have emerged from the ILO itself, as this makes it possible to consider the value-added by the new dimension of decent work. A brief sketch will have to suffice.

The early meanings of poverty focus on a range of deficits, whether material, social, or political, when they all coincide in an individual or in a class. Pioneering attempts to provide a "scientific" basis for measuring poverty can be dated back to the Poor Laws. Later independent and seminal contributions came from Dadabhai Naoroji (1901) in 1875 – who viewed poverty from the vantage point of the colonized people – and from Seebohm Rowntree (1901) in 1901 in his attempt to measure urban poverty in York, England, close to the heart of the first industrial empire. Despite these early contributions, however, the debate on absolute poverty, defined in terms of poverty lines, did not reemerge as a significant intervention until the 1960s in India. In the interim, poverty reduction was associated with modern economic growth, which was promoted through varying degrees of state intervention. The failure of such state-led development to alleviate poverty rekindled the debate. A key instrument in this was the absolute poverty line, which served to demonstrate the persistence of poverty even where economic growth had actually occurred. At UNRISD, Andrew Pearse (1984), Keith Griffin (1979) and Biplab Dasgupta were instrumental in demonstrating the inherent class bias in the patterns of diffusion and the accrual of benefits of the green revolution. At ILO, the trickle-down paradigm, promoted by the World Bank, was challenged, amongst others, by Dharam Ghai (cf. ILO, 1972), Gustav Ranis (cf. ILO, 1974), Keith Griffin, Azizur Rahman Khan and Eddy Lee (1984). In the ILO approach, explicit use was made of poverty lines on an international basis, and the concept of basic needs was installed as a key monitoring instrument. The policy objectives were widened to cover the impact of development processes and policies on deprivation, both relative and absolute. The ILO highlighted employment generation as the key policy variable; this was promoted through SAREC[1] support for the ILO's World Employment Programme (WEP). The WEP was highly inclusive and creative in setting its research and policy agenda, in that all structures, processes and policies that impinged upon employment outcomes, actual or potential, were incorporated within the scope of the research programme. It is therefore right to characterize it as a paradigm, where material and socio-economic deprivations were to be overcome.[2] This intervention set up an alternate agenda to that of the World Bank. Indeed, the basic needs programme effectively set the framework for a decade and more, with employment generation as the key instrument for achieving this objective. Predictably, the poverty line, with its associated measure of poverty incidence, became a key concept in targeting, monitoring and evaluating interventions.

This intervention constituted a turning point for the ILO, which had hitherto focused on its traditional mandate dealing with conditions of work, social protection, and workers' rights. Immediately, ILO became a significant and radical stakeholder in the global development arena. With the benefit of hindsight it can now be argued that remarkable as this shift was, it perhaps went too far in one sense, and not quite far enough in another. On the one hand, it created a platform for full employment policies, but the focus remained very much on the volume of employment, and the quality of the jobs created was generally ignored. On the other side, questions of participation and dialogue stayed in the wings, while the employment-income nexus held centre-stage. On account of this, the basic-needs approach was criticized for operating essentially in what Amartya Sen (1987) called commodity space. Participation-enthusiasts added to this by concluding that the approach was also top-down and paternalistic, since it implied a benign state authority distributing basic needs baskets to those below the poverty line. Another critique was that it took attention away from dimensions of inequality.

It is paradoxical that the income poverty approach was adopted by the World Bank – albeit within a rather different strategic agenda and theoretical basis. In the meantime, the wider debate – now set against the stark

---

[1] Swedish Agency for Research Co-operation.

[2] The early ILO Country Mission Reports provide ample testimony to this. Two classic reports are those for Kenya (ILO, 1972), and the Philippines (ILO, 1974).

background of structural adjustment and market-oriented institutional reforms under the influence of the World Bank and the IMF – shifted towards the concepts of social and human development. In an era when labour and social development were under sustained threat from neo-liberal monetarism, UNDP provided an umbrella for a critique using the fuzzy notion of capabilities and the fuzzier monitoring instrument of the Human Development Index. This shift to outcome-oriented social indicators drew on the earlier work of Jan Drewnowski (1974) and others at UNRISD in the 1960s and 1970s, Morris D. Morris & Michelle AcAlpin (1982), and of Donald McGranahan et.al. (1985). The focus on health and education was appropriate in a period when these sectors suffered under financial restraints. So of course did employment, the restructuring of which was closer to the central intentions of the structural adjustment programmes implemented virtually across the board in the developing economies under the tutelage of the World Bank. But the advocacy of employment atrophied in this phase, perhaps precisely at a time when it was most needed. The central axis of contention between development discourse and organizations was cast rather crudely as the reduction of income poverty (World Bank) versus the promotion of human development (UNDP). The ILO employment-income approach had closely followed macro-economic strategic issues, apart from lower sectoral and industry aspects of employment generation. The Organization had espoused programmes of deep structural reform, mostly in a direction opposite to that now holding sway. In contrast, the operational agenda of the human development approach, apart from seeking a greater prioritization of social sector expenditures, especially in education and health, was not systematic enough to serve as a critical bulwark against the neo-liberal approach being imposed by the WB and IMF on the developing economies generally. Arguably, ILO was shifted into the wilderness; along with this, labour and employment issues were largely silenced, and the ILO retreated into its traditional mandate, viz., the narrow focus on work conditions, technical cooperation, etc.

The next significant intervention was the concept of social exclusion, adopted and adapted by the ILO[3] from the ongoing debate in Europe inspired by controversy about social integration, though the essential core of the concept has been the subject of longstanding sociological research and reporting in the developing economies. This concept was used by some in a mechanical fashion as a synonym for basic needs deficits. Treated thus,

---

[3] See here the work conducted under the auspices of the research project of the International Institute of Labour Studies (IILS) of the ILO on the theme of social exclusion in developing economies. See Gore (1995) for an overview of the project and its findings, and Rodgers et al. (eds.) (1995) for an integrated interpretation. For another ILO-based attempt at achieving an overall synthesis, see Bhalla & Lapeyre (1999).

it added little value to ongoing debates. In a second angle, the concept was used to highlight the deeper causal and social dynamics of marginalization. As such, it was useful in highlighting the complex processes that led to the specific outcomes of which the poverty, or the human development approaches, provided snapshot images. Though this was not the thrust of the new work on social exclusion originating from the ILO or from Western academe, I would argue that the most significant potential contribution lies in its incorporation of identity-based forms of deprivation arising from discriminatory practices embedded in society, culture and polity. This could apply to gender, to ethnic groups, migrants, religions, castes, etc. Viewed thus, the approach provided genuine new purchase on the structural causes of deprivation while also bringing into the frame the notions of political participation, rights, dignity, social equality, citizenship, legal and customary frameworks of inclusion and exclusion. It also provided a universalistic orientation, since social exclusion and integration were at the heart of European and North American social policy debates. The spotlight shifted from labour and employment to citizens and the quality of citizenship; from poverty per se to political and de facto rights; from protection of material well-being to protection of identity-based rights as an equal citizen. While this was quite compatible with ongoing mainstream discussions over deprivation, it did not alter their orientation, since it was an agenda that could be adopted, at least in principle, by all participants.[4] It did, however, add a third concept to that of absolute poverty reckoned in terms of poverty lines, and human development reckoned in terms of the hugely oversold human development index (HDI).[5] Some efforts were made to operationalize the concept, though without great success.

The ILO's decent work concept and associated policy agenda has marked a major intervention in the discourse on deprivation since the late 1990s. Of course, it can be criticized for its synthetic, composite nature, rather like the earlier concepts of human development and social exclusion. Yet, with its four distinct components, it does stake out a lot of ground, even if not in a theoretically satisfactory manner. Despite this, it qualifies

---

[4] See Hills et al. (eds.) 2002 for an extensive discussion of the multiple meanings attached to this contested and fuzzy concept in Western European academic and policy discourse and debates.

[5] At this juncture, it is appropriate to note the voices from the ILO that have emphasized the dimension of socio-economic security as being a key element. A closer look at the interpretation of such insecurity reveals that the ambit of the interpretation adopted is very wide indeed, and embraces virtually all the three other dimensions of decent work. Also worthy of note separately is the strong case being developed for a universal Basic Incomes programme in general but for European countries in particular (see Standing (ed.) 2003). It is argued that access to such a Basic Income should be a universal claim of every citizen, and not a means tested benefit delivered to a narrowly targeted constituency. The overlaps and tensions between this position and other approaches mentioned remain to be explored.

as an attempt at setting a new paradigm. It is worth noting some of the ways in which it opens up space for partially redefining the terms of the development debate, and in the process resurrecting important dimensions that had been obliterated by the neo-liberal bandwagon.

First, the four components include economic dimensions, but they also include social aspects which qualify as ends in their own right. This widens the analytical and policy framework considerably. Dimensions such as participation and dialogue which were previously grafted on in the form of optional extras, are given equal weight with other mainstream economic dimensions such as employment. This implies that aspects of agency are included, and the concept does not exist in commodity space alone.

Second, this may allow the decent work framework, broadly interpreted, to incorporate the agendas of poverty reduction, human development and social integration. It has the potential to become an all-enveloping concept, although this would inevitably lead to a diffusion and fuzziness of theoretical meaning.

Third, the concept is fundamentally labour-ist in nature. Its point of entry into current discourse and debate is through the status, rights and role of labour. In a world where the ideas and images, processes and policies of development are overwhelmingly dominated by capital and its protagonists, this intervention opens up some countervailing strategic space. It potentially reclaims visibility and voice for silenced and subordinated labour.

Fourth, the decent work agenda reasserts the role of employment. This is timely and valuable, since this aspect has atrophied since the neo-liberal attack on employment as a development policy instrument.

Fifth, through extending the employment dimension beyond the simple volume of employment to include the quality, productivity and remuneration of work, the concept meaningfully engages with parts of the economy and debates which it had been shy of earlier. Thus, the fourth constituency of the informal economy, hitherto effectively excluded from the ILO triangular table, finds validation. Through this, the issue of gender is also made prominent, since the informal economy employs a disproportionate number of women workers. Again, through questions of the quality of employment and social protection the decent work agenda is capable of bringing international labour standards into its domain. This provides a more appropriate context for a discussion of ILS than the WTO frame of reference.

Sixth, the decent work concept extends the ILO agenda beyond its traditional inherited mandate. It also breaks away from the narrowness of the poverty line discourse and policy approach. The concept makes it possible to address virtually the full gamut of development concerns, and to question the nature of the structures and processes that reproduce the cycles of deprivation and exclusion. Much, of course, depends on the conceptual refinement and skilful use of the notion, without which it is likely to lapse into a buzz word.

Seventh, it needs to be recognized that this widening of the mandate and the agenda or, at the very least, the lexicon, of the ILO generates some inherent contextual tensions. Many of these are political, organizational, or operational in nature. Some, as indicated above, are conceptual.

1.2 From decent work for employees to decent living for all

There are two ways of looking at decent work. The narrow interpretation focuses on employment, and here the concept refers to remuneration, conditions of work, voice, dialogue. This is good as far as it goes, but clearly it does not go far enough. Some people, or even many of those enjoying decent work, might find that it does not necessarily guarantee decent living (which requires the fulfilment of conditions beyond the employment domain). Work for these employees could remain an island of decency embedded, even guarded vigorously, within an ocean of flagrant indecency. More importantly, the employment relation is far from universal; indeed in most developing economies, the majority of workers would be excluded from the frame of reference. This is exemplified by a comparison between the so-called classical model, and the development model, with the transitional model fast polarizing and gravitating towards the latter in the majority of economies in transition. Even with the classical model there is a clear tendency for the formal long-term employment relation to lose its general applicability with the risc of casual, flexible work and part-time, home-based, mobile workers.

In the broader interpretation of decent work the main focus could be on work, not employment. This broadens the coverage enormously in the developing and transitional economies. But it still falls short of universality: some home-workers, including women, child and elderly workers, tend to be conceptually (and statistically) invisible. So work needs to be appropriately defined in an inclusionary manner. But this is not enough: we must not ignore young people who are not yet in the workforce, or those who have left the workforce after a lifetime of labour (the retired and elderly), or those who are involuntarily excluded from the workforce (the unemployed, the disabled). This wider sweep immediately includes all care workers (many of whom are themselves invisible), since they are engaged with people in the groups who are formally "not working". It is a short step from this position to the assertion that in order to be meaningful, the coverage must really be universal. The decent work concept therefore needs to relate to the entire population.

To retain significance the concept of decent work has to underwrite decent living. Since decent living involves elements which fall outside the sphere of employment and work, this also widens the agenda and the range of actors involved; it effectively implies the existence of social mechanisms which successfully transform decent work into decent living, with gaps being bridged by other players, e.g., the state. Many basic needs, such as health, education, security, citizen rights, cannot be automatically read into the employment or work relation; and the failure of even good incomes to translate into good social services is a ubiquitous and familiar reality.

This raises the need to define decent living. In abstract terms, it could perhaps be defined at a universal level. But in material terms it inevitably implies different absolute levels of fulfillment across rich and poor countries. While some elements of decent work, such as voice, dialogue and the quality of employment relations, could be defined universally, other economic elements, such as remuneration, realistically could not. This introduces the need for a degree of relativism into the definition of decent living.[6] Arguably, the agenda of decent work for those in employment must be embedded in, and analytically linked to, the agenda of decent living for all.

1.3 The constituents of decent work: Synergetic and sequential relationships

Is there a trade-off between decent work and economic growth? Or are there synergies between them? How do these equations play out over time: are the effects realized immediately in the short term, or do they unfold through more complex long-term interactive processes? The answers could have implications for the phasing of policies addressing different components of decent work.

Whether one turns to the constructions of theory, or to the lessons of history, or to the gleanings from the more recent practice of development, it is difficult to arrive at a consensus. Though such exercises lead to more nuanced and qualified ideological and policy stances, there appears to be a persisting divide between two generally opposed views. The first is the instrumentalist stance which regards economic growth as the crucial means to achieving the ends of decent work in the longer run, while arguing that this long-term objective would be jeopardized by a premature prioritization of decent work over economic growth. A failure to make the economy the first development concern would undermine the very growth mechanism through which decent work could eventually be achieved.

---

[6] The paper questions the usefulness of a universally applied global social floor in the form of the ubiquitous $1/day poverty line (World Bank, 1990; Ravallion, Datt & v.d.Walle 1991.)

The other, essentialist view asserts that there are no trade-offs, only positive synergies between decent work and economic growth; and further, that each component of decent work constitutes an end in its own right, and should not be viewed instrumentally as a means for economic growth. Indeed, the achievement of decent work could well be regarded as contributing to higher economic growth. Laudable as such a stance might be on ethical grounds, it still needs to demonstrate its financial viability and sustainability.[7]

A comment on each of three different interactions might be appropriate. The first is the possible trade-off between growth and employment. While rewarding and fulfilling work is intrinsically desirable, how is this to be achieved for all? Conventionally, the demand for labour is a derived demand, and the level of employment is determined primarily by the level and pattern of investment. While the claim that full employment is automatically attained through free and flexible labour markets has long lost its credibility – if ever it had any – the alternative of achieving full employment through macro-economic management does not have many real supporters either. In any event, through its withdrawal from the economy, the state has lost the key instrument for influencing the overall level of investment in the economy. It can be argued that the lost ground has been partially reclaimed by the policies of labour market flexibilization which have led to a wider distribution of employment opportunities, though this is clearly at the expense of the quality of such employment which is often dominated by low-paid insecure jobs in the lower rungs of the service sector. Against the backdrop of contemporary policy debates which tend to reject employment as a valid, viable, or politically realistic direct policy objective, the decent work paradigm modestly reasserts the centrality of employment.

The debates over the trade-off between economic growth and labour rights (in the form of voice and dialogue), or more widely, between growth and democracy, are equally fraught and unsettled. The conservative view typically relies on historical examples where rapid growth has preceded the attainment of rights and democracy, and according to this view, has laid the foundations for it. The Republic of Korea and Taiwan (China) are the usual examples cited here. The argument has claimed legitimacy from the discourse of the strong developmental state. India, for example, with its democracy, could not make the hard choices necessary to attain

---

[7] This is analogous to the open debate on the relationship between economic growth and human development: while the long-run correlation between levels of human development and economic growth are clear enough, the causal equations underlying the achievement of those long-term positions are debated. For instance, would prioritized investment in human development components in a poor country lead to sustained economic growth that in turn could finance these human development expenditures? Or in other words, apart from being desirable ends in themselves, do the components of human development constitute sufficient instruments for achieving economic growth of an order that would underwrite sustainability?

rapid and sustained economic growth, and thus has persistent widespread poverty. On the other hand, it is argued that the East Asian tigers, and their Southeast Asian cubs, first attained rapid growth albeit under harsh political regimes; they then managed the successful transition to mature democracies, and now enjoy both economic as well as political freedoms and rights. Of course, this kind of argument can be further supported by noting the very late arrival of political democracy (in the form of full electoral participation) in the advanced market economies, with Switzerland achieving this status only a couple of decades ago.

There are several problems with such an approach. First, it regards political voice as a universal and unconditional right which cannot be delayed. Second, there are myriad examples where so-called strong states which have denied political rights to the people have not been successful in developmental terms. Third, the examples cited cannot shed light on the possibility of simultaneously attaining political rights and material advancement. The issues involved are far more complex, and do not lend themselves to the simplistic rejection of rights due to their supposed negative implications for economic growth. Fourth, such examples do not travel well in the presence of a very high degree of path dependence. And fifth, there could be counter arguments where the provision of political rights might make a significant contribution to the attainment of economic objectives through generating ownership and commitment among previously excluded sections of the population.

Parallel arguments carry over to the provision of social protection and the trade-off with growth. Indeed, a second trade-off is also frequently posited between different components of decent work itself: between the employment objective in terms of remuneration productivity and the extent of social protection enjoyed by the employee, and the objective of increasing the number of jobs, albeit of lower quality and lacking adequate protection.

The instrumentalist argument would say that risk-taking is a crucial dimension of investment and growth; that risks are only taken by individuals when there are adequate personal rewards. To the extent that social protection schemes involve a redistribution of income from successful risk takers to risk avoiders, the rate of investment could be negatively affected. This argument is often used to oppose fiscal and resource mobilization policies that would transfer income from the returns on investment to finance social protection programmes. High levels of inequality are often condoned on these grounds. Tax and transfer programmes would reduce the incentive and willingness to invest; would lead to an out-migration of the risk-taking, investing, richer sections of the population; and also lead to the break-up of communities with the rich deciding to leave. In short, risk and inequality feed investment and growth, and thus become the instruments of social protection gains – but in the longer term.

Predictably, there are significant arguments on the other side as well. First, a fluctuating and uncertain environment – which itself is potentially a source of socio-economic vulnerability for the poorer sections of the population – could also act as a disincentive for investment. Thus, systemic upheavals and transitions often preempt investment. Peace, stability and institutional reliability can be vital preconditions for investment. Second, technological change and market reorientation, such as in the process of agricultural development, also involve new risks; where these are substantial, the innovation and investment process is curtailed. Farmers, especially poorer ones, opt for low-risk and low-return strategies. Where local institutions, contractual arrangements, and insurance mechanisms are responsive, such risks can be preempted; so social protection programmes can help support investment in risky environments, especially for poorer agents. And of course there are many spillover effects from social protection to development, through the well-being of women, universal basic education, public health and disease control, or through the impact of pensions-for-the-poor on fertility behaviour, and through the positive effect of social protection systems on labour productivity. These arguments have been supported from Adam Smith in the classical tradition, to Alfred Marshall within the neo-classical framework, to Douglas North within the rubric of NIE. And quite apart from the instrumentalist arguments in favour of extending social protection to all in order to promote economic growth, there remains the argument for universal social protection as a right *per se*.

1.4 Social protection and security: Some frequently asked questions

We will start with a string of frequently asked questions about different aspects of social protection. The scope of these questions is enormous, and even the brief answers provided demonstrate the complexity of the field.

Why social protection?

This question seems innocuous, even unnecessary, yet even here there are grounds for controversy. The immediate justification must be in terms of the human costs of the absence of security and protection, in the form of losses, anxieties, and the too-often realized risk of a slide into penury and indigence. The justification then is similar to that for poverty reduction. This can be cast in the framework of a development-rights based approach, where the security of life, livelihood and citizenship needs is taken as a basic right of all individuals in all societies.

For those who worry about the resource implications of such a right, the pill can be sweetened by invoking instrumental or functional reasons for the provision of universal socio-economic security. The origin of this argument can be readily traced back to Adam Smith and his French classical contemporaries, all of whom frequently used this instrumental justification to underpin what they elsewhere acknowledged as a universal norm of civilized societies.[8] Thus, the protected worker would be more productive and profitable, which means that social protection is a good investment. A more potent argument addressed the fears of those who remained unconvinced: the security and protection of capital and wealth could be jeopardized by the poverty and vulnerability of the poor. Social protection policies were therefore also investments in political stability.

Opposing arguments cite the dependence created by the cocoon of security, leading to a loss of initiative, incentive and risk-taking capability. There is a loss of individual creativity in the economic sphere, and a high platform of social security is held to raise the supply price of labour, reduce competitiveness, and thereby investment growth as well as employment. Any drive to over-protect is rendered unsustainable by undermining the growth that has to finance such a policy. Apart from this, some take exception to what they characterize as a nanny state which is overly interventionist and directive. Thus some have argued that institutional arrangements which evolved as devices for underpinning socio-economic security on a universal basis within a community tended over time to undermine the spirit of entrepreneurship and the growth process, thereby rendering these societies non-viable as economic entities.

While these debates continue and are likely to remain unsettled, it is worth noting that almost as a rule, wherever state authority has passed to the erstwhile disempowered groups, their immediate preference has been in favour of installing systems that ensure socio-economic security and protection.

Of what?

What is to be made secure and protected? This is a vital question, and too often the answer is given too quickly without any consideration of the wide range of alternatives.

Should we protect equality of opportunity or of outcomes? Is it enough to ensure a level playing field in the market, or should there also be concern for inequalities in the resources brought by the various players to the market? Should the focus be on protective policies, i.e., to compensate for losses, or to provide safeguards against such effects? Or should

---

[8] See Rothschild, E. (1996).

the emphasis be on promotional policies which enhance the general economic and political strength of the individual (household, group, community, country) giving it the capacity to look after itself even if it encounters bouts of insecurity? Should the focus be on the outcomes as experienced by the subject, or on earlier points in the chain of causation that generates the insecurity? Should policy makers worry about protecting the quality of health, education, environment, etc., or should the focus be on the employment, incomes and livelihoods which underpin these outcomes?

The traditional mandate of the ILO would call for a focus on the employment-related forms of insecurity, e.g., unemployment insurance, occupational hazards, work-related conditions, pensions, etc. However, the broader decent work agenda implies a dramatic widening of the domain.

For whom?

The answer to this depends on the social protection agenda. In the conventional narrow sense, the natural constituency of social protection has been the employee or worker in the formal sector. This agenda might be appropriate for the classical model economies, but loses its salience in the developing and transitional economies where the focus needs to include the informal economy and home-based workers. If the focus is only on the poor, new issues arise over definition, measurement and operationalization: at what level of aggregation are these groups to be identified? Are such exercises to be conducted each year? Should attention be given to those at risk of sliding into poverty as well? If so, how are they to be identified? What about the specially disadvantaged groups, such as women, children, the elderly? What about the migrants, internal and international? The paradox about migrants, and one which helps to illustrate the dichotomy between poverty and socio-economic security, as well as between income and rights, is that many migrants are well above the poverty line, but nevertheless suffer some of the worst forms of vulnerability and rights violations. They also tend to become invisible in both the sending and the receiving regions, for reasons of expediency.

It is increasingly apparent that large population groups are rendered vulnerable on account of their religious, cultural or political identity. Thus, in the absence of interventions addressing these citizenship-related dimensions, it might be impossible to ensure their socio-economic security. This again widens the agenda for definition, as well as intervention.

What is the meaning of universalization? Should it apply to entire populations? Or only to sub-populations, such as those in poverty? It has been argued from a cynical, or realistic perspective that interventions that are based on targeting the poor alone might look good on paper, but might not be supported by the middle and upper classes whose acquiescence is required for the successful adoption and implementation of such programmes. This argues in favour of total universalization, rather than a more limited universalization in favour of the poor alone, which might lead to the exit of the collaborating, rent-seeking middle classes. In short, factoring in some leakage of benefits is thought to ensure institutional sustainability. Clearly this cost of targeting depends very much on the local political and institutional scenario – the argument has perhaps been derived from Bihar-like situations, characterized by endemic rent-seeking and widespread violence and corruption at local level, but would not be relevant in a Kerala-like scenario, marked by a high level of local account- ability of politicians and public officials based on pre-existing popular mobilization.

Independently of this type of reasoning, there could be legitimate grounds for including the non-poor in the domain of socio-economic pro- tection. A human right cannot really be limited to poor people, though there are obvious and difficult equity issues to be resolved.

How much?

If a policy of universalizing socio-economic security for the poor were to be adopted, what would constitute sufficient cover? Some have taken shelter behind the term "basic". But this only begs the question of what is "basic". Often, this is determined by financial resources, i.e., it is not related to the actual deficit or need of the target group as such. Some- times, basic refers to an inferior, lower level of income that corresponds to the $1 per day idea applicable to the poor. Here, basic means something good enough for the poor but not for the rest of the population; inequality and status differentiation are implicit in this reasoning. Is this acceptable? It is necessary to adopt some norm which does not marginalize the poor, but which can provide a rational basis for including resource constraints. Naturally, the prevailing degree of inequality, the political culture, and the presence or absence of egalitarian normative practices are key determi- nants of the balance that is struck. Typically the balance is weighted against the excluded precisely where the exclusions are extreme and intense. It becomes necessary therefore, almost always, to struggle to raise the level at which such norms are set. Often the so-called negative economic effects of "too much" security on productivity and incentives are used by the rich to legitimize the adoption of low norms for the poor.

Some of the argument parallels the debate over where precisely to draw the poverty line. In addition, the agenda of ensuring socio-economic security might argue that the poverty line would need to be raised further to say, PL(1+f) where f represents a fraction which covers observed fluc- tuations in the level of income at low levels.

How?

Social protection for all might be a defensible proposition, but how is this right to be claimed? There are two issues here: Who provides, and who pays for social protection programmes and services?

When the earlier queries have been tackled, one needs to consider the mechanisms and methods through which to intervene. The first question is whether there is any need to intervene at all. Those who believe in the Kuznetsian Inverted U curve hypothesis could argue that the best method might be to let growth do the job over time. There are several good reasons for rejecting this passive position. The U curve already incorporates the outcomes of policy interventions as well as of the mobilization and agency of various social groups, especially the excluded. It could be argued that current labour market tendencies might be unable to compel the provision of social protection programmes. So there could be a need to accelerate and catalyse this structural process through targeted policy and institutional interventions. In any event, if a right is worth achieving, it is worth achieving sooner rather than later.

In the "normal" course of capitalist development, responsibility for providing services had been assigned to the state in view of the long-term unaddressed insecurities of the poor. Of late, the redesigning of the government's role in developing economies has emphasized the function of the market in providing social protection services, effectively implying the privatization of public goods. Given the time-proven weaknesses of the market, and the rising inefficiency and corruption of state mechanisms and programmes the focus has shifted towards the third sector as a service provider. NGOs and civil society organizations, which used to develop prototypes for potential replication, have increasingly been drawn into relationships with the state as proxy service providers. The case of the Bangladesh Rural Advancement Committee (BRAC) and primary education in Bangladesh is an example. Key issues concern the quality of services in situations where the richer sections of the population exercise their option to resort to high quality and high price services offered on the open market. The issue concerns the financial mechanisms that could be used to access this type of supplier. The financial instrument needs to be flexible and mobile in view of the locational and occupational instability of the target population, and the question of subsidies. One extreme approach recently promoted is to hand out a dollar every day to all individuals below the poverty line, and leave it to them to find their own social protection supplies and suppliers. There could be several problems with this, including dependency and the stigma that might be generated through such handouts. There is also the vexed issue of identifying the poor in every time period. A second approach is to develop insurance mechanisms for the poor, based on the individual, or preferably, on self-help groups formed for the purpose. The problem here is that market insurance systems tend to exclude the needy who are perceived to take out more than they put in to the scheme. Further, poor people might only be able to pay very low regular premiums, which might only permit very low benefits and cover, with many exclusions and limitations. The challenge then is to devise a fair and adequate insurance scheme for the poor, and this introduces the role of the state in providing subsidies and topping up in order to guarantee services conforming to an acceptable norm.

Whichever combinations are taken up, the underlying objective is to provide universal cover for a list of specified aspects of socio-economic security, to a standard that matches the social norms for that population as a whole. Such norms should apply universally to all citizens, not just to the poor.

1.5 Three types of economy, and the problem of generalization

International organizations tend to address their mandate using the language of universalism, invoking concepts and terms which are considered to be generally applicable. This tendency is also apparent in usage of the term "decent work". However, there is a need to exercise extreme caution in this regard. The notion of decent work does not carry a single universal meaning, and any artificial generalization made implicitly or by default could have serious negative implications at a programmatic level. The discussion below is designed to highlight the question of difference.[9]

1.5.1 The classical model: Erosion of hard won gains of labour struggles

The classical model applies to the North-West, but also to Japan, and some other late entrants such as Taiwan (China), the Republic of Korea and Singapore. But it is worth noting the exceptions as well. The United States is not a perfect match. And, generally in the North-West, the drift in the neo-liberal era has been steadily away from the classical model. There are now substantial areas of informality in the labour market, and quite serious deficits with regard to pension contributions, which is especially worrying amongst the younger flexible workforce. The combination of private schemes relying on equity investments, and the global destabilization of stock markets has obvious negative consequences. Dimensions of vulnerability are being reinserted into the system in a context of ageing populations and rising dependency ratios.

---

[9] The discussion of the three "models" follows the typology suggested by Ghai (2002a).

1.5.2 The transitional model: Collapse of socialist welfare regimes

The transitional model is a useful description of a particular group of economies. But in some senses, it parallels the structure and trends of the classical model. During the socialist era most of the transitional countries displayed full employment, and all social entitlements were essentially linked to the employment relation which embraced the entire workforce. This has collapsed, and there has been a dramatic rise of the informal sector with diverse forms of casual employment, and the wide range of self-employment that is characteristic of developing economies. The slide from comprehensive, employment-based social protection systems to partial coverage and large deficits mirrors the trend in the developed market economies, except that it is more precipitate, ongoing and with no clear sign in many countries as to how and at what level it will stabilize. A special feature is the general demise of the state-owned enterprise sector – the original home of formal permanent employment and the concomitant social protection system. To some extent, the massive relocation of manufacturing activities away from the developed market economies into the developing economies provides a parallel to this. But while the collapse of the state-owned enterprise in the transitional model might be a temporary phenomenon – with new and more competitive manufacturing expected optimistically to kick in "soon" – the shift away from manufacturing to services in the North-West is clearly a more secular structural development.

1.5.3 The development model: Atrophy of community and commoditization of welfare

The development model economies are a diverse group. What is significant is that formal employment in the organized sectors accounts for a very minor fraction of the total workforce. In many of these economies the formal sector has withered, rather than developed healthily, in the period since structural adjustment programmes, although some have clearly benefited from the concentrated nature of the global relocation of manufacturing. But even in these positive performers, the majority of the workforce remains outside the formal sector.

1.5.4 The risk of misleading generalizations

It is worth noting that in the classical and transitional groups, poverty, social deficits and vulnerability are closely associated with employment (and its quality); but in the development model group, the majority of the poor are active workers in some form of self- or wage-employment relation.

The clear indication is that it would be inappropriate to use the social protection systems of the classical model as a template for systems in the development and transitional economies. While it might be important to salvage whatever is viable of the old social protection systems in the transitional countries, there is a need in all three groups, but especially in the development model, to base systems on an explicit recognition of the structural heterogeneity and diversity of these economies. Such an acknowledgment has wide-ranging implications for the design of social protection systems, and also for instruments of monitoring and evaluation.

Social policies have to address/reflect the forms and patterns of vulnerability; in turn, these derive from the internal/external interactions influencing the survival/accumulation strategies and paths of economic agents, players and units; these are embedded in and specific to particular economic and institutional structures and processes. What are the tolerance levels of any such global convergence in agendas or approaches with respect to divergences in the structures and processes that generate vulnerability? Is it meaningful to speak of a convergence of agendas or approach between the (early or late) retiree in Western Europe and the laid-off state enterprise worker in China? Or between the *gastarbeiter* and the floating migrant? Or between the new casualized self-employed worker and the working poor? Or between the insecurity of family farmers in Western Europe and peasants in Andhra Pradesh? Or between children working to buy Nike equipment and children working to produce it? At what level of aggregation does a convergence emerge in the lexicon? What is the price in terms of lost meaning?

During the post-structural adjustment decade, there has been a steady drift towards universalism at the level of organizational discourse and the policy design of international development agencies; there is seemingly credible discussion of convergence about the design of a global development agenda, the division of labour with regard to its formulation, implementation and monitoring; the rules of engagement between north and south including conditionalities and triggers for these; the role of national governments. The drift applies also to the universalization of basic socio-economic security. While building a global alliance behind the objective of universalizing basic socio-economic security is extremely useful in advocacy, promotional and political terms, there could be strong diminishing returns to carrying notions of convergence into the specific approaches, conceptualization and design of countervailing intervention policies and programmes. What emerges is the uncomfortable juxtaposition of convergent social protection discourse with disparate forms of vulnerability across countries. Hence plurality, reflecting the diversity of ground realities, must remain the byword; policy intervention packages need to recognize basic differences in the types of socio-economic insecurity in different locations and contexts. Otherwise, there is a likelihood that the global convergence of purpose might fall short when evaluated at the level of outcomes for a significant part, perhaps even the majority, of the world's population.

2. Socio-economic vulnerability: Patterns and processes

Four different categories of fluctuations, shocks and crises can be loosely distinguished.

First: those that take place within the "normal", "stable", "regular", "trend" process of social reproduction, which occurs in any system. This could be classified as an aspect of structural or endemic deprivation and poverty. These fluctuations could exist at various levels; they arise from a variety of sources, and manifest their effects on social entities from the individual to the family and household, to wider social, occupational or other groups.

Second: those that take the form of systemic transitions or *transformations*, representing rapid, dramatic, profound changes in the social and economic framework of society. Such fundamental changes have occurred in the erstwhile socialist world, including the former Soviet Union and China.

Third: those that could be described as major systemic *reorientations* which constitute a clear break from earlier paths, but which remain *within* an unchanging overall political and economic system. Examples are provided by the monetarist break with Keynesianism in the advanced Western economies during the Reagan-Thatcher era, and the structural adjustment programmes and associated institutional reforms imposed on the poor countries by the World Bank and the IMF since the 1980s.

Fourth: those that occur within the system but which could be regarded as episodic events, shocks, dislocations, disturbances, fluctuations. This group would include famines, wars, ethnic conflicts, natural and man-made disasters, economic crises.

These four types of vulnerability are obviously interrelated, and the distinctions made above are somewhat arbitrary and arguable. Yet there are insights to be gained from the exercise, which attempts to impose a framework on a vast array of seemingly disparate sources and forms of vulnerability observed in the three different "models" of economy outlined earlier.

2.1 Structural or endemic entitlement deficits

Endemic entitlement deficits refer to shortfalls in the crucial dimensions of well-being, such as nutrition, health and housing, that persist and are regularly reproduced in the economy. Thus, the regular reproduction of food insecurity and hunger for a large section of the population – even in the absence of famines or major fluctuations in harvest, the weather, or prices – would fall into this category. Such deficits are reproduced fundamentally because the poor remain poor from year to year. Likewise, major health deficits are reproduced even when there are no epidemics or other mass diseases. This secular, attritional reproduction of vulnerability is realized and experienced in the form of structural, or permanent, or persisting, or chronic poverty. This underscores the important point that at the most basic and significant level, the agendas of social protection and poverty reduction cannot really be separated.

2.2 Systemic transitions

This category refers to vulnerabilities that are created by systemic upheavals. Three examples are cited: the transition to a full-blown capitalist system; the revolutionary transition to a socialist mode; and the more recent transition away from a centrally planned economy back towards a capitalist system.

2.2.1 The capitalist transition

The term "pure exchange system transition," was coined by Sen perhaps on account of its acronym, PEST. It refers to a process whereby previous, traditional, informal, family or community based systems of social provisioning are eroded by processes of commercialization and monetization, social differentiation, wider markets, labour mobility, etc. on the one hand, and by concomitant (or even consequent) sociological processes involving the erosion of family and kinship ties and networks, other patron-client systems, and communitarian networks based on shared identities. It is posited that the erosion of social provisioning occurs before the emergence of new state- or market-based systems of insurance or protection. This lack of synchronization between the two processes leaves an open and widening area of vulnerability, which falls disproportionately on the weaker sections of society. Whether it corrects itself depends on the historical and conjunctural circumstances within which it occurs. It is arguable that such wide gaps have emerged steadily over the past century in the developing economies, and have widened further in recent decades. At the same time, new forms of protection have not really emerged to any significant extent. This condition applies especially to the developing economies, and within these, especially to the poor.

2.2.2 Socialist transitions

The transition to a "socialist" system is usually considered to remove a wide range of inherited types of vulnerability, poverty and deprivation, and to lay an institutional and policy basis for the minimization of socio-economic insecurities. On the whole, this expectation is borne out by the unfolding of the socialist projects of the twentieth century.

Another aspect of this transition – one that has gained considerable attention in the literature – concerns the human costs of the transition to socialism. The case of forced collectivization in the Soviet Union under Stalin and the famine that coincided with the Great Leap Forward in post-liberation China are two examples that have been extensively analysed.

2.2.3 Post-socialist transitions

The collapse of the Soviet Union and the crises of transition in the former Soviet Union (FSU) countries, along with the transition away from socialism in Eastern European (EE) countries, represents a major source of widespread socio-economic insecurity and destitution. The high social floor which protected almost the entire population in these countries has virtually collapsed, and there are few economic or institutional substitutes which provide alternative cover. The results have been so dramatic that they have affected the fabric of society, social norms and value systems, as well as behaviour patterns, e.g., marriage and divorce, parental support, fertility, etc. Not only have the old systems of social protection disappeared, but also old patterns of livelihoods. The costs of this societal upheaval have not been adequately documented, perhaps because they do not conform to the rosy version of the market paradigm.

Even in China, where the post-socialist transition has been dramatically successful in economic terms, the reforms have opened wide the Pandora's box of new sources and patterns of widespread social insecurity and vulnerability. Increasing attention is now being paid to this by the Chinese government, belatedly and somewhat reluctantly. Paradoxically, it is the egalitarian system of access to land that has continued to provide an income floor for the rural population. This is in sharp contrast to the FSU and EE countries which had already been transformed into industrial systems.

2.3 Systemic reorientations

Here, the focus is on changing the rules of the game within any particular systemic specification. Such reorientations can sometimes take the form of powerful ideological and structural breaks, with wide ramifications for the conduct of economic and political life, often especially in the domain of social protection.

2.3.1 Structural adjustment packages
and atrophying welfare access

The introduction of SAPs in the developing economies virtually across the board from the 1980s involved a systemic reorientation. These programmes swept away state-centred regimes of accumulation and distribution operating mostly behind protective barriers, but did not always substitute a productive and dynamic source of growth. Subsidized systems of social provisioning were quickly rendered financially unsustainable, and atrophied. Extensive deindustrialization occurred in various economies, and the new economic processes, where they emerged, were not always strong enough or egalitarian enough to provide an alternative framework for social security. The general consensus is that this reorientation has intensified and increased the many forms of vulnerability and socio-economic insecurity, especially after the acceleration of processes of globalization.

2.3.2 Monetarism and the dismantling of the welfare state

Another fundamental reorientation within the framework of advanced capitalist market economies is denoted by the rise of monetarism, alongside the dismantling of the welfare state. Starting with the Reagan-Thatcher ideological and programmatic rejection of the Keynesian and welfare state, this reorientation has spread to virtually all developed countries. The consequences are restructured economies with dramatically reduced bargaining power for labour, the casualization of work, the atrophying of social benefits, the withdrawal of the state from the economy and from social support systems, the privatization of economic and social services, and the rise of the user-pays principle. The result has been a rise in the forms and intensities of socio-economic and psycho-social insecurity and vulnerability in these economies, often marked by an increase in traditional forms of poverty.

2.3.3 Reflexive modernity and globalization:
From external to manufactured risk

Giddens (1996) has theorized on the different forms of risk-related politics associated with globalization and high modernity. While probably intended to be of universal relevance or applicability, this notion is more credible in the advanced market economies, and loses much of its salience in the context of widespread poverty and deprivation in the poor countries. But like PEST, this process has an inexorably unfolding logic which steadily reshapes life concerns, social values and the nature of politics, away from what Giddens calls "emancipatory politics" to "life politics" –

from the identity-and social group-based politics of structural deprivation to the individual-based politics of constructing a better life in complex but flexible modern environments.

One theoretical characterization of contemporary transitions in the first world posits that a by-product of modernization is the progressive replacement of external forms of risk (mostly associated with nature), by forms of manufactured risk (man-made). Alongside the transition from traditional modernity to high modernity and from passive to reflexive modernity is the passage from emancipatory politics to life politics. This confronts the individual with new areas of decision making often without the benefit of an adequate scientific basis for assessing risk and thus of making informed choices. Implicitly, the agenda of emancipatory politics, with its unremitting focus on the basic material conditions for social survival at a decent level, has opened the space for, and induced the mode of life politics. While risk, insecurity and uncertainty continue in new shapes and forms and influence behaviour and well-being, they are not deemed to threaten basic material survival.

2.4 Mass entitlement failures

This type of macro vulnerability refers to sudden cataclysmic failures in levels of living which threaten the survival of large numbers of people. Predictably those who are already poor are usually more in jeopardy, and experience far greater distress than the non-poor, though the phenomenon itself typically pushes new swathes of the population below the poverty line, often permanently.

It is remarkable that theories of poverty and deprivation usually deal with the endemic form, and tend to treat mass entitlement failures as exogenous events which have to be dealt with as stand-alone emergencies. This position is untenable, and it is necessary to consider and analyse such mass entitlement failures within the same theoretical rubric as endemic development deficits. Simultaneous treatment is necessary for the two phenomena.

It is important to note that mass entitlement failures affect entire – or large sections of – populations. As such, it is only the rich economies that have the capacity to deal with this form of risk. In the poorer economies, such events usually exact a terrible toll in misery and mortality, as the system is unable to cope with simultaneous mass shortfalls.

Four different forms of mass entitlement failure are briefly reviewed below, and their respective implications for forms and patterns of vulnerability are elicited, together with possible policy responses. The events, episodes and processes implied have unfortunately become all too obvious and frequent, and do not call for extensive comment or illustration.

2.4.1 Complex emergencies: Famines, environmental and other man-made disasters

The term "complex emergencies" has come to denote a wide range of "disaster" events, usually in developing economies. They include famines and other man-made disasters, e.g., those caused by industrial pollution or "accidents" such as Union Carbide and Bhopal, Chernobyl, or Shell Oil in Nigeria, etc. Various natural disasters, such as earthquakes, El Nino, floods, or exceptional rains, are included in this category. These events manifest covariant risk on a scale which often overwhelms the capacity of the nation state. Complex emergencies usually have long-term consequences and create intensive poverty and dislocation. The origins of many seemingly "exogenous" events lie in processes of ecological imbalance and environmental destruction that are very much the products of economic growth policies. It is a moot point if a free press and electoral democracy are sufficient to ensure adequate food security measures, for example.

2.4.2 Financial crises: Asia and Latin America

The onset of globalization, including the dismantling of controls on the flow of finance capital, has led to very substantial financial instability in general, and provided many spectacular illustrations of the failure of capital markets. These crises have then widened to affect the economy as a whole. While the bale-outs that have followed have protected investors, the costs have been carried overwhelmingly by the local populations, especially the working people and the poor. These crises have become, in themselves, powerful episodes that have reduced large sections of the population to poverty, often of a persistent nature. Alongside this, social provisioning systems have virtually disappeared. It should be emphasized that the scale of losses, and especially of bale-outs, is so enormous that they could dwarf the social sector expenditure of entire blocs of Third World economies. Examples include the Republic of Korea, Thailand, Indonesia, Mexico and Argentina; the list can be extended. It is also worth noting that such insecurities have been avoided, or preempted through alternative policies with regard to capital market liberalization. Examples of these are provided by Malaysia and India, and they underscore the importance of widening the terms of reference of social protection strategies to include preventive steps, not just relief.

2.4.3 Health pandemics: Survival of the fittest?

No doubt health pandemics have always occurred. However, recent history documents the debilitating impact of early colonial encounters for the local population. Subsequent economic intensification repeated the experience, as for instance in spreading disease through the construction of railroad and irrigation systems. More recently, the obvious cases of HIV/ AIDS and SARS can be cited, though there are several other diseases that are mass killers. There are other forms of man-made diseases or ill-being that need mention; such as mad-cow disease. Health insecurities of this type also characterize wide sections of the population of rich countries: the high rate of coronary disease and mortality in the rich countries is linked to altered dietary and work patterns, and a massive latent health problem is being generated by junk food. There could be other risks associated with genetic interventions in the food chain. In all these cases, there are definite connections between the health issue and the industrial profit machine; these links need to be identified and analysed.

2.4.4 Armed conflict

Perhaps the single largest source of insecurity is generated by wars and conflicts within and between nations and ethnic or religious groups. The examples are too numerous to list. Recently, attempts have been made to theorize the causes and rationale of such wars, mostly in terms of the struggle for control of natural or other resources. Such explanations might have some validity but it would be naïve to look for a simple answer, given the complexity of each arena of conflict. The role of identity-based factors, and also the global agendas of hegemonic powers cannot be overlooked. For example, the wars in the Gulf and in West Asia have surely been the sources of sustained widespread destitution for large populations. The burden falls disproportionately on women and children.

It has to be emphasized that at the present juncture, a very significant proportion of the poverty and vulnerability in the world arises from systemic occurrences that have a sudden onset and a finite (even if somewhat unpredictable) timeframe. These are experienced simultaneously by large sections of the population, which makes it impossible for people to insure themselves against such events. This applies particularly to the poor, and to poor countries. This consideration calls for a widening of the agenda to address the issue of ensuring socio-economic security at the global level *per se*. Unfortunately, current global power structures are not oriented towards addressing these needs in any meaningful way, and prefer to take refuge behind piecemeal reactions to "crises". They set minimalist development targets which are far too narrow in their conceptualization to address the massive scale of socio-economic insecurity. Indeed, there is a school of thought which argues, not entirely without credibility, that some of the major forms of vulnerability and insecurity stem precisely from the economic and political strategies imposed by the hegemonic powers of the day. It is held that all the above forms of systemic vulnerability are manifestations of the playing out of these strategies. Such an argument has stronger and weaker forms.

3. Mapping social protection coverage: A classificatory device

In order to map the extent of social protection coverage for any population, a simple and sturdy framework can be constructed highlighting three elements, one on each axis of a cube.

The first of these represents the *multiple dimensions of social protection*, and would cover a full spectrum of phenomena or domains over which protection is sought. These could include, for instance, food and nutritional security, health, aspects of employment or work-related insecurity, old age cover, children's education, access to legal aid, etc. This list could be quite lengthy if it included most of the potential deficits against which protection or insurance was necessary.

The second element pertains to *different social constituencies* in the population. This axis of the table would list groups such as children, women, the aged, workers, migrants, excluded minorities, low castes, spatially marginalized groups, the unemployed, etc. Each of these categories could be further disaggregated: for instance, workers could be formal-sector employees, or those in the informal economy. Special interest groups could be identified and included, such as domestic workers, or particular occupational groups such as traditional fishers, miners, or small-scale farmers. Amongst children, different age groups could be specified by gender; and the category of women could be divided as well, with distinctions based on family, work and personal circumstances. Crossing this dimension with the earlier one would generate a matrix which would map the social coordinates or incidence of different forms of vulnerability of various sections of the population.

The third element lists the *alternative provisioning systems* (potentially) available for addressing the specific dimensions of social protection identified on the first axis: state based provision, market based systems, employer/enterprise linked systems, occupational welfare funds and schemes, trades union or member-based organizations, other solidarity or community based institutions, informal or non-contractual family/household/lineage/kinship mechanisms, intra-household and inter-generational transfer mechanisms, self-selecting mutual-help groups, locality/spatially delineated systems, targeted programmes, NGO/CBO based interventions, national universal coverage systems, various types of insurance schemes, etc. These are all mechanisms or devices that offer protection against any specific form of vulnerability or risk for any particular social group or constituency.

The matrix has a cubic form which allows us to investigate the modes and forms of cover enjoyed by specific population groups in order to address particular insecurities and deficits. Each cell of this cube provides a space defined by a particular group, a specific dimension of insecurity, and a particular mode of cover. Traversing along the three axes of the cube can help to identify the overall needs and gaps in social provisioning. Clearly some of these protection mechanisms would be traditional, or conventional systems embedded in the social fabric, not mediated by the state or external agents; others could be classed as modern, state-based. Over time, the former tend to erode and the latter have recently atrophied, leading sometimes to a partial revival of the "traditional" arrangements. As we have already noted, Sen has called one of these shifts the pure exchange system transition (PEST), but the pathways are myriad. Such a classificatory framework can facilitate a mapping of the social protection system in any given country at any point in time. It makes visible the plurality of provisioning systems with respect to specific dimensions of social protection. Many lower level mechanisms are nested in larger systems, with strong interdependence between the different levels. The framework could also help to identify gaps in the system, with regard to social groups, or to the specific dimensions of social protection. Of course, it is necessary to go further and verify the incidence of population coverage in any cell; the extent to which that particular dimension (e.g. health) is covered; and the quality of coverage provided. Thus, each cell contains a composite, and complex reality. Such a schema would also reveal the wide divergence between the SP scenarios in the three model groups of economies. Of course, the matrix does not reveal the interdependence and the evolutionary dynamics of the system, the logic of which needs to be analysed within an inter-temporal framework. It is also necessary to recognize that there could be considerable diversity in the profiles of different individuals comprising any particular social category – for instance migrants, or pregnant women, or widows. As such, a further disaggregation would be needed for a meaningful map which did not lump together diverse sub-groups simply because they share a single label.

4. Designing social protection systems

Viewed at a generic level, a comprehensive social protection system would need to connect an array of interdependent elements.

4.1 Some macro considerations

First: it would need to base itself on *norms* which give full visibility and recognition not just to food requirements but to all basic needs. In particular, basic education and health needs are generally not appropriately included, and this can only have serious negative consequences for equity, growth and sustainability.

Second: an income level that meets all fully recognized basic needs. This income need not all accrue in the form of cash; it could include a variety of claims, flows and benefits in kind. This could be read as a basic needs line, although $1/day is definitely not an appropriate proxy for this BNL.

Third: it would have to acknowledge that money income, even when nominally sufficient to meet basic needs, cannot always and everywhere be converted into realized basic needs. This applies especially to those needs that have the nature of public goods, such as education, health, the environment, communications and information. It is commonly acknowledged that the markets for such goods are virtually absent in large sections of the rural sector, and even where they do exist, they tend to shut out the poor. Hence, the second element is recognizing and meeting the government responsibility of ensuring *appropriate supply systems* for such services, even when they are not provided free. This consideration is especially relevant in the case of the transition and developing countries.

Fourth: the system should be able to avoid or bear shocks and fluctuations in the BNL arising from exogenous and endogenous factors which influence the various components of income separately. This implies that the unit (individual, family/household) should have an appropriate level of assets, savings, insurance and other compensatory mechanisms.

Fifth: appropriate norms that recognize full basic needs, and a guaranteed supply of health and education services, do not combine to enable the poor to access these services if they do not have the necessary resources. The fifth element therefore concerns the design and implementation of *financial accessing mechanisms* for the poor. These could take various forms, ranging from universal public provisioning, to market based sales of services. However, bearing in mind the extreme vulnerability of the poor to fluctuations in their livelihoods, these mechanisms would have to include an element of fair social insurance which ensures that the poor do not suffer from periodic basic-needs deficits.

Sixth: the system would need to arrive at a universal, or more likely, a plural set of institutional mechanisms and devices through which the social protection cover would be generated or delivered. Such institutional arrangements could include, for instance: residential, or locality based delivery mechanisms; employer-based systems; direct provision by government to individual units; informal community and other mechanisms; local government or village council based systems; other civil society or membership-based organizations such as trades unions, occupational schemes, or development programmes run by government or by non-governmental organizations, e.g., via micro-credit programmes, or, alternatively, membership in insurance schemes.

Seventh: the system would need to consider whether to work through income transfer mechanisms, or income-generating activities, or whether to provide the components of social protection directly, e.g., food-provision schemes, free schooling and medical facilities, etc.

Eighth: a choice has to be made between a package approach where a variety of social protection inputs are integrated into a single transaction, and an arrangement whereby each item is separately delivered and accessed.

Ninth: an expectation that some improvement in the quality of life should be a component of what has to be socially achieved and protected for all. Thus, the unit should have some endogenous capacity for sustained growth, so that it can rise steadily above the poverty level implied by the BNL. In addition, access to social protection has to provide a platform for investment through augmenting the capacity of the beneficiary to bear risk.

Tenth: it should be possible to achieve the basic needs line without socially unacceptable costs, such as overwork, exposure to hazards and accidents, stressful work regimes. This introduces the elements of labour productivity and conditions of work.

Eleventh: social protection systems must adequately cover the relations between work and citizenship, by underwriting security, identity, dignity and citizenship rights, all understood within the mutual obligations arising from peaceful multi-cultural coexistence. This dimension incorporates the specific relational aspects associated with employment (e.g., subordination, exploitation, as well as voice and dialogue).

Twelfth: the system should be based on the principle of universal basic socio-economic security for all as a right, and not on a narrowly motivated instrumental or politically inspired programme targeted at selected groups for selected items. But this immediately opens the Pandora's box of issues concerning the upscaling of social protection to cover the entire population.

Thirteenth: the system would also need to protect against risks which apply simultaneously to large sections of the population, and sometimes to the entire populace. This calls for a different strategy which involves macro-economic policies, and could also require regional or global arrangements for underwriting such covariant risks.

Fourteenth: it is necessary to create a real sense of local ownership of such systems, not just at the level of perceptions, but also through vesting specific implementation, monitoring and accountability instruments in local civil society or representational bodies. These instruments could provide corrective feedback on the functioning of the SP schemes.

The social protection agenda is traditionally limited to protecting the beneficiary from the consequences of downward volatility. This limited perspective arises in the first instance from the classical model, where it is implicitly assumed that the BNL has been successfully attained, that the economy enjoys sustained growth and successful modernization with good governance, so that the relational requirements of SP are satisfied. It is obvious that in the other economic models, this narrow interpretation is unsatisfactory, since there are shortfalls in all the other elements as well.

4.2 Some micro parameters

Both in the study of existing protection mechanisms, and in the design of new schemes, several parameters have to be considered at the micro level.

What form does the source of vulnerability take? Is it an event, or is it a condition that continues over a period of time, such as a phase in the life cycle of an individual (beneficiary), or an element in a dynamic socio-economic process?

How predictable is the source of vulnerability? Agricultural labourers and marginal farmers experience shortfalls each year on a seasonal basis. The need for schooling for a child is entirely predictable (whether or not the family can actually manage to achieve this). For an employee, retrenchment might not be a predictable event, but retirement from work would be. The marriage of a child could fairly be regarded as a predictable event. For many of these types of phenomena, the timing can be roughly predicted. But while death is fully predictable, its timing is capricious and uncertain. Bouts of ill health, and accidents, might fairly be expected over a lifetime, but their frequency, intensity and duration remain uncertain. A related question is the expected frequency of the event causing the vulnerability.

What is the pattern of incidence? Does the phenomenon affect only the individual (household/unit), or does it simultaneously and independently affect a larger number of units? The covariant nature of risks across units has direct implications for the design of protection and insurance.

Is the impact spatially and/or socially concentrated or are the affected units widely dispersed? Are the affected individuals or units contiguous, in the sense that they constitute a locality or a group sharing some identity, and (potentially) forming a network? Or are these units scattered across the population, and not directly linked or known?

Are there indirect effects on related units? When a single individual (unit) is affected by the phenomenon, are the negative effects limited to this individual alone, or is there a wider collateral impact, or external effect on other members of the unit, i.e., the family, or neighbouring units? This would mean identifying stakeholders who would be indirectly affected by the phenomenon and who would have an interest in the design of the intervention.

How stable is the population? High instability makes schemes involving long-term transfers and payoffs unpredictable and unattractive.

157

How large is the group over which the intervention applies? A large group is a positive factor for many risks, but not without its costs (monitoring and verification are sometimes more effective and less costly in smaller groups). The nature of the groups is also relevant: are these solidarity groups, shared-identity groups, or groups covering people in a residential neighbourhood; what is the degree of intra-group heterogeneity?

Can the potential need, or loss, be quantified and measured? Or can it vary over a wide range? These sums have to be scaled against the level of income, as well as of asset ownership, of the units concerned.

What are the extant mechanisms of insurance against the prevailing sources of vulnerability, and why do they not provide adequate cover? Information on these points would help to identify weak spots in the social and economic framework which would have to be taken into account in devising new, alternative arrangements.

4.3 Some strategic issues

In devising new provisioning systems, the specific characteristics of the different dimensions of social protection need to be recognized. Thus, there are different possibilities and advantages of risk pooling in different cases; different degrees of predictability, risk and uncertainty; different costs and returns to alternatives on the supply side; etc. And there is the issue of pricing: it is inherent in the nature of the problem that those in need of protection would in general be unable to meet the full costs of its provision. This could involve insurance or free-access systems which have to be subsidized. Issues of targeting versus universal coverage become pertinent, alongside resource-efficiency versus rights-based perspectives. At national level it is not possible to insure against certain types of risk, which call for international or global mechanisms of protection and compensation. This has been vividly demonstrated – even though in a regressive manner – in the recent financial crises, where private debt burdens have been socialized in the wake of the crisis, even as significant sections of the national populations concerned have been pushed into traumatic poverty. Regrettably, such global efforts have been noticeably absent in the face of global disasters and poverty.

The traditional social protection strategy treats the shortfall as a gap to be met by transfers, usually in the form of welfare payments made to those below the basic needs line. And where the main income source is usually wage employment, this usually translates into unemployment insurance and compensation mechanisms. But in the development model, the accent has usually been on interventions that raise the income of the beneficiary through a variety of mechanisms. Indeed, employment generation programmes play an important, even crucial role. But alongside these are various investment-oriented interventions which improve the physical and/or human capital of households below the BNL. This could involve land access programmes, health and education for mothers and children, improved information and access, micro-credit schemes and a range of other poverty alleviation programmes, many of which are based on work-fare principles. Thus, the egalitarian growth, development and poverty alleviation agendas interface closely with conventional SP programmes, and it is difficult, and perhaps counterproductive, to maintain a forced division between them at the levels of design, resourcing, implementation and monitoring. The challenge is to define the focus and domain of the social protection agenda.

5. Monitoring indicators of social protection

Are appropriate monitoring indicators available that cover the different dimensions of social protection? How effective are the indicators of deprivation that are currently being employed in policy discourse and in major development organizations? How far do they go in serving as meaningful indicators for monitoring the state and progress of the systems of social protection and their components? A selective discussion follows which looks in turn at the poverty line approach (largely used by the World Bank), the composite social indicators methodology and instruments used by UNDP, and some indicators used to assess the gender dimensions of deprivation and vulnerability. It will be argued that none of these are really satisfactory for the purpose of highlighting the forms, extent and incidence of the various types of vulnerability addressed by the social protection policy agenda.

5.1 What is wrong with the poverty line approach?

Measuring the incidence of poverty using the income poverty or food poverty approach has two sets of weakness. The first group of problems stems from the many detailed methodological assumptions or choices that have to be made in the estimation procedure. How should the food basket be made up? What adult equivalence scales should be adopted? How should inter-sectoral and inter-regional variations in diet and prices be handled? What type of income distribution data are used in the estimation process? Answers to these, and many other, questions are often dictated not by methodology but by data availability. The robustness of any poverty estimation using the poverty-line approach therefore needs to be checked for its sensitivity to variations in these choices and assumptions. These difficulties are real but they could not be said to overturn the approach itself. However, the second set of problems raises doubts about the fundamental meaningfulness of the poverty line. These criticisms go well beyond practical objections and suggest that the approach fatally distorts the very meaning of poverty. While the first set of weaknesses pertaining to "methods" has been widely discussed in the literature, the second group of issues concerning "meaning" remains under-emphasized. In view of the widespread heavy reliance on the income poverty line approach, it is useful to briefly highlight some major objections of the second type. This underlines the need to adopt a broader notion of human poverty in place of the narrow focus on income or food-poverty lines; above all, it argues that such poverty lines cannot be meaningfully used as proxies for vulnerability and socio-economic insecurity.

Energy expenditure. Food poverty lines usually make no allowance for differential energy requirements arising from hard physical as against non-manual work. Since the poor work much harder in physical terms than the non-poor, this sets up a bias towards the underestimation of deprivation. The standard assumption when constructing poverty lines pegs caloric requirements to the basal metabolic rate, which broadly corresponds to a passive physical state.

Cheap calories. In its concern for economizing on resources, the poverty-line estimation procedure usually assumes that the stipulated calorie requirements will be met through the purchase of the lowest priced calories available. Very often this demands that the poor find cheaper baskets than is possible in reality, or than they would themselves prefer to consume. The requirements of a balanced diet, as well as the choices and preferences of the poor are usually overlooked; the poor are not allowed to enjoy dietary tastes and preferences! The result of this procedure is that in reality, those with incomes precisely on the poverty line (thus set) are usually found to be consuming far fewer calories than the level on which the poverty line is set in the first place.[10]

Non-food basic needs. Usually, different procedures are used to estimate the food and non-food components of the poverty line basket. While dietary requirements are calculated on a "scientific" basis according to bodily needs, the non-food component of the poverty threshold is not calculated on a *needs* basis. Instead, the procedure essentially identifies households whose expenditure on food exactly matches the cost of the

---

[10] For example, in India, while about 30 per cent of the population is deemed to be below the income-poverty line, it is only above the 70th percentile of income that, on average, the calorie levels implicit in this poverty line are met.

food component in the poverty line basket, and then checks how much such households *actually* spend on non-food items. Thus, the food component is needs based whereas the non-food component reflects the poverty of the poor with no guarantee that basic non-food needs are satisfactorily met. This is a very serious shortcoming, and could have the effect of suppressing the visibility of such crucial basic needs as health, education, housing, transport and communications, fuel etc. There is reason to believe that this is the case in China.

Public provisioning. Logically, the expenditure profile should include the imputed cash value of goods and services received in kind as gifts or transfers; "expenditure" records the value of all consumption items, not just those on which cash outlays are made. In reality, the poverty line typically limits itself to private expenditure. The public provision of goods and services is excluded. This is a significant gap when it comes to health and education services, particularly in developing economies, where the role of public provision is usually substantial. In the absence of such information, one can only speculate over actual outcomes with respect to these key basic needs. Since access to public provision is often heavily unequal across locations, and within communities, this gap constitutes a significant weakness, especially when it comes to cross-sectional or inter-temporal comparative analysis. In many situations, even households which have the financial capacity might find it impossible to obtain adequate education and health services simply because these are not available locally; in contrast, these facilities might be available in the open market, but many cannot afford them on a regular or satisfactory basis. The poverty line approach implicitly assumes that money can buy health, education and other services at any time in any place.

Household assets base. The economic strength of a household, family or individual depends not only on the income, but also on the asset base. If there was a uniform and stable relationship between asset ownership and income (like a fixed capital: output ratio), additional information on assets might be redundant. Even here, the assets would imply a store of value that could be converted into income through encashment. But levels of asset ownership vary, and many unproductive assets are held as stores of value. The level and pattern of assets also determine the staying power of the household unit in the face of income fluctuations. On the other hand, many poor households are deeply in debt, and the profound implications of this fact are ignored by focusing only on the level of income. In reality, poverty lines are typically drawn in terms of expenditure not income levels, and as such incorporate another weakness: they are silent on how this expenditure was financed, i.e., were there positive or negative savings?

Intra-household disparities. The unit of analysis adopted for the estimation procedure is the household. This raises a host of estimation problems concerning the economies of scale in consumption, the choice of appropriate adult equivalence scales, etc. While these issues can be carefully addressed, the use of the household as the basic unit ignores the crucial question of intra-household disparities in access, consumption and other entitlements. Thus, the welfare of women, children and the elderly might not be adequately reflected in the average level for the household. This is a potentially serious gap. For instance, gender inequality in consumption is often reflected in malnourished pregnant women, resulting in low birth weight children, and these children are known to have inferior life chances. Similarly, gender inequality in education could also affect the life chances of the children of under-educated women, thus leading to the reproduction of deprivation.

Annual fluctuations. The poor are especially vulnerable to vicissitudes in their livelihoods, and this is reflected in fluctuations in their annual levels of income. Thus, while the poverty line itself is held constant, and even if the statistical incidence of poverty remains the same over two periods, the composition of the poor could be quite different, with some of the "old" poor climbing above the poverty line even as other "new" poor slip below it. Thus, the annual poverty line estimates of poverty cannot indicate what percentage of the population experienced poverty, say, in the previous 3 or 5 years. Is poverty a transitory or a relatively permanent state for the household concerned? This important question remains unanswered. Similarly, the annual average for consumption hides the possibility of extended periods of hunger that cannot be compensated by the possibility of consuming above the norm in the plentiful season.

Marginalization and exclusion. The poverty-line approach treats each household independently and rates it on the basis of average per capita expenditure level. In this approach, all relational dimensions are missing. The fact that poor households suffer from high levels of spatial and social exclusion and marginalization is omitted. There is no reference to the issues of inequality and to power relations in the community where the poor live. The approach is one-dimensional and is blind to the socio-political dynamic that underlies the persistence and reproduction of poverty. This masks the weakness and continuous erosion of the claims of the poor with regard to community or social resources, or in their access to government services.

Self-perception of the poor. It is widely acknowledged that the subjects themselves usually have a different perspective on the sources, forms, nature, and intensity of their various deprivations and development deficits from the analyst armed with a particular indicator, especially an absolute income or food poverty line. These insights are unheard and unseen in the mechanical poverty line approach, but are crucial to the design of effective development interventions.

Narrow policy focus. The narrow income-poverty line approach does yield some important information on its chosen scale, but it is fundamentally one-dimensional and overlooks the multi-faceted nature of human deprivation. This can easily lead to a superficial and misleading understanding of the nature and causes, as well as the cures of human poverty. A grave danger posed by the income-poverty line approach is that it leads to the adoption of targeting, monitoring and evaluation criteria which are equally narrow, thus carrying the many blind spots in the concept of deprivation into the operational phase of interventions.

All these difficulties apply to the use of the standard poverty line approach in any specific location. Protagonists of the approach will no doubt point to the theoretical possibility of checking or compensating for many of these objections; in reality, this requires vast quantities of additional information, which is usually unavailable, or impossible to process in time and resource terms. Therefore, the above criticisms maintain their validity with regard to current practice. The fundamental question that arises is whether there is sufficient "poverty" in the poverty-line approach, or whether there is so much noise on some channels and silence on others as to render this a dangerously misleading instrument for listening to the voices of the poor, or for finding out about poverty and the poor. It can be seriously argued that such fears are justified when data are aggregated and cannot be supplemented with additional information on the dimensions and gaps listed earlier. Yet, the global community has agreed to halve the incidence of poverty by 2015, *using precisely such an imprecise measuring rod.* [11]

5.2 Other indicators

What about other mainstream indicators of deprivation, such as the human development index, or others in that family? Even a quick reflection on the structure and content of the HDI confirms that it is far too aggregated and blunt an instrument to shed light on the socio-economic insecurity of a population. This is not surprising since it was not really designed for this purpose. In varying degrees, this also applies to several other indicators.

---

[11] It is worth noting that on official Chinese data and estimation procedures, no more than about 30 million Chinese are presently below the poverty line. China is therefore well ahead of the Millennium Development Targets (MDTs), having achieved its goals in this regard more than a decade ahead of time! However, other stories have other data and methods. Likewise, it has recently been argued that the global MDTs for poverty reduction have already been met. Such deductions fly in the face of a direct appreciation of the forms and extent of deprivation at present, and only add further doubts about the use of the poverty line methodology.

In contrast, non-aggregated approaches, especially those that involve the participation and self-perception of the poor themselves, are capable of providing extensive insights into the expressed needs of the poor with regard to the types of insecurity that they themselves prioritize. While such approaches are extensively used, they are known to have several serious flaws which can bias the findings, especially with regard to the voices of the poorest and the weakest. Nevertheless, at micro level, these methods, when carefully applied and qualified, constitute a powerful and effective instrument. But the findings from these methods are inherently incapable of being aggregated without external bias, and recent attempts (by the World Bank) to arrive at aggregated "voices of the poor" can only lead to a cacophony of noise, with no common theme.

While the more general indicators of deprivation and poverty are not suitable for monitoring dimensions of social protection, a number of standard indices are usually consulted in this regard. How strong are such indicators? They tend to be drawn from the data systems of modern industrial economies, and focus on the status of the formal workforce. For instance, regular data are generated on the coverage of unemployment insurance schemes, accident insurance, indices related to working conditions and unionization. Further information can be obtained, often on an economy-wide basis on pensions, health insurance cover, education, etc. Where the social framework matches the conceptualization implicit in these indicators, the result is broadly satisfactory. However, we have argued that socio-economic insecurities vary widely across the three groups of economies, and within each type of economy. These formal sector indicators would cover a very small fraction of workers in a typical developing country. Further, many of them are not fully applicable to the labour market specifications of these economies, when such markets are understood to include the entire working population. A significant proportion, even a majority, of workers might be self-employed, for instance. It also becomes difficult to interpret the statistics for some standard dimensions such as pensions. For instance, the coverage might be high in a classical type economy, but very low in a development model economy. But the latter might rely on family and community networks for old-age care, whereas such "traditional" systems might have atrophied in the classical model economy in its transition to "modernity". How can such statistics be compared in the context of old-age care across these economies? The examples can be multiplied at will, almost.

The trouble arises mostly from attempting to collapse complex and wide notions of insecurity into narrow indicators corresponding to rather precise concepts which might not reflect the complexity and diversity of social reality.

Two other observations are pertinent here.

First: an indicator of coverage of some particular dimension of social protection does not in itself provide an adequate measure of the extent of persisting insecurity even with regard to that particular dimension. Consider the need for crop insurance and its provision in two economies, one prone to high fluctuations in output and prices, and the other where these are relatively stable. A similar incidence of crop insurance cover for the two economies would not imply equal coverage of the need, since one of the economies clearly has a far greater need than the other, and is likely to be left with a larger deficit or residual uncovered need in this regard. Similarly, a poor country might have a very low rate of formal pension cover, but in reality have good quality elder care provided by the family. The system might be superior to that in a modern economy where the family tends to break up and leave the elderly exposed. In the latter system, a higher rate of pension cover might automatically transfer into better old age care. The recent deaths of older people during the heat wave in Europe illustrate this point. It is necessary to determine the need for social protection, i.e., the extent of the original insecurity, and to measure coverage of the need. The two indices together would then yield some meaningful information about the gaps that persist. Put notionally:

Gross need − cover = Residual or gap

where it is recognized that a variety of mechanisms and arrangements could provide cover. This would produce a cross-sectional snapshot of the system at a point in time.

Second: it is necessary to go beyond the snapshot and investigate the dynamics of the different elements of the above equation for each of the main dimensions of insecurity, and/or by specific social groups and constituencies, or by types of economy. This would provide information on trends in the three different elements. For instance, in the modern European economy, the casualization of labour means that a significant number of younger people are not adequately covered for old age through pension contributions, and this gap is likely to manifest itself increasingly over time. The family system might be weakening before new systems of elder care can be constructed in poor developing economies, implying here as well a widening of insecurity, although formal sector pension cover might well be rising. Such dynamics need to be captured in order to clarify the processes at work. Without such information, it is likely that the available monitoring indicators will be misinterpreted.

5.3 Profiling gender-related insecurity: A taxonomical illustration

It has been argued that the standard mainstream indicators of human development or poverty cannot adequately reflect the status of a population with respect to socio-economic security. Given the multiple dimensions of insecurity, and the diversity of the social groups that comprise any large population, it is inevitable that every summary statistic or indicator of socio-economic security will be heavily reductionist in nature. In order to find more accurate meanings, and more informative indicators for summarizing, comparing or monitoring socio-economic security, it is necessary to work at a much lower level of aggregation, focusing perhaps on a specific group or a single dimension. Here, an attempt is made to convey the difficulty of the task by sketching a framework for an inventory of gender-related socio-economic security.

The matrix in the table demarcates the phases in the life cycle of a woman, from pre-birth to old age. Of course it is possible to split the phases or to choose different points of separation. Within these phases one can take cognizance, notionally, of various events or episodes – birth, puberty, marriage, childbirth, divorce or separation, widowhood, etc.

Profiling gender vulnerability

B: Domains of vulnerability	A: Life cycle phases					
	Pre-natal	Infancy & childhood	Girlhood & adolescence	Young woman	Middle age	Old age
Reproduction						
Empowerment						
Knowledge, education, learning						
Consumption, nutrition, health						
Personal security, survival						
Work, labour, employment						
Property, assets, endowments						

A: Life cycle phases

- pre-natal
- infancy and childhood
- girlhood and adolescence
- young woman
- middle age
- old age

On the journey through life, the woman enters or operates in various domains: the home, the school, the workplace, public space, her home after marriage, etc. She does so in a variety of roles and at different ages. In each domain, she encounters different fields of gender bias and disadvantage with which she has to contend. Such fields are categorized in the columns of the table. Within each category, it is possible to list more specific sub-fields in order to capture more specific forms of insecurity.

B: Domains of disadvantage and vulnerability

Seven broad domains are used, though these could well be defined in other ways.[12]

- reproductive sphere: family: wife, mother, widow: sexuality, marriage, reproduction

- empowerment: personal, cultural, political – culture and socialization, discipline, behavioural regulation; authority, decision-making power; independence, autonomy, life-choices, freedoms; mobility, visibility, voice: public sphere participation; politics, representation, networks, information-access

- knowledge, education, learning

- consumption, nutrition, health, well-being

- personal security, survival, legal status and cover, rights and redress, institutional support

- work, labour, employment; at home and in the labour market

- assets, endowments, entitlements, access, control

A and B together create a matrix whereby a woman's journey through disadvantage and vulnerability can be charted. This can be done variously for different social groups, cultures and individuals. The table generates a

---

[12] For two other specifications, see Kabeer (1994, ch.6) and Nussbaum (1990).

refined and comprehensive inventory of the threats and experiences that the social protection agenda needs to address. To make this visible for policy makers, it is necessary to carry through this disaggregated analysis to the level of indicators and measurement. It is clear that the so-called gender sensitive human development index and the gender empowerment indices are utterly unable to cope with such complexity, and fail to provide significant monitoring signals for a very wide range of phenomena reflecting gender insecurities.

Such a matrix could be specified and filled in variously for different contexts defined by different time periods, cultures and societies, or social groups. It also allows for comparison across these contexts. Alternatively, it permits the construction of indicators which focus on specific domains, going across the different phases of the woman's life. Or the focus could be on the different phases of life, i.e., the girl baby, the girl child, the young woman, the widow, and so on. Within each cell of the matrix, it is possible to provide an elaboration and/or illustration. It is also possible to check against such a matrix the scope, coverage and adequacy of various indicators which attempt to capture these gender disadvantages. Such an exercise would immediately show the exceedingly limited scope and coverage of the major gender-sensitive indicators that continue to dominate the discourse, for no good reason.

Such a scheme allows, indeed, requires a holistic perception and analysis of gender disadvantage. It also makes visible phases, events, domains and biases in a fashion which permits connections to be made and chains of causality to be identified.

Similar matrices can also be constructed for other target constituencies or entities, e.g., migrants, children, minority groups, particularly vulnerable occupational groups and the elderly.

6. Concluding observations

In lieu of conclusions, the paper closes by noting four tendencies in the policy discourse on poverty reduction and social protection. All four pertain to the manner in which resource needs are strategized, and each could be problematic.

First, there is increasing acceptance of the idea that the poor should pay for their social protection. The "bankability" and the "financial maturity" of the poor are presented as positive attributes of their worth and their potential for self-help. Ironically, this is widely accepted by those who were until recently staunch opponents of the principle of user-costs levied on the poor for access to basic needs. The shift to the money metric approach goes hand-in-hand with a shift in favour of the open market as a provider of services on the user-pays principle. This is further supported by the argument that such payments create a sense of ownership amongst the poor which leads to their empowerment, and also raises the level of accountability. Of course, these would be positive outcomes, should they actually occur on any widespread scale. Overlooked, however, is the body of argument and evidence that shows that such methods tend systematically to exclude the poor, who form the target group in the first place.

Another manifestation of the increasing reliance being placed on the money metric, whether at the level of concept, policy design or monitoring, is the ubiquitous dollar-a-day line that has come to dominate development discourse. Virtually by default, this line has started setting goal posts for targeting and monitoring.

Consider for instance, the recent somewhat "Luddite" call from an eminent economist (with a penchant for courting controversy) to dispense with the entire range of poverty alleviation programmes, and instead resort to the singular device of ladling out one dollar each day to every person under the poverty line, leaving the recipients to spend their dollar on their daily bread, or their daily fix, or tobacco or whatever else.

There are several motives behind this call: that the poor should be allowed to express their own preferences in using the poverty-reduction budget; or that the high delivery costs of government programmes should be reduced; or that the high rates of leakage and rent-seeking should be controlled. But the cure might be worse than the malady in many cases, since it overlooks the entire range of supply side issues, pertaining to access, institutional exclusion, market failures and information gaps.

Second, there is increasing emphasis on using micro-insurance mechanisms, both formal and informal, to provide social protection for the poor. Just as the poor are now deemed to have become bankable, they could also be capable of handling their protection needs through market-based insurance mechanisms, or through using their accumulated "social capital". Attractive as this sounds, the approach has several lacunae. Where there is extensive poverty, and risks move together, all sink or swim together. Tawney (1932) noted that when there was a shortfall in one feudal village in China, the next village was also likely to be affected and in deficit, as was the next district, leaving little possibility of insurance across units. Two: many units, or members of units might be unable to meet the insurance premiums, and be left hopelessly vulnerable. Three: these arrangements often break down precisely when they are most needed, as in the case of patron-client, or landlord-tenant relations in bad harvests. Insurers deny and default on payout claims. Even families split up, the strong repudiating the weak. Four: the implications of such exposure are dramatically worse for the poor, who can be, and usually are, reduced to destitution with little chance of recovery; if the basic norm constitutes the social floor, they fall through to the ocean bed. Five: not all informal insurance mechanisms for income smoothing and sharing might be generally regarded as reflecting socially desirable or laudable motivations, behaviour or values; for instance, intra-familial insurance mechanisms often involve forms of control, emotional black-mail, or outright coercion, as well as some reprehensible practices, mostly against dependents, whether women, children, or the aged. An institu-tional theorist might be tempted to explain some of the most flagrant violations of gender rights in these terms. Six: insurance mechanisms are essentially designed to provide financial access, but they do not guarantee the availability of the goods and services required to meet the specific insurance need. Thus, the poor might join health insurance schemes, but health facilities might be unavailable. Between a non-existent market, and dysfunctional or atrophying informal insurance arrangements, there is an expanding area of vulnerability; but there are many people in this no-man's land. Thus, there is a good chance that, as with other things, the poor will also beget poor insurance. The emphasis on insurance is partly driven by a desire to take the pressure off the state as a provider of universal social protection. Given the widespread experience of market failure in this area, the scattered stories of successful prototypes of micro-insurance for the poor should not be a platform for relieving the state of the role of ultimate underwriter of the social protection needs of the poor. No doubt, there is a need to conceptualize universal coverage in terms of plural systems of cover, which incorporate the roles of the market, the state, and other solidarity organizations of and for the poor. However, the market cannot be relied upon to provide universal coverage for the poor – markets cater to money demand, not human need.

Third, there is virtually universal acceptance of the new rules of the fiscal game, and somewhat perniciously of the idea that there is a sharp budget constraint on government social protection expenditure. This argu-ment lends support to the user-pays principle even when applied to the poor. The corollary is that a blind eye is turned to the possibilities of domestic resource mobilization, even in societies characterized by high levels of poverty and inequality. The possibility of redistributive taxation is not examined, nor is the potential of alternative fiscal and macro-eco-nomic policies which are not predicated upon acceptance of fiscal con-straint. Together, the state is rendered even more passive, and the status quo with respect to inequality goes unquestioned. These trends need to be challenged.

Fourth, there is a damaging tendency to frame the argument for uni-versal social protection in terms of resource availability. The constraint of resource limitations, whether at national or household level, cannot be wished away. However, the myriad possibilities of responding better to social protection needs through institutional and behavioural changes that are contingent not on the injection of more money, but on different ways of doing things are overlooked. This applies to the economy as a whole, but also to the local community or village level.

Finally, there is a tendency to problematize social protection, and consequently to frame policy interventions, in an isolated manner. Usually this involves focusing on an enterprise, an organization, a specific scheme, or a local community. Even when wider interventions are considered, the issue is the replication of some prototype micro-scheme. There is no doubt that many forms of socio-economic vulnerability need to be addressed at the local level in this manner, and also that local institutional structures are crucial in the successful design, implementation and monitoring of these interventions. However, there is a risk of marginalizing social protection if the wider context is ignored. More than ever before, the sources of insecurity and vulnerability lie well beyond the boundaries of the local space, and arise from processes which are national, and usually global in nature. Not taking this explicitly on board in the design of policy would relegate social protection interventions to the level of rescue operations. Clearly, attention also needs to be simultaneously on the sources and origins of the vulnerability. The role of preemptive and preventive policies should not be overlooked, especially in the current global environment. This paper has attempted to highlight the relevance of these wider dimensions. This also provides a stronger and multi-channel bridge between social protection dimensions and the agenda of decent work as a framework for development interventions.

In general, this paper has argued that the notion of decent work – and social protection, which is one of its four constituents – needs to be considered within a broad development context, rather than in a narrow focus on the workplace or enterprise alone. Hence the agenda for decent work – and for universalizing social protection – must engage with wider processes and policies of development. It is essential to remain aware of the wide structural differences between different groups of economies, and to ensure that the search for universality does not generate a false uniformity in concept or policy.

References

Agarwal, Bina, 2000, *Gender inequality- Some critical neglected dimension*", Presentation at the Symposium on decent work for women, Friday 24 March 2000. Geneva: ILO.

Anker, R. et al., 2002, M*easuring decent work with statistical indicators*, Statistical Development and Analysis Unit, Policy Integration Department, ILO, Geneva. 24 July 2002.

Baccaro, Lucio, 2001, *Civil society, NGOs, and decent work policies: Sorting out the issues*, Decent Work Research Programme, Discussion Paper DP/127/2001, ILO, Geneva.

Bhalla, A.S.; F. Lapeyre, 1999, *Poverty and exclusion in a global world*, Macmillan, Basing-stoke, UK.

Dasgupta, Biplab, 1977, "India's green revolution", in *Economic and Political Weekly*, Annual Number, February, Vol.. Xii, Nos. 6,7 and 8.

Drewnowski, Jan, 1974, *On measuring and planning the quality of life*, Institute of Social Studies, The Hague.

Egger, Philippe 2002 "Towards a policy framework for decent work", in *International Labour Review*, 141(1-2): 161-174

Fields, Gary 2001, *"Decent Work" and development policies*, Paper prepared for the ILO, mss. September.

Fields, Gary S., 2002, *International labor standards and decent work: Perspectives from the developing world*, Paper prepared for the Conference on International Labor Standards, Stanford Law School, May.

Ghai, Dharam, 2002a *Decent work: Concepts, models and indicators*, DP/139/2002, Education Outreach Programme, IILS Discussion Paper, Geneva, ILO.

Ghai, Dharam, 2002b. *Social security priorities and patterns: A global perspective*, DP/141/2002, Education Outreach Programme, IILS Discussion Paper, Geneva, ILO.

Giddens, Anthony, 1996, "Affluence, poverty, and the idea of a post-scarcity society", in *Development and Change*, Vol.27, No.2, April.

Gore, Charles, 1995, "Markets, citizenship and social exclusion" in Rodgers et al. (eds.) 1995.

Griffin, Keith; A. R. Khan, 1978, "Poverty in the world: Ugly facts and fancy models", in *World Development*, Vol. 6, No. 3, pp. 295-304.

Griffin, Keith, 1979, *The political economy of agrarian change: An essay on the green revolution*, Macmillan, London.

Hills, J., J. Le Grand; D. Piachaud (eds.), 2002, *Understanding social exclusion*, Oxford University Press, Oxford.

ILO, 1972, *Employment, income and equality: A strategy for increasing productive employment in Kenya*, Report of the ILO Country Mission, World Employment Programme, ILO, Geneva.

ILO, 1974, *Sharing in development: A programme of employment, equity and growth for the Philippines*, Report of the ILO Country Mission, World Employment Programme, ILO, Geneva.

ILO, 2000, *Decent work and poverty reduction in the global economy*, Paper submitted by the ILO to the 2nd Session of the Preparatory Committee for the Special Session of the General Assembly on the Implementation of the Outcome of the World Summit for Social Development and Further Initiatives, April.

ILO 2001, Report of the Director General: *Reducing the decent work deficit – A global challenge*, International Labour Conference 89th Session. Geneva June.

Jose, A.V. 2002 *Decent work in a development perspective*, IILS Discussion Paper, Geneva, ILO.

Kabeer, N., 1994, *Reversed realities: Gender hierarchies in development thought*, Verso Press, London.

Khan, A.R.; E. Lee (eds.) 1983. *Poverty in rural Asia*, ARTEP, ILO, Bangkok.

McGranahan, D.; E. Pizarro; C. Richard, 1985, *Measurement and analysis of socio-economic development: An enquiry into international indicators of development and quantitative interrelations of social and economic components of development*, UNRISD, Geneva.

Morris, Morris D.; M. B. McAlpin, 1982, *Measuring the condition of India's poor: The physical quality of life index*, Promilla & Co. Delhi.

Naoroji, Dadabhai, 1901, *Poverty and un-British rule in India*, Swan Schonnenhein & Co. London.

Nussbaum, M, (1990), *Women and human development: The capabilities approach*, Cambridge University Press, Cambridge.

Pearse, Andrew, 1984, *Seeds of plenty, seeds of want: Social and economic implications of the green revolution*, Clarendon Press, Oxford.

Ravallion, M.; G. Datt; M. v.d. Walle, 1991, "Quantifying absolute poverty in the developing world", in *Review of Income and Wealth*, Series 37, pp.345-362.

Rodgers, Gerry, 1995, "What is special about a social exclusion approach", in Rodgers et.al. (eds.) 1995.

Rodgers, G.; C. Gore; J.B. Figueiredo (eds.) 1995, *Social exclusion: Rhetoric, reality, responses, A contribution to the World Summit for Social Development*, International Institute of Labour Studies, (IILS), ILO, Geneva.

Rothschild, Emma, 1996, "The debate on economic and social security in the late eighteenth century: Lessons of a road not taken", in *Development and Change*, Vol.27, No.2, April.

Rowntree, B. Seebohm, 1901, *Poverty: A study of town life*, Macmillan, London.

Saget, Catherine, 2001, Poverty reduction and decent work in developing countries: Do minimum wages help?" in *International Labour Review*, 140(3): 227-269

Sen, A.K., 1987, *Commodities and capabilities*, Professor Dr. P. Hennipman Lectures in Economics, University of Amsterdam, 1982, Oxford University Press, Delhi.

Standing, G. (ed.), 2003, *Minimum income schemes in Europe*, Socio-Economic Security Programme, ILO, Geneva.

Stiglitz, Joseph E. 2002, "Employment, social justice and societal well-being", in *International Labour Review*, 14 (1-2): 9-29.

Tawney, R.H., 1932, *Land and labour in China*, George Allen and Unwin, London. World Bank, 1990, *World Development Report*, Washington, D.C.

Chapter V
Social dialogue for decent work

Sarosh Kuruvilla

Executive summary

The goal of this paper is to develop measures (indicators) of social dialogue to help assess the progress of nations on this important dimension of *Decent Work*. The ILO's definition of social dialogue covers various types of information exchange (e.g. negotiation or consultation), between representatives of governments, employers and workers, on any issue of common interest, and includes both bipartite and tripartite mechanisms. However, partly because the ILO's structure is tripartite, tripartism has been seen as the primary avenue for social dialogue.

More recently, the growing size of the informal sector, the continuing decline in the living standards of large sections of the world's population, and the decline in union density internationally, have all prompted the ILO to articulate the concept of *Decent Work,* comprising four basic principles or core rights that are universally applicable. Since social dialogue is one of these core labour rights, there is renewed interest in developing measures or indicators of social dialogue.

The paper argues that any effort to develop measures of the social dialogue concept should take account of its current limitations. First, overwhelmingly, social dialogue has been operationalized in terms of collective bargaining between employers and workers (bipartite), and social concertation, i.e., tripartite talks between representatives of labour, employers, and governments. Other actors (e.g. civil society) have been ignored in this process. Second, there is no guarantee that collective bargaining rights do in fact lead to discussions about social policy at national level, although this is implied in the ILO's practice of developing social dialogue.

Third, the focus on "representatives" is also limiting, in that great numbers of the world's workers (and in some cases, employers) do not have the right to representation, which raises the question of how the practice of social dialogue could apply to these populations. Finally, there is the implicit assumption that an "employment relationship" between workers and employers is necessary for social dialogue to occur. This assumption excludes large numbers of workers who are in the informal sector, or who are self-employed, or in contractual relationships, since social dialogue as currently defined does not apply to them. Any attempt to develop measures must be sensitive to these problems.

Numerous efforts have been made to develop measures and indicators of social dialogue (these are reviewed in the paper). Overwhelmingly, the focus has been on the rights underlying bipartite collective bargaining and the way it is actually practised. Measures regarding the rights and practice of tripartism have also been developed, but these have largely been based on research in Western Europe (the one region of the world in which tripartism is significantly developed). The advantages and problems of the various different measures that have been used in prior efforts are also examined in the present report.

The design of the social dialogue indicators described here takes account of the conceptual problems mentioned above as well as the lessons learned from previous approaches. The guiding principles are as follows: the measures developed must be linked with earlier approaches to preserve continuity; measures of the rights underpinning social dialogue are clearly necessary but they are not sufficient, as we need good measures of the actual practice of social dialogue as well; since social dialogue is a complicated process, there is also a need for subjective interpretations of the elements involved by experts who have an intimate knowledge of national systems: the measures developed must take account of the large portions of the world's population who do not have representation rights, as well as those who are not in traditional employment relationships; the measures must be dynamic, comprehensive, valid and transparent; and finally, the costs involved in collecting data for the measures and the actual assessment exercise must be lower than those required for alternative forms such as national surveys.

The methodology advocated here involves the creation of "National Social Dialogue Data Sheets" that incorporate information on 28 quantitative and qualitative indicators/measures of social dialogue. Section 4 of the paper defines each indicator and provides a detailed justification for including it in the overall assessment instrument. The National Social Dialogue Data Sheets should be prepared by national or regional experts, who should also carry out the basic research required to collect, analyse and present this information. Each National Social Dialogue Data Sheet will thus reflect the state of social dialogue in the country concerned and also indicate ways in which it could be improved. In that sense, these are dynamic, rather than static indicators. To increase uniformity in the data sheets, detailed guidelines are developed for national experts in respect of each indicator. These guidelines mitigate problems with the subjective interpretation of labour and industrial relations institutions and the way they operate (an essential aspect of social dialogue in practice), since they provide a stable comparative basis on which national experts can make their evaluations.

The approach taken in developing this framework of 28 indicators deals with the conceptual issues noted above as well as the problems with prior approaches. It is comprehensive, since it covers the rights underpinning social dialogue as well as the actual practice; it is reliable since it draws upon experts who know social dialogue practices well in each country or region; it is cost efficient, since it is cheaper than carrying out national surveys in every country; it is relatively simple to understand; it is real, given that the measures are based on the variation in rights and practices in the world rather than on abstract and unmeasurable concepts; and it is dynamic in that it shows how each country could improve on different dimensions of social dialogue. A unique aspect of this approach is that each national data sheet is made up of both quantitative and qualitative information that provides a broad picture of the operation of social dialogue in that country, but which does not permit crass (and needless) "comparative rankings of countries". Rather, the overall focus is on helping countries improve on social dialogue. The primary limitation of the approach is that some of the indicators for the unorganized and informal sectors are not very clearly specified, given the lack of research on the new alternative approaches to social dialogue that have emerged during the last decade. The paper concludes with a discussion on the tradeoffs between validity and reliability in the measures proposed.

Introduction

This paper aims to develop usable indicators of the concept of social dialogue, as part of the ILO's effort to develop operational measures of *Decent Work*. Section 1 examines the concept of social dialogue. Section 2 looks at past approaches to measuring social dialogue. Section 3 discusses what we have learned from past approaches and the implications for developing indicators and collecting data. Section 4 describes and justifies the proposed indicators. Section 5 concludes the paper with a discussion of the implications of this methodology for practice, and an examination of the costs.

1. The concept of social dialogue and decent work

For the past six decades, the concept of social dialogue has been central to the ILO's core mission and organization. Social dialogue is defined by the ILO to include:

> all types of negotiation, consultation or simply exchange of information between, or among, representatives of governments, employers and workers, on issues of common interest relating to economic and social policy. It can exist as a tripartite process, with the government as an official party to the dialogue or it may consist of bipartite relations only between labour and management (or trade unions and employers' organizations), with or without indirect government involvement. Concertation can be informal or institutionalized, and often it is a combination of the two. It can take place at the national, regional or at enterprise level. It can be inter-professional, sectoral or a combination of all of these. The main goal of social dialogue itself is to promote consensus building and democratic involvement among the main stakeholders in the world of work.[1]

While social dialogue as defined above encompasses both tripartite and bipartite relationships, in practice it is more closely linked to tripartism for a variety of institutional reasons. The conceptual glue linking social dialogue and tripartism is the notion of participation, which is fundamental to the tripartite structure of the ILO itself.

Tripartism has assumed a centrality in the ILO that bipartism does not enjoy. However, the key problem with both concepts is that they define and often limit the ILO's sphere of influence. For instance, it can (and has) been argued that the traditional agents (employers' federations and trade unions) represent only a very small part of their constituencies. In particular, trade unions do not represent a significant percentage of the world's workforce. Although there is great variation in trade union densities (measured by union members as a percentage of the non-agricultural workforce) across the world, it is only in very few cases that unions represent a majority of the workforce (see table below).

The data in the table are obviously not perfect, and do not include density figures from all countries. But the table is suggestive of the limitations of the concept of social dialogue and tripartism articulated by the ILO. First, a sizeable majority of the world's population does not have access to avenues for social dialogue. Second, and even more important, many non-European countries have not developed tripartite structures, given that bargaining is

---

[1] ILO, 1994; 1996; 1999.

Average union density and bargaining coverage

Region	No. of countries for which union density data is available, as of 1995	Average union density	Average collective bargaining coverage % for countries for which this data is available (number of countries)	% of world population in each region (2000)
Americas	23	14.50	30.90 (12)	13.7
Asia and Oceania	16	15.58	18.53 (10)	61.3
Europe	33	42.64	72.89 (13)	12
Africa	25	14	30 (8)	12.9

Source: World Labour Report, ILO, 1997/8.

decentralized in many nations. Third, even if we only look at the result of bipartite negotiation, collective bargaining coverage rates are low. Fourth, we must remember that most countries do not allow every member of the non-agricultural workforce to be represented by unions…there are significant exclusions such as workers in small enterprises, workers in supervisory positions, workers earning above a threshold level of income, workers in essential industries, and workers in export processing zones. Finally, various data show that union membership all over the world has declined steadily during the last two decades (in some cases from a high base, in others from an already low base). Although the reasons for lack of union penetration or collective bargaining coverage are many, the basic conclusion from the table above is that only a minority of the world's population enjoys the right to social dialogue via tripartism or bipartism.

Clearly, therefore, the traditional governance structures and the policies deriving from these structures were based on the assumption that urban industrial society (the organized sector) is an enduring model for job creation and worker protection. However, today's reality shows a growing "unorganized" sector in most developing nations. The ILO has not been blind to this reality, and through the ILO Declaration of 1998 and the subsequent articulation of its decent work concept, the office is attempting to broaden its focus beyond the organized sector. The decent work approach is aimed at all workers, even those outside the organized sector. The main element is to establish a universal "social floor" based on four principles or core rights; freedom of association and effective recognition of the right to bargain, elimination of forced labour, abolition of the worst forms of child labour and elimination of discrimination. The concept of decent work requires institutions and rules in all nations to promote these rights. In the case of social dialogue, however, the ILO has not yet articulated new "pathways to the periphery", as its concept of social dialogue remains

rooted in traditional bipartite or tripartite terms, and its structure, programmes and projects continue to reflect that traditional orientation.

The key problems are the low and declining levels of union density
and the increasing proportion of the world's workers who do not have the
right to participate (the concept underlying social dialogue). Since there
is no sign at all of unions increasing their membership in most countries,
worker participation must occur through alternative institutions or means.
This is the "grey" area that the ILO has to consider in developing indicators of social dialogue.

The above background raises several fundamental questions. Must the
concept of social dialogue be restricted to "representatives of governments,
employers, and workers on issues of common interest relating to economic
and social policy"? We have already pointed out that many workers do not
or are not allowed to have representatives. Another question...do bipartite
negotiations, which form the basis for collective bargaining in many countries, count as social dialogue since they do not involve the government
or the general public? Yet another question....do bipartite negotiations
ultimately lead to tripartite negotiations? The common element in these
questions is that they hinge on the existence of *representatives* of employers
and unions. This forces us to focus on social dialogue ONLY in arenas
where such representation occurs. Second, focusing on representatives of
employers and *unions* suggests that the *employment relationship* is at the core of
social dialogue. The discussion that follows will explain in detail how these
two concepts limit social dialogue.

As long as the ILO defines social dialogue as "involving all types of
negotiations, consultations, or exchange of information between or among
representatives of employers and workers on issues of common interest
relating to economic and social policy" (Jose, 2002, p. 2), then democrati-
cally elected trade unions are the best vehicle for providing workers with
"voice" or participation. However, in the absence of the principal-agent
relationship we need to cover alternative approaches.

In many countries, individual workers have the right to raise industrial
disputes. Arguably this provides individual workers with some degree of
"voice" without "representation". However, this "voice" at the workplace
does not necessarily provide workers with any voice over public policy that
is of interest to them. Recently, a number of other alternatives have arisen,
which do not require "representation by unions" but still provide employees
with some degree of voice at work, and perhaps even in making policy relevant to them. These include NGOs purporting to provide workers with
some voice in decision making, through a variety of means, or corporate
codes of conduct that lay down basic standards or guidelines for worker
consultation, or regional-level guidelines and codes, voluntary industry
codes and in a few cases, agreements on working conditions for factories

where there is no union representation. Some examples include the Global Reporting Initiative (GRI), the UN Global Compact and certification systems. There have also been efforts that look beyond labour-standards compliance to worker development. Consider the following examples. There is an NGO called Global Alliance, a tri-sectoral alliance (World Bank, Nike, Gap, and Universities) which provides training to workers and supervisors in garment and sportswear factories. The partners offer worker education in a number of areas such as health, safety, nutrition, financial planning, communication skills, presentation skills, while simultaneously providing supervisory training to employers' representatives in the factories. As a result, some real "empowerment" is taking place, and many factories have established health and safety committees or worker committees to discuss workers' problems. This is an example of introducing "participation" where no "voice" existed before. Similarly, the ILO has a Factory Improvement Programme that consists of training factory managers in the apparel industry to follow good work practices. This approach is based on the idea that managers can be persuaded to establish good and participatory work practices if it is demonstrably in their interest to do so. The results of these training programmes are encouraging.

Such alternatives are open to a number of criticisms. The most important one is that workers often do not participate in drawing up the codes of conduct that apply to them. Second, the evidence that they really provide voice is not very compelling. It is still too early to draw the conclusion that workers in these factories have adequate voice. However, they certainly have more say than they did in the past.

Another relevant issue is whether providing voice at the workplace leads to some degree of voice at the policy level. Put differently, do collective bargaining rights necessarily lead to tripartite rights and practice? We do not have clear answers to this question. Many countries have little or no tripartite consultation over social policy issues, but considerable collective bargaining. On the other hand, for example, the international agreement on working conditions in the toy manufacturing industry fundamentally concerns workplace issues, i.e. health and safety in toy factories, but it has had wider effects on safety and health policy in some developing countries. The alternatives briefly mentioned above tend to increase workers' voice at the workplace, and in some cases in a wider context, without traditional notions of representation.

Yet these avenues do not solve the problem of social dialogue for those who are not in an *employment relationship*. Arguably, there is no "employment relationship" in many parts of the informal sector, the largest sector in the world economy. Many in the informal sector are actually self-employed, and often engaged in contractual relationships with other people or institutions. Without representation, and without an employment relationship, how can we provide social dialogue to the informal sector? This is the critical problem that definitions of voice do NOT address.

Thus, when we consider how to improve social dialogue in the world (note that this is a more critical need in developing nations) there are three problems. First is the question whether many developing nations today have the institutional framework that gave rise to unions, collective bargaining and tripartite negotiations. Second is whether there is enough trade union representation for workers, given the low levels of union density in most third world nations. Third, the size of the informal sector shows that there is very little of the "employment relationship" which is so necessary to the ILO's definition of social dialogue. These problems may not be easily surmountable.

What is the implication of the above discussion for developing measures of social dialogue? The paper takes a three-pronged approach. First, measures of social dialogue are developed in ways that are consistent with the ILO definition, i.e., assuming an employment relationship and requiring representation by unions and employer federations, incorporating both bipartite collective bargaining and tripartite negotiations. Although this does not address the various limitations noted above, especially in relation to third world nations, it still is a relevant approach, given (a) the current nature, composition, and focus of the ILO; (b) the relatively large percentage of countries where representation and the employment relationship exist; and (c) as long as our model of economic development is geared towards increased formal sector industrial employment (which is the case today). Thus, assuming that development will take place, the traditional approach involving unions, employers' associations, and governments remains valid. Therefore, the bulk of the measures developed in this paper are based on the conventional approach.

Second, the paper includes measures of worker voice where there is no representation by unions. These include the plethora of alternative approaches that are emerging such as corporate, bilateral, and multilateral codes of conduct, certification programmes, NGO activities, worker development and training programmes, and pressure from consumers. Given that these efforts are expanding, while trade unions are shrinking, it is important that the concept of social dialogue should take account of these alternative voice mechanisms. They are not perfect measures to be sure. For example, a key pillar of the ILO, the international trade union movement, is divided over how best to deal with these alternative approaches and is sometimes opposed to them on the grounds that they are poor substitutes for unions. They are right, in that they are poor substitutes for the degree of participation provided by trade unions, but in the absence of trade unions, they are a significant development: any measure of social dialogue then, must take into account these developments, however imperfect.

Third, the paper attempts to deal with the issue of social dialogue where there is no representation and no employment relationship, which characterizes a significant part of the third world today. As several authors have pointed out (e.g. Jose, 2002), the basic requirement here is a highly decentralized participative democratic regime. Unless there is grassroots democracy, there can never be social dialogue, especially where informal sectors are large and without the institutional conditions that favour the development of workplace, or tripartite institutions. As is patently obvious, there has to be a long-term revision of the ILO's definitions and objectives to be consistent with this approach. In sum, despite the various problems noted, the bulk of the measures developed in this paper are consistent with the ILO's current definitions of social dialogue.

2. Prior approaches to measuring social dialogue

This review of previous efforts to measure social dialogue provides more detail on each of the measures used in the table which appears in Annex I.

The review highlights the major types of measure and examines the implications of each category for the future development of indicators. It also illustrates the point that no measure is perfect – they all have significant advantages and disadvantages. Those interested in a more complete discussion should refer to Lance Compa's paper (2002). The present review concerns social dialogue at national level. For measures at the individual firm level, the reader might consult the reports of companies under the Global Reporting Initiative of the United Nations.

In general, the various measures listed in the table can be broken down into five major categories: *(a)* common and universal measures; *(b)* particular measures of institutions, processes, and outcomes; *(c)* measures focusing on rights and violations thereof; *(d)* measures focusing on implementation; and *(e)* descriptive reports from various institutions.

Common and universal measures

These measures have been commonly used by the ILO and independent writers for decades, they are generally easy to collect, they are quantitative or can be used in quantitative comparisons, and they are available for most member countries of the ILO.

The first and most commonly used measure is union density, i.e., the number of union members expressed either as a percentage of the non-agricultural workforce or as a percentage of wage and salary workers. Union density has sometimes been used as a measure of union strength. This measure has been seen as an important indicator of the potential for social dialogue, the argument being that higher union density is associated with more social dialogue at tripartite or bipartite level. Union density data exist for most countries, and experience in the European countries has invariably shown a positive correlation between union density and almost any other measure of tripartism or bipartite industrial relations. Nonetheless, the measure has also had its problems. First, not all countries outside Europe evidence the positive correlation noted above. Second, union density as a proxy for union strength and as a basis for dialogue is questionable in countries where unions are not independent and are subject to authoritarian control. Third, there have been several problems with the quality of data, both in terms of the data collection methodology and in the calculation of density. For a detailed review of the problems with using union density as a proxy for social dialogue and/or union strength and influence see Kuruvilla et al. (2002), and Compa (2002). An important question is whether union density as a percentage of the agricultural workforce (a measure commonly used in North America) is appropriate, since agricultural workers in many countries do have unionization rights, and are, in fact, unionized. In this context, the percentage of union members amongst wage and salary earners (the measure used by the OECD) might be more appropriate.

A second indicator – collective bargaining coverage – has also gained popularity over time. Collective bargaining coverage was seen as a measure of bipartite industrial relations in countries where bargaining was invariably conducted at the industrial or workplace levels; and it was considered to be a measure of tripartite industrial relations in countries where bargaining was conducted at national level. Collective bargaining coverage was a tangible measure of the real degree of social dialogue (or participation) since it provided a quantifiable indicator of the number of workers who are actually covered by collective bargaining agreements i.e., in some sense a real measure of the effectiveness of collective bargaining. This measure is not as widely available as union density, and in some countries, the information is very difficult to collect. For example, many countries require that all collective bargaining agreements be registered yet there is no effort to consolidate the total number of agreements – thus, the data are available, but not collected and collated in usable form. In addition, there is a danger in assuming that collective bargaining coverage adequately represents the right to bargain, since in many countries collective bargaining agreements at the apex level are extended to cover workers in the entire industry, whether unionized or not. Kuruvilla et al. (2002) have combined indicators of collective bargaining coverage with levels of bargaining to arrive at a measure of union influence and effectiveness of representation, but this approach has not yet taken root.

A third indicator that has been commonly used is whether countries have ratified the ILO Conventions relating to freedom of association and collective bargaining. The assumption here is that ratification denotes a country's basic commitment to social dialogue and can serve as a basis for the ILO to persuade members to increase social dialogue or at least to avoid repressing social dialogue possibilities. These data are easily collected and are already in the ILO databases e.g. the reports of the Committee on Freedom of Association. Several studies have used these data to examine growth (Rama, 1995), export performance (Mah, 1997) and trade performance (Rodrik, 1996). Chau and Kanbur (2001) even find that standards are higher in countries which ratify Conventions than in countries that do not. The disadvantage of the measure is that not all countries have ratified the relevant Conventions (the United States for example), and even amongst those which have, there are many violations. Despite the problems, this indicator has tactical value, because such data make it possible for the ILO to use its powers of persuasion to convince countries to implement the Conventions in practice. For a detailed treatment of this measure, see Hepple (2003).

A fourth measure, less commonly used than the others but still relatively easy to collect, concerns the existence of national tripartite structures or institutions. The data are easy to collect using national legislation, but the existence of tripartite structures and institutions does not always guarantee that tripartite social dialogue actually takes place, nor does it tell us much about the quality of that dialogue.

Particular measures of institutions, processes and outcomes

These measures are highly variable. They reflect the approach of individual researchers, data are often not readily available, and the measures are usually based on interpretation and judgement by academic researchers.

The nature, processes, institutions, and outcomes of tripartism are the focus of this set of measures: for a detailed review see Kenworthy and Kittel (2002). One group of measures reflects the degree to which unions (or employer associations) are concentrated or centralized, which is arguably a precondition for successful tripartism. A second group reflects the process of tripartism, for example, the levels at which bargaining takes place, the degree of corporatism in national decision making, the degree of policy concertation, or the level of involvement by different actors in the wage setting process (see Annex I for examples of these measures). A third group of measures reflects employer or union activity, such as the degree of wage coordination, and the locus of authority in bargaining. In general, these three groups of measures focus on different aspects of the interaction between the tripartite, and in some cases, bipartite actors. A fourth group focuses on the outcomes of tripartite processes. The most common outcomes that have been studied are strikes and lockouts (this measure gives rise to several interpretation issues), wages (e.g. wage drift as a measure of tripartite bargaining or wage centralization), or the relationship between wage centralization (an outcome measure) and macro-economic performance. Many variants of these measures can be found in the literature on corporatism which has been very popular in the realm of political science.

Despite the variation in focus, these measures share some characteristics. First, they have the advantage of being integrated in the national institutional framework – thus, they are largely "accurate" even if they are not quantitative in nature. A related point is that several of these measures require interpretation and judgement by researchers with deep institutional knowledge of the country's industrial relations systems. Much of the industrial relations literature is case-study oriented, either national- or industry- or workplace-level case studies. These qualitative measures certainly tell us more about how tripartism actually works than the traditional quantitative measures, although data on wages tell us a lot too. On the other hand, a significant disadvantage is that these measures tend to relate primarily to the Western European countries, largely due to the prevalence tripartism has enjoyed in many countries in this region. For example the link between wage centralization (a tripartism measure) and macroeconomic performance can be demonstrated only in countries where there is serious and active tripartism. Although these measures have been used in comparative research, much of that research focuses on Europe. The measures do not transfer well to countries without strong tripartite arrangements or to those with decentralized bargaining regimes. However, this group of measures indicates that national experts must play a key role in depicting the practice of social dialogue.

Measures focusing on rights

A third set of measures focuses on the rights underpinning social dialogue. These measures go beyond ratification of ILO Conventions, as they indicate whether the rights to freedom of association and collective bargaining actually exist in member States. While the ILO has focused on this issue for decades, working quietly with each member State, these measures are slowly becoming more popular with recent debates about trade and labour standards and various monitoring efforts. At least one organization, Verité,[2] assigns points on a number of measures pertaining to the rights (laws) underpinning social dialogue. For example, do workers have the right to freely elect their own representatives? Are union activists adequately protected from discrimination? Are unions free from government control? Is there legal protection for the right to strike? As Compa (2002) notes "Threshold evaluations can examine laws with relative ease to determine whether the right legal framework is in place to afford freedom of association to workers. However, most countries' laws are not clear cut". He cites the example of the United States, where law forbids discrimination against workers for union activities, but goes on to exclude large swathes of the labour force from this protection. Thus, beyond a superficial level of analysis, the use of laws as indicators of social dialogue requires very careful analysis and expert knowledge of national labour law.

Another method of approaching the rights question lies in the examination of violations. The OECD follows such an approach, coding and assigning numerical values to countries regarding compliance with freedom of association. This is based on qualitative and descriptive data drawn from a multiplicity of sources, including the ICFTU annual survey, US State Department Section 6 reports and ILO committee reports (Committee of Experts on the Application of Conventions and Recommendations-CEARC) and Committee on Freedom of Association-COFA. These are discussed in greater detail in the fifth category below. The problem with this approach is that the numerical scores are only as good as the input data. These suffer from several problems, especially the fact that they are not comprehensive reviews of freedom of association in any given country. The OECD classifies countries into four categories, on a four-point "favourable to critical" scale.

Similarly, another approach has been taken by Kucera (2001), who codes and assigns numerical values to instances and seriousness of violations of freedom of association using seven different data sources (unionization rates, Freedom House indices, findings of violations in EPZs, and weighted and unweighted indices based on textual analysis of ICFTU's

---

[2] Established in 1995, Verité is an independent, non-profit social auditing and research organization (an NGO). Verité's mission is to ensure that people worldwide work under safe, fair and legal working conditions. Verité accomplishes its mission through monitoring independent factories, linking with local humanitarian and advocacy organizations to interview workers and report on workplace conditions. Where Verité auditors identify exploitation of workers or health and safety violations in the workplace, Verité develops concrete steps to correct them through a combination of training for management and workers, education programmes and remediation programmes. Since 1995, they have completed over 700 factory evaluations in 61 countries. Their management team is comprised of individuals based in five countries with backgrounds in organizations such as Oxfam, Save the Children and Amnesty International. Recently, Verité completed its report to CALPERS (California Public Employees Retirement System). The report ranked countries on 44 separate indicators connected with labour conditions. The website is www.verite.org

annual surveys, US state department Section 6 reports and CEARC and COFA reports. This research develops 37 detailed criteria on freedom of association, yet the data gaps for any country are considerable as Compa (2002) points out.

The focus on rights is clearly important because they are the foundation on which the concept of social dialogue stands. There are some major implications of using this set of measures however. First, the collection of such information requires a good knowledge of national labour law systems; there are differences across nations in terms of labour law, but also considerable variation within nations on how the law is established and administered, which means that a knowledge of the administrative rules surrounding these rights is critical. Second, judgement is required, especially in the interpretation of legal positions and opinions. Third, interpretation and judgement are important in examining violations and using violations as a basis to score countries. For example, not all violations of the law are reported or documented, the nature of the violations differs within and across systems, and violations may only take place within one or two sectors within a country, (thus it would be wrong to "tar" the entire country with a low score on rights because of these limited violations). Alternatively, it may be that a high incidence of complaints pertaining to violations indicates the vibrancy and robustness of the rights regime in that country. Hence, judgement is important in deciding whether the number of complaints is healthy or unhealthy. Fourth, the availability of data regarding labour law systems is not uniform – we know a lot about some countries' systems but less about others. Finally, many of the qualitative databases that underlie quantitative measures and scores are complaint-driven, so they do not constitute a comprehensive survey in each country.

Measures focusing on implementation

Our fourth category of measures reflects the way in which labour laws are actually implemented in different countries. This is similar to examining how social dialogue works, but the focus is on whether the rights are respected. Two groups of measures are involved. The first includes assessments by researchers or other experts on how things work – for example are there non-formal restrictions on the right to organize? Or is collective bargaining allowed without government interference? Do works councils or factory committees actually work? Some types of industrial relations outcomes may be useful here, such as the number of collective bargaining agreements, or strikes. The second group of measures relates to the institutional capacity of governments to enforce laws, and generally takes the form of recording the number of inspections, or the number of fines for violations of laws, or the adequacy of government inspection staff.

The disciplines of industrial relations and industrial sociology have a long tradition of examining practical implementation issues and outcomes, and there is a considerable body of published research. On the negative side, this research is diverse, since it focuses on different levels of IR institutions within countries; there is little uniformity in approach (except in regard to some outcomes); and there is variation in the countries which have been studied. Very little is known about labour institutions in at least a third of the ILO member States, partly because there is no academic tradition of studying these subjects.

Here too, national expertise and informed judgement is critical to assessing the way in which IR systems work in practice, and to evaluating the degree to which governments are capable of implementing labour law. There is also the question of dealing with different expert interpretations of cases and events, and of identifying national experts. A major criticism of Verité's approach has been a lack of expertise in national industrial relations systems.

Descriptive reports

These fall into two categories, comprehensive and occasional. Compa (2002) has examined these in great detail. The best examples of comprehensive reports are those published by the US State Department (Section 6 reports) that examine all labour rights, not just freedom of association; ICFTU's annual survey of violations of labour rights; and the ILO's CEARC and COFA reports. The State Department approach is to provide a yearly account of human rights in each country, based on a variety of sources, including document analysis, interviews with local experts and site visits by the labour attaché. Many of the questions require interpretation and judgement, and the responses are not easily quantifiable. ICFTU's report provides an overview of labour law and practice and then describes specific violations during the year reported; their primary sources of information are national labour movements. The third important group are the ILO's CEARC and COFA reports. These describe the situation in countries under scrutiny with respect to ILO Conventions Nos. 87 and 98. The COFA reports are complaint driven.

The advantage of these studies is that they are prepared at regular intervals (except COFA). The disadvantage is that in some cases they do not make an in-depth analysis of social dialogue, and where they are complaint driven, they are not necessarily comprehensive. This tends to skew country assessments towards those whose trade unions avail themselves of the COFA complaint procedure. But they do provide a "rich mosaic" of information (Compa, 2002) and should be part of any assessment of the right to social dialogue.

The second category, occasional descriptive reports, covers a large variety of documents that are not annual or comprehensive. These include government agency reports (USILAB, USTR Trade Policy Committee, OPIC, NAALC, Congressional Research Service), International Agency Reports (e.g. UNHCR, GRI, and World Bank occasional reports) union reports (e.g. AFL-CIO) and private agencies and NGOs (AFL-CIO, Freedom House, Human Rights Watch, Lawyers Committee on Human rights, International Labor Rights Fund, Amnesty International, Solidar, Asia Monitor Resource Center, Code of Conduct Reports, FLA).

The comprehensive and annual reports are more useful than the occasional reports since they provide consistent information regularly. They can be integrated in the present effort to develop indicators, and they are a useful source for national experts as well. The occasional reports also serve as a basis for further detailed and regular information-gathering efforts.

Summary

A wide variety of measures and indicators have been used to assess and demonstrate the social dialogue concept. There are quantitative and qualitative measures and a host of descriptive reports. In general, the measures exhibit tensions between quantitative approaches and subjective interpretations, breadth and depth of coverage of issues, complaint driven and comprehensive approaches, and static and dynamic indicators. The measures are also "skewed" geographically, towards countries where unions are strong and free, and have tripartite systems, or where the study of industrial relations is well developed. Descriptive reporting seems to dominate over comparative scoring schemes. All these measures have significant disadvantages, and many "quantitative indicators" such as union density, collective bargaining coverage and strikes are open to different interpretations. The next section examines the implications of these past approaches for the further development of indicators, and for data collection and use.

3. Implications for indicator development, data collection and use

The first principle is that any new effort must be connected with the old, to preserve some degree of continuity. Thus, despite their disadvantages, measures that have been used frequently in the past, such as union density, will continue to play a part, although the data may be used in new ways. This principle also means that greater weight will be accorded to traditional bipartite and tripartite institutions in the development of measures.

A second principle is that it is essential to measure the rights underpinning social dialogue. Because these rights are varied and numerous, we must select some over others. But this also implies that national or regional experts who are very familiar with the labour law systems must be involved in assessing these rights.

Third, it is clear that a focus on rights alone is necessary but not sufficient. We must measure how rights are implemented and how they are exercised in practice. Here too, local knowledge of the institutions and how they work in each country is essential to drawing conclusions.

Fourth, it is clear that subjective interpretation by national experts is key to assessing social dialogue. As the data in Annex I suggest, the work of experts has resulted in more in-depth reporting which is more useful in assessing how social dialogue works than the quantitative indicators of union density, bargaining coverage, or wage drift. Since industrial relations institutions, rules, and outcomes are socially embedded in their unique institutional contexts, progress on social dialogue must be evaluated by experts with a deep institutional knowledge of those countries. This principle, however, has one major implication. It is likely that arguments and differences of opinion will arise because of the subjective interpretations of national experts. There are two ways in which this can be minimized. First, it is advisable that all national experts follow a basic framework of assessment that is flexible and sensitive to cross-national institutional differences. The present paper will develop this framework and issue detailed guidelines for national experts. Second, it is important that assessments of social dialogue in each country be made public and available on the internet, so that dissenting voices and views can also be aired. In the long term, *transparency* is key to measuring progress on social dialogue.

Fifth, it is clear that there must be a dynamic focus when developing social dialogue indicators. We must move beyond static indicators to provide a sense of where social dialogue is headed – at the minimum our measures must indicate trends or the direction of progress.

Sixth, and consistent with the new interpretation of social dialogue as a mechanism to increase workers' voice, it is necessary to develop indicators of social dialogue in a non-union setting or in places where unions do not exist.

A seventh principle pertains to the quality of information and the cost of data gathering. We know that easily available data (such as union density) tell us very little about social dialogue in practice. We also know that detailed descriptive studies tell us the most. Many information-rich approaches use multiple methods, including case studies, complaints, interviews, analysis of documents and so on. It seems likely that a qualitative research approach may yield the most useful information. Surveys are less useful because they are not always sensitive to how institutions work and the extent to which rules are followed. It is also likely that a qualitative approach using national experts will cost less than country surveys.

Finally, the choice of indicators depends heavily on how the data are likely to be used. One type of usage (indeed, the majority of previous work) is to determine whether there is, in fact, violation of the freedom of association in member countries and the extent of violation. The CEARC and COFA reports of the ILO are good examples here. A second type of usage is embodied in the OECD approach, which is explicitly comparative and seeks to group countries according to the severity of violation. Similarly, organizations like Verité have focused on the development of comparative scoring and ranking systems, which are then used to drive investment decisions. A third type of usage has been to link measures of social dialogue to broader constructs such as economic development and trade performance, and some of these studies have been comparative in nature.

The key purpose of developing indicators of social dialogue is to help nations make progress on social dialogue and decent work. This is the ILO's interest as well. Thus the indicators should be used for longitudinal comparisons *within* nations, rather than cross-sectional comparisons *between* nations. The present paper therefore develops the concept of "national social dialogue data sheets" which make it possible to assess the nature of social dialogue at a glance, and to assess progress over time. The approach includes both scorable and non-scorable criteria to present a comprehensive picture of social dialogue, and therefore yields enough information to make comparisons on some issues. However, the primary focus is on measuring national progress.

4. Indicators for the national social dialogue data sheet

This section presents the indicators, provides a rationale for each one, and develops guidelines for reporting and assessment. The indicators are listed in Annex II.

A. Basic control information

The indicators in this group provide some basic information that is relevant for the operation of social dialogue. Such indicators have been widely used in the past; they link up with earlier approaches and facilitate longitudinal comparisons.

A1. Union density and changes in density

Rationale. This is a widely used measure that is available for most countries. It is not an indicator of social dialogue, although it has been used as such in past work. It is included as basic control data, although we do not make any interpretations from this measure.

Guidelines for national experts. It is necessary to report three aspects of union density data. First is the denominator used (some countries calculate density as part of the wage and salaried workforce (e.g. OECD countries), while others calculate it as a percentage of the non-agricultural workforce (United States). Second, it is also necessary to report the data source. Many countries use unions as the primary source for union membership data, while others use national surveys. Third, it is important to indicate the trend in union density – perhaps over the last five years, or at least to report the percentage change, so as to provide a dynamic picture.

A2. Whether countries have ratified ILO Conventions Nos. 87 and 98, and the number of violations of these Conventions during the last five years.

Rationale. Monitoring and reporting this information might induce more countries to ratify the Conventions. Although this does not guarantee social dialogue, ratifying countries can be persuaded to uphold these rights. It is also important to report trend data, since we are interested in progress.

Guidelines for national experts. It is necessary to use multiple sources of information here. National statistics are the obvious first stop, though not all countries keep figures on violations of these two Conventions. The second stop must include CEARC data and COFA data from the ILO, which can be made available to national experts. Third, other sources of data can be consulted. The key issue here is for the national experts to report the data, but also to give an opinion on whether they think this is a partial or comprehensive picture of violations. A comprehensive picture is collected from a source where most if not all violations are reported.

> *Example:* For the United States, the data sheet might look like this.
> – Ratified ILO Conventions Nos. 87 and 98: No
> – Violations of ILO Conventions 2000: 14 2001: 12 2002: 10 (These figures are not real.)
> – Violations information based on data that is: Comprehensive

A3. Labour force statistics

Rationale. To provide basic information about the labour force in absolute numbers and as a percentage of the population, as well as the size of the labour force in different sectors. The sector-wise distribution is important because some sectors tend to evidence more social dialogue than others (e.g. manufacturing over services).

Guidelines for national experts. Sector-wise employment data are easily available from national or international statistics for most countries. It is necessary to report employment in each sector rather than the contribution of each sector to GDP. However, it is also necessary to provide some measure of unionization or collective bargaining by sector, if possible.

A4. Who does the legislation on freedom of association and collective bargaining apply to? Which categories of people are excluded from this legislation? What percentage of the non-agricultural population has rights with regard to freedom of association and collective bargaining?

Rationale. This is critical information. It is a dynamic measure, since it allows us to see whether countries progressively expand the proportion of workers who have access to social dialogue. For example, in the Republic of Korea teachers have recently been given the right to form unions and bargain collectively.

Guidelines for national experts. Calculations must be based on the laws in each country, and on labour force statistics. In many countries this information is not easily available, so researchers will have to make the calculations themselves. Experts must make clear the denominator that is being used.

Example: In the United States, roughly 27 per cent of the civilian labour force does not have the right to bargain collectively. A smaller percentage does not have the right to freedom of association (this is largely because a number of public sector employees have the right of freedom of association but are not allowed to bargain collectively).

B. Rights underlying social dialogue

If the basis for freedom of association and collective bargaining is not strong, then social dialogue (either tripartite or bipartite) will not function well. A large number of indicators are relevant here.

B1. Freedom of association

The right of workers to form representative organizations of their own choosing is a primary determinant of social dialogue. This section focuses on how employer and union organizations are formed, whether they are free to operate without government supervision or interference, whether members of these organizations are protected against discrimination, and whether these rights can be taken away either temporarily or at government whim.

B1A. Union and employer association formation

Rationale. There is great variety in the laws and processes of union formation around the world. In some countries the process is simple and easy; in others it is long drawn out and difficult. This often has significant implications for the unions' ability to bargain collectively, as in the United States. In that country, 30 per cent of workers must indicate their preference for a union, in which case the NLRB conducts elections. Until the elections are over, both sides (union and employer advocates) try to persuade the workers to join or not to join. In addition, allegations of unfair labour practices must be investigated. It is possible for the employer to legally delay the process of union formation through tactical actions. In some countries, unions can only be formed if the government permits and the government has the absolute right to grant union registration or withhold it, as is the case in Malaysia.

There is generally less variation in the formation of employers' associations and the process is quite simple. Moreover, often there is no legislation limiting the formation of employer associations. Hence, we focus only on the formation of unions.

Guidelines for national experts. A categorization scheme is provided below to guide the judgement of national experts.

Category	Description
Category A: Simple process	Where the process of union formation is simple and direct; where there is no supervision by government bodies and no need to conduct elections; where there is no scope for employer opposition.
Category B: Lengthy process that is open to influence (de jure) by employers	Where the laws prescribe a lengthy and time-consuming process; where employers can influence the outcome of elections through campaigns or can influence the speed at which a union can form through tactical but legal actions.
Category C: Difficult process where employers (de facto) have great influence over union formation	Where employers can influence the outcome of a union election though legal and illegal actions; where these type of action are widely used (substantiated with figures); where the punishment for violations of the law is not a sufficient deterrent.
Category D: Process where prior government permission is required de jure	Where unions must seek government permission to form: where governments have a history of denying permission (figures needed here).

Example: The United States would fall into category C on this scale (since the union formation process is quite complex and can be challenged on various occasions by the employer) while Malaysia (where the Registrar of Trade Unions has near absolute power to accord or withhold registration) will fall into category D.

B1B. Independence of unions and employer associations

Rationale. Social dialogue depends heavily on unions and employer associations being independent of government control. There is variation here as well. In most countries unions at the local or national level are independent but in some countries they are heavily controlled by government, which limits their ability to voice the concerns of workers effectively. Assessing the degree of government control is not easy. Verité, for example, has created a four point scale in which a score of 3 means that multiple unions can organize without government interference, 2 indicates some interference, 1 means that unions are closely affiliated with the government and 0 means that they are not independent. The literature on corporatism is particularly relevant here since different models of corporatism tend to evidence different levels of government control over unions, as noted by Kenworthy and Kittel (2002). The literature on corporatism is used as a basis for developing categories here; a three point scale is recommended.

Guidelines for national experts. A categorization scheme is provided below.

Category A: Independent	Where it is clear from historical studies, case studies, and the national expert's own research, that unions are independent of government control, where the government or ruling party is not a significant source of union finances, and where the government or ruling party does not control the union's strategic goal articulation.
Category B: Unclear	Where previous studies, case studies, or the national expert's research shows that there is notional independence but that there is still some degree of government influence over national or local union decisions (examples should be provided). Or when one federation is controlled by the government while other federations are free of government control.
Category C: Not independent	Where it is clear that the unions in general are controlled by government, or that only one federation friendly to the government is permitted to exist.

Example: The United States would be classified in category A; Singapore would be in category B (there is much controversial research that links the People's Action Party and the Singapore National Trade Union Congress, making this arguable); the Republic of Korea before 1997 would be a good example of category C.

B1C. Protection from discrimination against union members or activists

Rationale. The key issue here is whether nations provide protection from employer or government retaliation against workers who join unions or who are union activists. Without such protection, social dialogue cannot move forward. Here too there is variation, although the extremes are easy to measure. There are many Western European nations with no explicit legal protection but with no violations because of the country's institutional history and structure. The long list of unfair labour practices outlined in US legislation might merit placement in category A: but the general ineffectiveness of the law as a deterrent to such behaviour and the continuing evidence of violations would give at best, a place in category B. Malaysia gives some protection against discrimination but a variety of other actions are de facto permissible under the law (e.g. the practice of closing a factory because of union activity and then reopening it with non-union employees – indirectly discriminating against union members) would merit, at best, a place in category C. Countries where no protection exists would be placed in category D.

Guidelines for national experts. The following categorization will help national experts to place countries.

Category A: Strong protection with full recourse or institutional conditions which do not permit such violations.	Where a broad set of anti-union activities are illegal; where the law provides procedural recourse that is generally considered effective (previous research/case studies) or where the number of violations has steadily declined in the past five years (NE to provide data), or where such violations are non-existent due to wider institutional forces in the country.
Category B: Partial protection with full recourse	Where a much narrower set of practices are illegal; where there is a system of resolution provided by law that is generally considered effective (research/case studies), and where the data show a declining trend.
Category C: Partial protection with partial and ineffective recourse	Where the law does not clearly prohibit anti-union practices; or where there is no effective system to resolve alleged violations, and where the data show persistent violations (report data).
Category D: No protection	

B2. Bipartite free collective bargaining

Union formation is necessary for social dialogue but it is not sufficient. For social dialogue to occur the parties, once formed, must be able to bargain freely. Category B2 indices concern the ability to bargain. Note that in countries which lack an environment congenial to the development of unions and collective bargaining, alternative representative structures might accomplish the same objectives. We deal with these later.

B2A. Union recognition and obligation to bargain

Rationale. Once unions have formed, bargaining cannot necessarily start automatically. In some countries there is a distinction between union formation and recognition of the union as the bargaining agent, an intermediary step before the employer is obliged to bargain. In other countries recognition as the bargaining agent takes place at the formation stage. Second, even after formation and recognition, there is variation in the duties imposed on the employer. Some countries impose an obligation to bargain. Others impose the obligation, but the process is riddled with loopholes which can delay the start of bargaining. Several countries do not impose an obligation to bargain on the employer. Social dialogue on a bilateral basis cannot take place if there is no obligation to bargain or if bargaining can be delayed. For instance, in the United States, research shows that in roughly 25 per cent of the cases where unions win the representation election, there are delays in bargaining.

Guidelines for national experts. The following schema may be used by national experts in assessing their countries on this dimension.

Category A: Clear rules on recognition and obligation to bargain	Where there are clear rules regarding union recognition, and where the law imposes a clear duty on the employer to bargain; where data show no violation of the obligation to bargain; where data show no delays in union recognition.
Category B: Problems in recognition or problems with the obligation to bargain	Where the rules regarding bargaining and recognition are clear but where practice shows delays in one or both.
Category C: No recognition or no obligation to bargain	Where there are no rules regarding recognition (in cases where recognition is required) with consequent delays in the start of bargaining, and/or where there is no obligation on the part of the employer to bargain.

B2B. Scope and subject matter of bargaining

Rationale. The obligation to bargain does not in itself guarantee that successful social dialogue will take place. Countries differ on what they will allow the parties to bargain about. At one end of the continuum are countries (e.g. Sweden) in which co-determination legislation mandates that any subject of interest to either union or management is subject to bargaining. In the middle of the continuum are countries that make a distinction with regard to bargaining subjects. The United States, for example, uses the "mandatory" versus "permissive" distinction. Mandatory subjects such as hours, wages, and working conditions are normal subjects of bargaining, while permissive subjects such as management rights or union security issues will be bargained only if both parties agree that they are negotiable. This approach also gives rise to continual debates on what is a mandatory subject and what is permissive. At the other end of the continuum are countries which prohibit bargaining on certain issues. Singapore and Malaysia do not permit bargaining on transfers, promotions, job assignments, retrenchment and lay-offs. Taiwan (China), does not permit bargaining on the introduction of new technology. Thus, the scope of bargaining directly affects the extent of social dialogue.

Guidelines for national experts. The following table is based on the variations identified in the literature.

Category A: Broad scope	Where any item of interest to either party is bargainable.
Category B: Intermediate scope	Where the rules suggest that some subjects may be bargained only if both parties agree that they are negotiable.
Category C: Narrow or restricted scope	Where the subjects of bargaining are restricted by legislation.

B2C. Right to strike, restrictions on the right to strike, and weakening of the right

Rationale. Free collective bargaining requires the right to lockout (for employers) or strike (by unions). Many countries have procedures that restrict the right to strike in national emergencies, but we will not consider that here. Similarly, strikes are often banned in essential services in most nations, and that is also excluded from the present discussion. We will simply note that some countries choose to take such a broad view of "essential" that it could be a significant threat to the right to strike.

At one end of the continuum are countries that freely permit the right to strike for non-essential service workers, or at least the private sector. The Western European countries are good examples. Then there are countries that permit workers to strike if they are directly involved in an industrial dispute, but which do not permit sympathy strikes. The United States and the United Kingdom are good examples here. Then there are countries that permit the right to strike, but significantly weaken the right in certain ways. The United States is a good example here since it allows employers to permanently replace striking workers where the dispute does not involve unfair labour practices – wage disputes fall into this group. Other countries permit the right to strike, but then de facto take away that right through a plethora of administrative rules and restrictions. In India and Singapore, for example, dispute resolution rules require 14 days notice of strike. If either party calls for mediation, then the strike must be withheld and the parties must enter the mediation process. If mediation is not successful, the government may refer the dispute to binding arbitration, or to an industrial court or tribunal (the two countries differ on this approach). Theoretically then, strikes will not take place if this procedure is followed. Singapore has not reported a strike in the last 12 years, while India reports strikes on a daily basis (which shows that the procedure does not work well in India). Finally, some countries, such as China, still do not permit the right to strike. Apart from the legal provisions in force, it is necessary to take account of subtle variations in rules that cannot be captured by a simple scoring mechanism, thus requiring national experts to exercise their judgement. One rule that is prone to much variation is the definition of legal and illegal strikes under national law.

Guidelines for national experts. The following guidelines do not place great emphasis on data regarding strikes, since the number of strikes and lockouts is affected by issues other than rules, such as the economic cycle and shifts in bargaining power. We also know that the number of strikes has decreased steadily in most countries with the decline in trade union membership.

Category A: Unfettered right to strike	Where workers may strike even if they are not directly linked to the dispute (e.g. sympathy strikes).
Category B: Normal right to strike	When workers directly connected with the dispute are free to strike.
Category C: Weakening of the right to strike	Where industrial relations rules permit the replacement of striking workers, thus weakening the ability of labour to exercise the right to strike.
Category D: Circumvention of the right to strike	Where the right is curtailed by provisions that require the strike to be withheld, or the use of compulsory arbitration or adjudication for private sector workers. Each country is likely to have different rules that affect the right to strike.
Category E: No right to strike	When there is a ban on strikes.

B2D. Parallel workplace representation

Rationale. Social dialogue is improved if employees have avenues (besides unions) for participation at work. In the absence of unions, these avenues are particularly important. The best known example of parallel representation is the works council, which is common in most Western European countries. There is great variation in the scope and function of works councils or similar institutions across countries, however. In addition, there is a debate on whether works councils in fact substitute for unions, and this argument has been cited by many unions to oppose government plans to introduce works councils (the United States). On the other hand, European experience shows that unions can work well with works councils, often exercising significant control over them. It should be noted that works councils evolved long after unions were formed in most European nations. It is possible that they represent an evolution in traditional industrial relations concomitant with "new forms of work organization" which are accompanied by high flexible wages, wages tied to skill acquisition, high participation, and flexible deployment or "functional flexibility".

Guidelines for national experts.

Category A	Countries where the law prescribes the works council or committee and mandates regular meetings covering a wide range of issues.
Category B	Countries where the law prescribes some form of workplace level committee, even if the scope is restricted. Safety and health committees are good examples.
Category C	Countries with no provision for workplace representation.

B3. Tripartism

This section focuses on a series of rights that underpin tripartism.

B3A. Right to tripartite processes

Rationale. Tripartism depends heavily on whether the law provides for it. Many countries explicitly provide for tripartism in their national legislation. It is also possible that there is no legal provision for tripartite relationships, but that they are practised (hence the differentiation between rights and practice). It is also possible that countries provide for tripartism in a limited form, i.e. for specific subjects. In addition, the enactment of legislation regarding tripartism is often the result of demands by strong unions. It is clear, however, that tripartism flourishes when it is backed by legislation, whatever the origin of the right to tripartite processes.

Guidelines for national experts. Three categories are relevant here.

Category A	Where national legislation explicitly requires some form of tripartite consultation.
Category B	Where the law does not specify any requirement or form of tripartite practice and does not prohibit it in any form.
Category C	Where tripartite processes are explicitly prohibited.

B3B. Limitations on tripartite rights: Affiliation

Rationale. Even if countries explicitly require or do not prohibit tripartism, there are several ways in which the ability of actors to effectively engage in tripartite activity is reduced or enhanced. One issue is whether unions or employer associations have the right to affiliate to federations or industry level bodies. There are two ways in which the right to free affiliation is limited. The first is a ban on affiliation. As an example, Malaysia permits enterprise level unions in its electronics industry but does not permit them to affiliate with industry level unions. In other cases, unions are only allowed to affiliate with a specific federation, which is often sponsored by the government, without the freedom to affiliate with alternative or competing federations. This is also a limitation of tripartite rights.

Guidelines for national experts. There are two categories here. Category A relates to countries which do not prohibit affiliation to higher level organizations or federations. Category B countries explicitly prohibit such affiliation or require affiliation to a preferred federation.

B3C. Limitations on tripartite rights: Politics

Rationale. Tripartite social dialogue is generally understood to mean that employer organizations and unions participate broadly in economic and political discourse. Yet many countries restrict the ability of unions and employer organizations to do so. One method is to limit their ability to affiliate with political parties. The second is to expressly forbid apex trade union or employer organizations from participating in politics. Malaysia is a good example of this, as the apex federations are registered as societies rather than unions.

Guidelines for national experts. There are three categories here.

Category A	Countries where there are no restrictions on union or employer abilities to participate in politics or affiliate with higher level organizations or federations.
Category B	Countries where there are restrictions on the ability of unions and employer organizations to affiliate with higher level bodies.
Category C	Countries where unions and employers are prohibited from political activities and debate.

C. Social dialogue in practice

This section focuses on indicators of both process and outcome, so that we can assess how social dialogue is working.

C1. Bipartite process and outcome

C1A. Collective bargaining coverage

Rationale. A measure of coverage is essential since it indicates how many employees are covered by collective bargaining agreements. The number of union members or union density may not be closely related to collective bargaining coverage for a variety of reasons. In many developing countries (e.g. Philippines), the number of union members (according to union records) is much higher than the number of employees covered by collective bargaining agreements. This is due to overstatement of union members on the one hand, and the presence of unions of unemployed persons, on the other. In France, for example, collective bargaining coverage is very high (almost 80 per cent), although union density figures are very low. This is because agreements reached by some unions and employers are extended to the rest of the industry. A second problem with collective bargaining coverage is that while some countries have the data, others do not.

Guidelines for national experts. For this indicator to be useful, the national expert should report the data over time (e.g. for the last five years), identify how the data were collected, and explain any variance between this measure and union density.

C1B. Number of collective agreements

Rationale. The number of collective bargaining agreements tells us whether bipartite social dialogue is increasing or decreasing. It is a direct measure of the growth of collective bargaining. Although the number of agreements might be related to coverage, note that coverage is partly due to other institutional forces, as in France. It is also possible that coverage may be high even with a low number of agreements, if the size of the workforce covered by each agreement is large. Hence, both measures are necessary. Note that the number of agreements in any given year will vary with the length of the agreements, which typically ranges between one and five years.

Guidelines for national experts. Report the number of collective bargaining agreements for each of the last five years, at least.

C1C. Parallel workplace arrangements

Rationale. Since we have a measure of rights regarding parallel workplace arrangements it is also necessary to see how those rights translate into practice. The international variation here is great, as is the availability of good data. Some countries (e.g. Japan) report the number of joint labour/management councils in firms, while others do not. In most Western European countries works councils are mandatory, yet there is no systematic information on what they do in practice. These institutions also differ substantially in terms of scope. Works councils in Europe are typically involved in all aspects of the employment relationship except for wages. There is some evidence in Germany for example, that over time the works councils have increased the scope of their decision making activities. In contrast there are many countries where the scope is limited. In the Philippines, for example, labour/management councils typically discuss only safety health, and welfare issues. Thus, the national experts must draw on previous research and data to make an assessment.

Guidelines for national experts.

Category A	Where parallel workplace arrangements generally exist in most firms, and where these institutions take substantial decisions regarding day-to-day workplace issues i.e. where the scope is broad. Where possible, data on distribution should be provided.
Category B	Where only a minority of firms have parallel representation arrangements and where they take substantial decisions, i.e. where the scope is broad. Where possible, data on the distribution of such institutions should be provided.
Category C	Where parallel representation institutions commonly exist, but have limited scope (e.g. safety and health only, or welfare only or some other combination that suggests limited scope).
Category D	Where parallel representation with limited scope exists but only in a minority of firms.
Category E	Where parallel representation institutions do not exist, or they exist but are not routinely used.

C1D. Number of strikes and lockouts

Rationale. This is one measure of healthy social dialogue, as the right to strike and lockout is a key element in practice. The actual number of strikes and lockouts is open to different interpretations. For example, countries that recognize the right to strike but report no strikes either have very good labour-management relations or place administrative restrictions on the right to strike. A dramatic increase in the number of lockouts can suggest a change in relative bargaining power between employers and unions. Strikes may occur for a number of reasons including political motivations.

Guidelines for national experts. Report the number of strikes and lockouts over time.

C1E. Data on grievances or industrial disputes

Rationale. This is yet another (and more important) measure of the health of bipartite labour relations. Unions may not strike because of weak bargaining power, and employers may not lockout for the same reason. However, disputes between labour and management are best resolved through means other than the strike. For social dialogue to work well, it is essential that employees and employers use these alternative means to settle their differences. In addition, in countries where the right to strike is administratively restricted (see Hebdon and Stern, 2003) the number of disputes and grievances may be high, as employees seek alternative ways to settle their disputes.

There is great variation in the availability of data. Most countries report the number of disputes or grievances that go to arbitration or other third-party resolution mechanisms. Some countries also report disputes by cause, which provides even more information regarding the health of social dialogue, since it tells us which aspects of freedom of association and collective bargaining are being violated.

Guidelines for national experts. Report trend data on the number of disputes and if possible the number of disputes by cause for the last five years.

C2. Tripartite process and outcome

C2A. Tripartite processes

Rationale. Even within Western Europe, where tripartism is most developed, there is wide variation in the way it works in practice. The literature on corporatism (which is heavily focused on Europe) is a good basis for developing and refining this measure, although the present paper relies on research in developing nations to create categories that take account of the variation across countries. This measure is also based on the judgement of the national expert, but backed up by research. (Annex I lists the large number of measures used in previous research that focus on the outcomes of tripartism).

Guidelines for national experts.

Category A	Where there is evidence of regular meetings and cooperation between the social partners, and there is clear and documented evidence of participation in key macroeconomic decisions. Data on the regularity of meetings is necessary but not sufficient here. It is important that the national expert provide concrete examples of national decisions. This could involve wages too.
Category B	Where there is no regular interaction between the social partners, but they come together when occasion demands; decisions regarding national economic and social issues emerge from tripartite discussion.
Category C	Where there are occasional meetings between the social partners, primarily for information and consultation; the social partners make recommendations, which may or may not be accepted by the government.
Category D	Where it is clear that social partners meet but not to discuss substantial issues (pseudo-tripartism).
Category E	No participation in any issue at the national level.

C2B. Tripartite outcomes: Wages

Rationale. It is useful to have an objective measure of outcomes as well as the subjective measure based on the judgement of the national expert. The simplest objective measure is wage drift. However, since this is only applicable where wages are the subject of centralized bargaining, this measure cannot be used in all countries.

Guidelines for national experts.

Category A	Report data on wage drift for countries in which bargaining is highly centralized at tripartite or industry level.
Category B	Does not apply: do not report data in countries where bargaining is primarily decentralized.

C2C. Tripartite outcomes: Income inequality

Rationale. An important indicator of the success of tripartism in industrial relations is the extent of income inequality. While it is true that inequality is caused by a number of factors (such as skill differentiation), there is also very strong evidence that inequality increases when bargaining systems become decentralized (see Kuruvilla et al., 2002). Thus, high inequality is likely to be associated with a decrease in tripartite activity or no tripartite activity at all.

Guidelines for national experts. The World Bank reports income inequality data for most countries. It is necessary to report the gini-coefficient over time, but also to report the source of the data, as multiple sources exist for several countries.

D. Alternative avenues for social dialogue: Codes of conduct, certification and reporting systems

D1. Descriptive measures of industry codes

Rationale. Alternative approaches are particularly relevant for third world countries with fairly limited labour movements, and with national legislation which has not been effective in providing opportunities for social dialogue. Some corporate codes of conduct have developed in response to pressure from northern unions and NGOs precisely because legislation in some countries was not sufficiently protective of workers' rights.

These emerging approaches require attention on the part of the national expert for two main reasons. First, they are often sector-specific or industry-specific and it is necessary to estimate how many workers are covered by these arrangements. Second, and most important, it is necessary to know if local workers are involved in drawing up the codes of conduct that apply to them. Research shows that this is generally not the case, but we do know that international unions are sometimes involved in designing multilateral codes of conduct or industry-specific codes. The different mechanisms (codes, certification schemes, reporting arrangements), the variations in application (countries, industries, sectors), and the variations in effectiveness do not permit the creation of uniform or objective assessment criteria. The approach is therefore to leave this as a descriptive measure. National experts should consider various issues (see below) when they report and assess these developments. Since these alternatives are just emerging, it is possible that future research on effectiveness will make it possible to develop classifications and scorable criteria.

Guidelines for national experts. National experts should report on each of the following issues.

(a) *Industry codes of conduct.* Attention should be paid to the scope of the code (broad or narrow), the number of employees in the industry who are effectively covered by the code, and whether there are any research studies on the code's effectiveness in improving workers' participation in decision making.

(b) *Company codes.* The national expert should determine whether a majority of companies in a particular industry (e.g. sports shoes or garments) are covered by corporate codes of conduct, whether monitoring is conducted by independent monitors; the number of workers in the industry who are covered by the codes should be noted. National experts should also report on the scope of the codes in terms of furthering social dialogue.

(c) *Certification and reporting systems.* National experts should report on the number of companies in the relevant industry that are part of general certification and reporting schemes, and whether these are monitored by independent monitors. They should cite case study evidence where available.

In general, the national experts should focus their assessments on the involvement of local workers in developing alternative practices, and the extent to which social dialogue opportunities for local workers have increased as a result of these practices.

E. Implementation and government capacity

National law has to be enforced in ways that make the practice of social dialogue possible. There are two main approaches to enforcement. The first is to impose high penalties for non-compliance. The second is to operate an inspection regime that is reliable and forces employers and unions to obey the law.

E1. Penalties for violating social dialogue laws

Rationale. The enactment of laws pertaining to social dialogue is not sufficient to ensure that social dialogue takes place. It is possible for actors to break the law or ignore it on a routine basis. For example US employers continually violate the law that prohibits firing union organizers. Research suggests that they do this because the penalties for violation are minor compared to the savings made by keeping a union from forming in their enterprise.

Guidelines for national experts. This subject requires the national experts to exercise their own judgement, but the following categories are proposed as a guide.

Category A	Where in the opinion of the national expert, the penalties for violation are not a sufficient deterrent. National expert to provide trend data for past five years on violations.
Category B	Where in the opinion of the national expert the penalties for violation are a sufficient deterrent. National expert to provide trend data for the last five years.

E2. Government administrative capacity

Rationale. For inspections to work, governments must have an administrative system to carry them out, a sampling procedure that is relevant to the needs of the country, an adequate budget and qualified personnel. These elements are all necessary if the inspections are to be an effective means of law enforcement.

Guidelines for national experts. National experts must exercise their own judgement, although that judgment should be based on the following issues:

(a) adequacy of personnel and budgets compared to the number of workplaces;

(b) sampling schemes: the frequency and adequacy of inspections;

(c) coverage of establishments;

(d) data on violations.

Many countries provide sampling schemes and annual data on the number of establishments inspected, so the necessary information is available. The national experts can use two primary categories:

Category A	Where the national expert feels, based on the above four sets of data, that governments have the institutional capacity to monitor labour laws in their country.
Category B	Where the national expert feels that the institutional capacity is lacking.

F. Rights and practice in the informal sector

It is essential to develop social dialogue indicators for the informal sector, given the growing size and centrality of this sector in the world. However, the diversity of occupational categories, and a lack of "descriptors" of the sector make it very difficult to decide what information is relevant to the creation of indicators. Thus, our approach focuses on basic general information, although some research would make it possible to create more detailed measures.

F1. Freedom of association

Rationale. The right to form associations and/or unions is a precondition to social dialogue. There are several instances where unemployed workers have formed unions (e.g. Philippines), or where informal sector workers have formed associations (although not always for collective bargaining purposes). The informal sector also includes a sizeable number of agricultural workers, and there are organizations of peasants in some countries. Broadly, the alternatives range from countries in which all workers (including informal sector workers) have the right to form associations or unions, countries in which the law is silent on the issue (associations and unions may or may not exist in practice), and countries where freedom of association is specifically prohibited or excluded for informal sector workers.

Guideline for national experts. The national expert simply reports whether the country recognizes the right or not. Thus

Category A	Countries which expressly allow freedom of association for the informal sector.
Category B	Countries where the law is silent on the issue and the right exists in practice.
Category C	Countries where the right is de jure or de facto prohibited.

F2. Collective bargaining and individual disputes

Rationale. While bargaining does take place either formally or infor mally in many parts of the informal sector, it is not clear that the right to bargain is uniformly available to informal sector workers in all countries. And in many cases, particularly in small establishments that are outside the scope of legislation regarding collective bargaining, workers can exercise their social dialogue rights individually through regular or specially created dispute resolution channels, by raising individual disputes. It is also desirable to know which types of informal sector workers have these rights. Thus, the guidelines for national experts are based on the variation in these approaches, but also stress the need to provide information on the types of workers in the informal sector who have or do not have these rights.

Guidelines for national experts.

Category A	Where collective bargaining is protected and encouraged in the informal sector generally.
Category B	Where collective bargaining is permitted only for some occupations within the informal sector, or for some types of informal establishments (national experts to state which occupations/establishments).
Category C	Where all informal sector workers may raise individual disputes even though collective negotiations are not applicable.
Category D	Where only some occupations or employees in certain types of establishment may raise individual disputes even though collective negotiations are not applicable. National expert to provide detail on the occupations and types of establishment.
Category E	Where the rights are granted in categories A-D, but only in respect of certain subjects (e.g. retrenchment).
Category F	Where no collective or individual rights are granted to the informal sector.

F3. Unionization

Rationale. It is important to examine the practice of freedom of association in the informal sector. There are two problems here; the variation across occupations and the lack of data. For example, in India construction workers are in the informal sector. However, construction workers in many states are heavily unionized. It is unrealistic to hope for estimates of union density in each occupation in the informal sector. What the national expert can do, however, is to list the occupations which are unionized and perhaps estimate (however roughly) the density of unionization in the informal sector.

Guidelines for national experts. Report on the informal sector occupations that are unionized, and estimate union density using these figures.

F4. Other informal sector organizations

Rationale. There are numerous informal sector organizations that provide some degree of voice for workers on a range of issues. In the Indian state of Kerala, for example, organizations of contract workers in the beedi industry have associations which manage social security funds. Cooperatives and NGOs are also active in the informal sector. It is not possible to devise guidelines for national experts with regard to this point. Instead the national data sheets should allow space for experts to report on unusual practices to enable some cross-national learning about informal sector work.

5. Implications and costs of this methodology

To summarize, the methodology adopted in this paper focuses on the creation of national social dialogue data sheets for each country. The guidelines for national experts mitigate the problems with subjective interpretation, since they provide a basis on which judgements can be made. The national experts are expected to provide data to support their judgement in many situations. The methodology involves a degree of transparency in that the NSDDS will be made available on the web so that interested parties can discuss the results and argue over the conclusions reached, which also helps to limit the degree of subjectivity. This transparency is important in itself, since it will promote discussion and raise awareness of social dialogue issues. However, it is impossible to completely eliminate subjective judgements from this process.

The NSDDS approach has several implications.

Construct validity. This approach identifies all the relevant issues (rights, practices, outcomes) connected with the operation of social dialogue. Thus, it certainly points to the most appropriate concepts and the most relevant measures for evaluating progress on social dialogue as defined currently by the ILO.

Reliability. There are several ways in which this methodology promotes reliability in data collection. First, it forces national experts to consider various issues as they make their judgements. Second, the guidelines are clear enough to enable any national expert to collect the data. Third, the national experts often have to report data to back their assessments. Fourth, there is a high degree of internal consistency. Yet, reliability is not perfect. There is no guarantee that two national experts will agree on how collective bargaining institutions actually work in practice. It is true that reliability would be better if we had measures that were more "objective", but this would reduce construct validity. Because social dialogue is a complex phenomenon some degree of qualitative judgement and interpretation is necessary for a realistic and meaningful assessment.

Relationship to past approaches. The indicators developed for the NSDDS are based on comparative research and earlier approaches to measuring freedom of association and collective bargaining. However, there is an important departure. A large number of measures have been used in previous research on tripartism as it operates in Europe, but tripartism is not well developed in the rest of the world (75 per cent of global population), and the NSDDS should not be overly biased towards European models. The indicators are designed to help countries make progress on social dialogue, and it is the rest of the world rather than Western Europe that needs to make the most progress.

Comprehensiveness. Although these indicators describe social dialogue in the formal sector very well, more work is needed on alternative approaches such as codes of conduct, certification and the informal sector. Codes of conduct and certification schemes are relatively new phenomena, and information is not yet available on the variation in how these approaches work. Some basic sets of information on these issues have therefore been developed for the NSDDS, with the expectation that more assessable indicators can be devised in future.

Comparative ranking. The essence of this approach is to yield national data sheets that provide a composite picture of the state of social dialogue. There is space for categorization, actual trend data, examples, judgements and so forth. It is possible to reorder the categories so that they can be scored (or ranked). However, not all the indicators are amenable to scoring. Thus, it is not possible to arrive at country rankings if all the indicators are used. If ranking is the goal, then a smaller subset of indicators could be used, but that would provide a less comprehensive picture of social dialogue. Nevertheless, comparing a national social dialogue data sheet over two points in time will allow policy makers to judge whether a particular country has made, or is making, progress on social dialogue.

Costs and frequency of data collection. An important issue in collecting data is the cost involved. The approach advocated by this paper of using qualitative data prepared by national experts not only captures the processes of social dialogue, but is cost efficient. Assuming that one national expert per country is engaged, and that data are collected and reported for 100 countries, the NSDDS would cost about US$500,000; i.e. much less than the same number of national surveys. This means that such data can be collected more frequently. Given the interest in monitoring progress, one suggestion is to have national experts prepare NSSDS for each country once in 4 or 5 years. Another way to reduce the cost would be to engage regional experts who would cover several countries, or to use ILO country experts (see below).

Nature and availability of national experts. The above figures assume that there are national experts in each country. That is not necessarily a valid assumption, as several countries do not have an academic discipline of industrial relations (hence no national experts). However, there are two other sources of national expertise. One is within the ILO. The ILO regional offices have staff who are experts on social dialogue in certain groups of countries and who are perfectly capable of collecting data according to the template provided in this paper. The second source of expertise is research on comparative industrial relations; there are scholars who focus on these issues in a set of countries or a region. Thus, it may not be necessary to identify a national expert in every country, as long as regional experts are available. A combination of ILO experts and comparative industrial relations scholars would be appropriate.

References

Boreham, P.; Comston, H.: "Labour movement organization and political intervention: The politics of unemployment in the OECD countries, 1974-1986", in *European Journal of Political Research*, 1992, Vol. 22, pp. 143-170.

Brown, D.: *International trade and core labor standards*, OECD Labor Market and Social Policy Papers, No. 43 (Paris, OECD, 2000).

Calmfors, L.; Driffill, J.: "Bargaining structure, corporatism, and macroeconomic performance", in *Economic Policy*, 1998, Vol. 6, pp. 14-61.

Cameron, D.R.: "Social democracy, corporatism, labor quiescence, and the representation of economic interest in advanced capitalist society", in Oglethorpe, J.H. (ed.): *Order and conflict in contemporary capitalism* (Oxford, Clarendon, 1984).

Chau, N.; Kanbur, R.: "The adoption of international labor standards conventions: Who, when, why?", in Collins, S.; Rodrik, D. (eds.): *Brookings trade forum* (Washington, D.C., Brookings Institution, 2001), pp. 1131-1156.

Compa, L.: *Assessing assessments: A survey of efforts to measure countries' compliance with freedom of association standards*, prepared for the Project on International Labor Standards (Washington, D.C., National Academy of Sciences, 2002).

Compston, H.: "Union participation in economic policy-making in France, Italy, Germany and Britain, 1970-1993, in *West European Politics*, 1995a Vol. 18, pp. 314-319.

—: "Union participation in economic policy-making in Scandinavia, 1970-1993", in *West European Politics*, 1995b, Vol. 18, pp. 98-115.

—: "Union power, policy-making and unemployment in Western Europe, 1972-1993", in *Comparative Political Studies*, 1997, Vol. 30, pp. 732-751.

Crouch, C.: "Conditions for trade union wage restraint", in Lindberg, L.; Maier, C.S.: *The politics of inflation and economic stagnation* (Washington, D.C., Brookings Institution, 1985).

Ghai, D.: *Decent work, concepts, models, indicators* (Geneva, ILO, IILS, 2002).

Golden, M.: "The dynamics of trade unionism and national economic performance", in *American Political Science Review*, 1993, Vol. 87, pp. 439-454.

— et al.: *Union centralization among advanced industrial societies: An empirical study*, version dated 11 Feb. 1998, data set available at www.shelley.polisci.ucla.edu/data.

Hall P.; Franzese, R.J: "Mixed signals: Central bank independence, coordinated wage bargaining, and European monetary union", in *International Organization*, 1998, Vol. 52, pp. 501-535.

Hebdon, R.; Stern, R.: "Do public-sector strike bans really prevent conflict?", in *Industrial Relations*, 2003, Vol. 42, No. 3, p. 493.

Hepple, R.: *Rights at work* (Geneva, ILO, 2003).

Hibbs, D.A.; Locking, H.: "Wage compression, wage drift, and wage inflation in Sweden", in *Labour Economics*, 1996, Vol. 3, 109-141.

Hicks, A.; Kenworthy, L.: "Cooperation and political economic performance in affluent democratic capitalism", in *American Journal of Sociology*, 1998, Vol. 103, pp. 1631-1672.

ILO: *Freedom of association and collective bargaining* (Geneva, ILO, 1994).

—: *Conclusions concerning tripartite consultation at the national level on economic and social policy* (Geneva, ILC, 1996).

—: World labour report 1997-1998 (Geneva, ILO, 1998).

—: Declaration on fundamental principles and rights at work (Geneva, ILO, 1998b).

—: Decent work: Report of the Director-General (Geneva, ILO, 1999).

Iversen, T.: *Contested economic institutions: The politics of macroeconomics and wage bargaining in advanced democracies* (Cambridge, Cambridge University Press, 1999).

Jose, A.V.: *The ILO Declaration on Fundamental Principles and Rights at Work: Role of social partners in South Asia* (Geneva, ILO, IILS, 2002).

Kenworthy, L.: *In search of national economic success: Balancing competition and cooperation* (Thousand Oaks, California, Sage, 1995).

—: "Unions, wages, and the common interest", in *Comparative Political Studies*, 1996, Vol. 28, pp. 491-524.

—: *Quantitative indicators of corporatism*, Discussion Paper 00-4 (Cologne, Germany, Max Planck Institute for the Study of Societies, 2000).

—: *Wage-setting coordination scores*, version dated 17 June 2001a, data set available at http://www.emory.edu/SOC/lkenworthy.

—: "Wage-setting measures: A survey and assessment", in *World Politics*, 2001b, Vol. 54, pp. 57-98.

—: "Corporatism and unemployment in the 1980s and 1990s", in *American Sociological Review*, forthcoming.

—; Kittel, B.: *Indicators of social dialogue: Concepts and measurement*, Report delivered to the ILO, 7 Feb. 2002.

Kittel, B.: "Trade union bargaining horizons in comparative perspective: The effects of encompassing organization, unemployment, and monetary regime on wage push-fulness", in *European Journal of Industrial Relations*, 2000, Vol. 6, pp. 181-202.

Kucera, D.: "Decent work and rights at work: New measures of freedom of association and collective bargaining" in Blanpain, R.; Engels, C. (eds.): *The ILO and the social challenge of the 21ˢᵗ century* (Kluwer Law International, 2001) pp. 125-135.

Kuruvilla, S. et al.: "Union growth, decline and revitalization in Asia", in *British Journal of Industrial Relations*, 2002, Vol. 40, No. 3, pp. 431-463.

Lange, P. et al.: "The end of corporatism? Wage setting in the Nordic and Germanic countries", in Jacoby, S. (ed.): *The workers of nations* (New York, Oxford University Press, 1995).

Layard, R. et al.: *Unemployment: Macroeconomic performance and the labour market* (Oxford, Oxford University Press, 1991).

Mah, J.S.: "Core labor standards and export performance in developing countries", in *World Economy*, 1997, Vol. 20, p. 774.

Rama, M.: "Do labor market policies and institutions matter? The adjustment experience of Latin America and the Caribbean", in *Labor*, 1995,

Rodrik, D.: "Labor standards in international trade: Do they matter and what do we do about them?", in Lawrence, R. et al. (eds.): *Emerging agenda for global trade: High stakes for developing countries* (Washington, D.C., Johns Hopkins University Press, 1996).

Schmitter, P.: "Interest intermediation and regime governability in comtemporary Western Europe and North America", in Berger, S. (ed.): *Organizing interests in Western Europe* (Cambridge, Cambridge University Press, 1981).

Soskice, D.: "Wage determination: The changing role of institutions in advanced industrialized countries", in *Oxford Review of Economic Policy*, 1990, Vol. 6, No. 4, pp. 36-61.

Traxler, F.: "Farewell to labour market associations? Organized versus disorganized decentralization as a map for industrial relations", in Crouch, C.; Traxler, F. (eds.): *Organized industrial relations for Europe: What future?* (Aldershot, Avebury, 1995).

—; Kittel, B.: "The bargaining system and performance: A comparison of 18 OECD countries", in *Comparative Political Studies*, 2000, Vol. 33, pp. 1154-1190.

— et al.: *National labour relations in internationalized markets* (Oxford, Oxford University Press, 2001).

Verité: *Report to the California Public Employees Retirement System (CALPERS)*, Emerging Markets Research Project, www.verite.org,2002.

Wallerstein, M.: "Wage-setting institutions and pay inequality in advanced industrial societies", in *American Journal of Political Science*, 1999, Vol. 43, pp. 649-680.

— et al.: "Unions, employers' associations and wage setting institutions in North and Central Europe 1950-1992" in *Industrial and Labour Relations Review*, 1997, Vol. 50, No. 3, pp. 379-401.

Annex I
Existing indicators/measures of social dialogue

Source	Measure	Comments
Universal (widely used)	Union density	+ Available for all countries − Density not necessarily related to existence of social dialogue
Schmitter, 1981, Cameron, 1984, Wallerstein, Golden and Lange, 1997, Traxler, Blaschke and Kittel, 2001	Union concentration (a) Inter-associational concentration (b) Intra-associational concentration	+ Data calculated for most European/advanced nations − While higher concentration scores are generally associated with social dialogue in Europe, there is no causal link
Traxler et al. 2001; Golden et al. , 1997, Kenworthy, 2000	Union centralization and employer centralization (authority that employer/union confederations have over their locals)	+ Data for advanced nations − No causal connection between degree of centralization and social dialogue, although associated in European countries.
Universal (widely used), ILO	Level of bargaining	+ Universal measure, general association between centralized bargaining and tripartite social dialogue
Wallerstein, Golden and Lange, 1997	Wage centralization measures The level of involvement by employers, union confederations in wage-setting	+ General association between centralization and tripartite social dialogue + Data calculated annually for advanced industrial economies
Iversen, 1999	Centralization of wage bargaining arrangements (locus of bargaining authority and degree of union concentration)	+ Advancement of the basic level of bargaining measure − Captures variation in the case of European countries where there is centralization to some extent, but most other countries are decentralized to plant level
Traxler, Blaschke, and Kittel, 2001	Bargaining centralization (includes level at which bargaining takes place and number of workers at each level)	+ Conceptual advance over basic level of bargaining measure − Requires extensive data that is generally available in advanced industrial countries of W. Europe − Subjective judgement of researchers important
Soskice, 1990; Crouch, 1985; Layard, Nickel and Jackman, 1991; Hall and Franzese, 1998	Wage coordination (degree to which there is harmonization by actors in the wage setting process)	+ Useful for measuring wage-related outcomes − Relevance to social dialogue low − Requires extensive annual data collection efforts

Source	Measure	Comments
Traxler et al., 2001	Wage coordination (identification of the modes by which coordination is achieved)	+ Useful for measuring wage-related outcomes − Relevance to social dialogue low − Requires extensive annual data collection efforts
Kenworthy, 2001a	Wage coordination index (characterization of institutional features of wage setting arrangements that might result in different types of coordination)	+ Focus on characterization of arrangements useful as predictor of coordination − Relevance to social dialogue low
Several studies, but in particular Boreham and Compston, 1992; Compston, 1995 1997, and Traxler et al., 2001	Corporatism: indices (based on qualitative assessments of authors) regarding the influence of employers and labour on government policy. The scope is wide ranging from influence to policy concertation.	+ Heavily researched in the European countries − Considerable variation in indexes based on different authors' focus includes influence, activities, and results − Requires extensive study of each country's experience
Kittel, 2000	Index of firm-level worker representation (includes legal basis for CB, rights and duties of works councils, and special veto rights of works councils)	+ Takes into account legal basis for firm-level dialogue + Appropriate focus on rights − Does not take into account practice − Rooted in European experience
Universal	Collective bargaining coverage (number of people covered under collective agreements in a country)	+ Universal measure that looks at the practical impact of trade union activity at the workplace − Does not evaluate the quality of collective agreements − Difficult and expensive data to collect, particularly in developing countries where there are no regular surveys
ILO (see also Verité for a scoring system)	Conventions regarding freedom of association and collective bargaining (focus on whether rights exist for social dialogue)	+ Easily available data from ILO − Ratifying the Conventions does not mean that the rights exist in those countries * Potential value as useful background information
Universal measure (ILO and national government statistics)	Strikes and lockouts (measured in number and indicative of the exercising of rights, but perhaps also of the failure of social dialogue)	+ Easily available − Construct validity issue. No strikes does not mean that social dialogue is good…..as there could be a number of reasons for lack of strikes.

Source	Measure	Comments
Verité	Conventions (freedom of association and collective bargaining) related laws. Laws focus on the independence of workers' organizations, freedom of workers to elect their own representatives, protection against discrimination for joining unions, freedom from government control, legal protection of the right to strike.	+ Positive and useful measures in that they assess the extent to which national legislation protects the right (in practice) to freedom of association and collective bargaining − Requires detailed and expert knowledge of people making the assessments/or of respondents to surveys
Verité	Effectiveness of implementation of laws. Assessments regarding the independence of trade unions, de facto non-formal restrictions on right to organize, and extent to which collective bargaining is allowed without government interference.	+ Positive in that these measures focus on practice, and how well the laws are actually working − Requires detailed country knowledge
Verité	Institutional capacity of government to enforce laws, measured by inspections, scale of corruption, fines for violation of laws, and adequacy of inspection staff.	+ Positive hitherto unutilized measure − Requires expert knowledge
Kucera, 2001	Violations of workers' rights to produce worker rights scores on 37 variables using a large variety of qualitative data sources (ICFTU, US State Department, etc).	+ Positive in that it focuses on violations and codes available evidence on violations − Difficult to obtain comprehensive data on a number of issues, and a lot of missing data in the textual source documents
Kuruvilla et al., 2002	Union influence scores (an index comprising levels of bargaining and collective bargaining coverage)	+ Provides a counter-measure to union density by looking at the actual influence of unions on workers' rights − Does not examine rights/violations
Freedom House	Civil liberties, (including the right to organize)	
Ghai, 2002	Economic democracy	

Source	Measure	Comments
US government agencies	Compliance with freedom of association Agencies: USILAB, USTR, OPIC, NAALC, CRS	+ Detailed reports using multiple methods of data collection − Only for selected countries − Occasional coverage
US State Department	Descriptive reports on workers' rights in every country (section 6 reports). Relies heavily on multiple methods including use of local labour attaché.	+ Universal, systematic, annual − Quality is mixed
AFL-CIO	Core labour standards country assessment	+ In depth − Few countries so far
Freedom House	Civil liberties, democracy and political rights, and questions on Conventions Nos. 87 and 98	+ Focus on freedom widely defined is good, multi-method approach − Shortfall in terms of labour rights
Human Rights Watch	Descriptive reports on human and labour rights in selected countries	+ Multimethod approach − Focus on workers' rights is idiosyncratic − No comprehensive coverage of countries
International labour rights fund	Descriptive country reports	− Occasional
ICFTU	Annual survey of trade union rights (focus on violations during the period)	+ Annual and survey based + Quality improving − Only trade union perspective
ILO-CEARC	Focus on application of Conventions. Analysis of national labour laws and consistence with ILO Conventions	+ Technical reports, detailed − Careful diplomatic language obfuscates
ILO-COFA	Violations of freedom of association	+ Detailed − Complaint driven (not all unions complain/use this procedure)
OECD report	Index of compliance with freedom of association based on ILO, ICFTU, and US State Dept descriptive reports	+ Places countries in different groups with respect to compliance − Problems using subjective judgement regarding which violations are more severe

Annex II
List of indicators advocated in this report

Indicator number	Type and description of indicator
A	Basic control information
A1	Union density and changes in density
A2	Ratification of ILO Conventions 87 and 98
A3	Labour force statistics
A4	Percentage of population covered by FA and CB legislation
B	Rights underlying social dialogue
B1	Freedom of association
B1A	Union and employer association formation
B1B	Independence of unions and employer associations
B1C	Protection from discrimination against union members or activists
B2	Bipartite free collective bargaining
B2A	Union recognition and obligation to bargain
B2B	Scope and subject matter of bargaining
B2C	Right to strike and restrictions on this right
B2D	Parallel workplace representation
B3	Tripartism
B3A	Right to tripartite processes
B3B	Limitations on tripartite rights: Affiliation
B3C	Limitations to tripartite rights: Politics
C	Social dialogue in practice
C1	Bipartite process and outcome
C1A	Collective bargaining coverage
C1B	Number of collective agreements
C1C	Parallel workplace arrangements
C1D	Number of strikes and lockouts
C1E	Data on grievances or industrial disputes
C2	Tripartite process and outcome
C2A	Tripartite processes
C2B	Tripartite outcomes: Wages
C2C	Tripartite outcomes: Income inequality
D	Alternative avenues for social dialogue
D1	Descriptive measures of industry codes
E	Implementation and government capacity
E1	Penalties for violating social dialogue laws
E2	Government administrative capacity
F	Rights and practice in the informal sector
F1	Freedom of association
F2	Collective bargaining and individual disputes
F3	Unionization
F4	Other informal sector organizations

Annex III
Glossary

AFL-CIO	American Federation of Labor-Congress of Industrial Organizations
CALPERS	California Public Employees Retirement System
CEARC	Committee of Experts on Application of Recommendations and Conventions
COFA	Committee on the Freedom of Association
CRS	Cost Reduction Strategy
EPZ	Export Processing Zone
FLA	Fair Labor Association
GDP	Gross Domestic Product
GRI	Global Reporting Initiative
ICFTU	International Confederation of Free Trade Unions
ILC	International Labour Conference
ILO	International Labour Organization
IR	Industrial Relations
NAALC	North American Agreement on Labor Cooperation
NE	National Expert
NGO	Non-Governmental Organization
NLRB	National Labor Relations Board
NSDDS	National Social Dialogue Data Sheets
OECD	Organisation for Economic Co-operation and Development
OPIC	Overseas Private Investment Corporation
UN	United Nations
UNHCR	United Nation High Commission for Refugees
USILAB	US International Labor Affairs Bureau
USTR	US Trade Representative

Profiles

Dharam Ghai

Dharam Ghai is Advisor to the International Labour Organization. His previous positions include Director of the United Nations Research Institute for Social Development, Research Director of the World Employment Programme at the ILO and Director of the Institute for Development Studies at the University of Nairobi. He served as coordinator of the Transition Team of ILO Director-General Juan Somavia in 1998-99. He was also a member of the Pearson Commission on International Development, Visiting Fellow, Economic Growth Center, Yale University, and Chief of the Secretariat for the World Employment Conference in 1976. He has written extensively on employment, poverty, rural and social development, social indicators, structural adjustment and social dimensions of globalization and the environment. He is a member of the advisory boards of several journals and research institutes.

Bob Hepple

Sir Bob Hepple, QC, FBA is Emeritus Master of Clare College and Emeritus Professor of Law in the University of Cambridge. He is a practicing barrister at Blackstone Chambers, London, and has acted as an independent expert for the ILO, UNCTAD, and the European Commission. His special interests include labour law and anti-discrimination law. He is the author of over 20 books and a large number of other contributions on labour law, equality law and human rights. His most recent books are *Labour Laws and Global Trade* (Hart Publishing, 2005) and *Rights at Work: Global, European and British Perspectives* (The Hamlyn Lectures 2004, published by Sweet & Maxwell, 2005).

Martin Godfrey

Martin Godfrey has long experience as a researcher, consultant and teacher/ trainer in the Institute of Development Studies, Sussex University, UK (including managing a multi-country research project). Recent experience includes analysis of labour markets and the economics of education and training in transition economies (including Armenia, Hungary, Moldova, Russia, Romania, Serbia, Tajikistan and China), and preparation of papers on labour-market and employment implications of the HIV/ AIDS epidemic (ILO), employment dimensions of decent work (ILO), and youth employment policy in developing and transition countries (World Bank). He received his Ph.D. in economics from Manchester University.

Ashwani Saith

Ashwani Saith is Professor of Development Studies at the London School of Economics and also at the Institute of Social Studies, The Hague, Netherlands. His research interests include studying reforms and transitions in developing economies, rural development processes and policies, poverty, agrarian institutions and reforms, the non-farm economy and rural industrialization, village level studies, international and internal migration in Asia (especially India and China).

Sarosh Kuruvilla

Sarosh Kuruvilla is currently Professor of Collective Bargaining, Comparative Industrial Relations and Asian Studies at Cornell University. He obtained his doctorate in business administration from the University of Iowa in 1989 and joined the faculty at Cornell in 1990. His research interests focus on comparative industrial relations and, specifically, on the linkages between industrial relations policies and practices, national human resource policies and practices, and economic development policies. Much of his work concerns the developing world. He is the author of over 50 journal articles and has served as a consultant to the ILO, the World Bank, and Asian governments.